T0230738

Network and Data Security for Non-Engineers

Network and Data Security for Non-Engineers

Frank M. Groom
Kevin Groom
Stephan S. Jones

CRC Press
Taylor & Francis Group
Boca Raton London New York

CRC Press is an imprint of the
Taylor & Francis Group, an **informa** business

AN AUERBACH BOOK

CRC Press
Taylor & Francis Group
6000 Broken Sound Parkway NW, Suite 300
Boca Raton, FL 33487-2742

First issued in hardback 2017

© 2017 by Taylor & Francis Group, LLC
CRC Press is an imprint of Taylor & Francis Group, an Informa business

No claim to original U.S. Government works

Version Date: 20160426

ISBN-13: 978-1-4987-6786-6 (pbk)
ISBN-13: 978-1-138-43680-0 (hbk)

Library of Congress Cataloging-in-Publication Data

Names: Groom, Frank M., author. | Groom, Kevin M., author. | Jones, Stephan., author.
Title: Network and data security for non-engineers / Frank M. Groom, Kevin Groom, and Stephan S. Jones.
Description: Boca Raton : CRC Press, Taylor & Francis Group, an Informa Business, [2017] | Includes bibliographical references and index.
Identifiers: LCCN 2016008261 | ISBN 9781498767866
Subjects: LCSH: Computer networks--Security measures.
Classification: LCC TK5105.59 .G78 2017 | DDC 005.8--dc23
LC record available at https://lccn.loc.gov/2016008261

Visit the Taylor & Francis Web site at
http://www.taylorandfrancis.com

and the CRC Press Web site at
http://www.crcpress.com

Contents

Preface

This book has been developed to support the graduate Network and Data Security course offered by the Center for Information and Communication Sciences at Ball State University. The book was stimulated by the numerous break-ins at national enterprises including JP Morgan Chase, Sony, and a number of government agencies, including the military. It was further stimulated by the spread and various mutations of the Stuxnet worm, which initially affected Iran's centrifuges; and, finally, by the break-in and persistent presence in Anthem Blue Cross and Blue Shield's computer systems.

The book includes my own research into the various methods and techniques employed by the hacking community as well as the approaches that have proved most successful in detecting and eliminating such invasions. It includes information gathered from various national security enterprises as well as materials from the data security courses taught at major universities across the country. My graduate students have helped condense portions of my Network and Data Security class to appropriate material for the various chapters of the book. As a consequence, the book follows my course topic sequence quite closely and will be used as reference material for future offerings of this class.

Frank M. Groom, PhD

MATLAB® is a registered trademark of The MathWorks, Inc. For product information, please contact:

The MathWorks, Inc.
3 Apple Hill Drive
Natick, MA 01760-2098 USA
Tel: 508 647 7000
Fax: 508-647-7001
E-mail: info@mathworks.com
Web: www.mathworks.com

Authors

Frank M. Groom is a professor of information and communication sciences at the Center for Information and Communication Sciences at Ball State University. He conducts research into high-bandwidth networking and the storage and transmission of multimedia objects. Dr. Groom has conducted research into multiprotocol label switching (MPLS)-driven fiber networks, intelligent agents, network-based data deployment, and firewall-based security. He has conducted a number of national research projects using surveys, focus groups, personal interviews, and student research culminating in two of his published books. Furthermore, he has conducted many specialized statistical research studies for AT&T, McDonalds Corp., and Nth Dimension Software. In addition to his graduate level networking, information systems, network security, and advanced database courses at Ball State, Dr. Groom annually conducts a graduate research methods course for Ball State graduate students where he teaches many of the methods he has employed in his own research. His research has been conducted both in industry and at the university studying both big data problems as well as smaller situations. Dr. Groom has presented networking and data processing courses to major American corporations, including PricewaterhouseCoopers, IBM, AT&T and its various units, Motorola, Digital Equipment Corp. (now HP), Unisys, Ford Motor, Hillenbran Industries, and McDonalds.

AT&T has twice sponsored Dr. Groom to present advanced data processing and networking courses to the graduate students and faculty of Beijing University of Posts and Telecommunications (BUPT) and the People's Republic of China Government Office of Telecommunications. He was honored with having two of his papers presented at the Plenary Session of the 1996 International Conference on Information Infrastructure (ICII'96) in Beijing, China, and another paper presented as the Plenary Session for the Broadband 2000 conference in Tokyo. Furthermore, in 1996, 1998, and 2006, Dr. Groom presented papers on ATM networking, Multimedia, and VoIP at the leading French Graduate School of Telecommunications (Ecole Nationale Superiore des Telecommunications [ENST]) while consulting with research professors and reviewing the PhD dissertation research of current candidates.

In addition to publishing over 120 technical papers concerning networking, systems design, corporate re-engineering, and object-oriented storage, Dr. Groom has published a number of books, including *The Future of ATM and Broadband Networking*, *The Future of IP and Packet Networking*, *The ATM Handbook*, *The Basics of Voice over Internet Protocol*, *The Basics of 802.11 Wireless LANs*, and *Multimedia over the Broadband Network*. Further, he has authored two chapters in other books: *Network Manager's Handbook* and *Knowledge Management*. He is the coeditor of the four-volume 2006 Annual Review of Communications, and is one of the coauthors of the second edition of *The Fundamentals of Communication for Non-Engineers* with Stephan S. Jones and Ronald J. Kovac for Taylor & Francis.

Dr. Groom has a PhD in management information systems from the University of Wisconsin, was division manager in charge of the Information Systems Division of Wisconsin Bell, and is the retired senior director of information systems for Ameritech (now once again part of AT&T).

Kevin Groom is a project manager for AT&T's network projects for large corporations. He is a former senior network engineer in AT&T's Network Service Division, supporting AT&T's national backbone network for 15 years. He has a BS in telecommunications and an MS in information and communication sciences from Ball State University.

Stephan S. Jones spent over 16 and a half years in the communication technology industry while operating his own teleconnect company, providing high-end commercial voice and data networks to a broad range of end users. Later, Dr. Jones was district sales manager for the Panasonic Communications and Systems Company, providing application engineering and product support to distributors in a five-state area.

Since joining Ball State as a professor of information and communication sciences, Dr. Jones has served as the codirector of the Center for Information and Communication Sciences Applied Research Institute and has conducted research in the development of broadband delivery systems, unified communications, and health-care information technologies, and he has written/edited 15 books and authored numerous book chapters. In his current role as the director of the Center for Information and Communication Sciences, he is charged with external funding development, student career development and placement, the pursuit of new curriculum ideas, graduate student recruiting, and the out-of-classroom learning experience of the Student Social Learning Program.

Dr. Jones received his PhD from Bowling Green State University, where he also served as the dean of continuing education, developing a distance-learning program for the College of Technology's undergraduate Technology Education program.

Chapter 1

Introduction to Security Threats

Our world is increasingly descending into the ancient vision of "good" versus "evil," or at least the opposites of "ying" versus "yang." The concentration of fresh talent in hot spots around the globe is resulting in innovative products and apps providing enhanced capabilities for an increasing number of users. From smartphones to smart cars, the "Internet of Things" is now upon us. The great companies of our times continue to experiment and introduce connective technologies that satisfy human needs and frequently create those needs. But simultaneously, the "evil" side is growing even faster in its capability, employing those very same technologies for malicious purposes.

Where technology users were previously merely annoyed by individuals and small groups who identified themselves as "hackers," the software and techniques used for unwanted entry into systems are now readily available to groups aligned with nation-states (China and Russia being prime examples). Moreover, these widely available tools are constantly mutating into more complex versions. Programs generated for a specific strategic purpose, such as the Stuxnet worm, have been reverse engineered, and their complex code has now been altered to facilitate an attack on the control systems of any of our structural systems, including electrical power grids, water purification systems, air traffic control systems, and even our planes and cars. And this is just the beginning. A wealth of enabling tools is still to come with robotic, intelligent devices at our beck and call, while malicious agents will surely remain bent on attack, diversion, and destruction. The purpose of this book, then, is to apprise the reader of the various components that have enabled the services we use, as well as to explain how these very same tools have simultaneously been diverted for malicious purposes.

Our first example is a case study of the 2014 Anthem break-in by a Chinese hacking group in Shanghai and the step-by-step process by which the attackers gained entry, placed hidden software, downloaded information, and hid the evidence of their entry. Subsequently, we provide a discussion of the tools they employed, as well as the intent to establish a persistent presence in the systems they entered, the ability to use those sites as testbeds to determine successful variations of their software that elude detection, and the ability to reach out across "trusted connections" to the entire health-care system of the nation.

Next, we examine the components of technology that are being diverted. We start with application code and how it can best be protected with isolation approaches. We look at the general principles of a secure system and then how hackers approach such systems. We follow with an examination of the various forms of infection, including viruses, worms, bots, and Trojans. We then examine encryption, using the Rivest–Shamir–Adelman (RSA) algorithm as our working example. Internet Protocol Security (IPSec)—which is at the heart of the secure virtual private network (VPN) connectivity widely employed by American businesses—is discussed, along with the contrasting use by Chinese hackers of their own undetectable VPN, the Terracotta VPN, which makes the hackers' activity appear to be normal traffic entering and traversing "protected" systems.

We examine web applications, complete web systems, domain name systems (DNSs), and the general structure of the public Internet. And, given that the world has rapidly migrated into a totally mobile, Steve Jobs–inspired world of instantaneous communication and download, we examine the present vulnerability of the ubiquitous "smart" devices. As the Stuxnet worm has gained such wide press, we examine the stepwise process of that particular infection and show how the electric grid system is a similarly exposed target for destruction by such a worm.

Finally, we conclude with RSA's layout of the various forms of cyber warfare that the world is currently experiencing, many of which take advantage of the false sense of security into which many of us have lapsed.

Chapter 2

The 2014–2015 Anthem Blue Cross and Blue Shield Break-In Case Study

Anthem has stated that their systems were entered into during December 2014–January 2015. Anthem is an insurance company. It has 12 State Blue Cross and Blue Shield Healthcare Insurance Companies, and a Life Insurance Company and a number of Affiliated Companies. It seems clear, however, that this unauthorized entry occurred between January 2014 and April 2014 (Brian Krebs, *Krebs on Security* Blog, February 9, 2015). We believe that the attackers are based in Shanghai, China, and are loosely aligned with the Chinese military. They have a mature set of tools, are exceptionally skilled, and intend to gain a persistent, long-term presence in the systems that they enter. It is not yet clear what they intend to do with this presence, what information they have downloaded, what they will do within the Anthem systems, or what they will do to the various health-care providers that have "trusted connections" with the Anthem systems, be they businesses, customers, hospitals, drug companies, pharmacies, medical practitioners, or other insurance companies (including the U.S. government Medicare/Medicaid system). However, the combined vulnerability of these entities is clear.

Such hacking groups, variously identified as "Deep Panda" and variations on that name, must be self-financed. Their source of income for supporting their operation comes from the sites that they attack. Thus, they offer for sale on the anonymous sites of the "dark web" bundles of between 2,000 and 10,000 IDs, including social security numbers, wage information, and location information. For example, the Anthem customer file contained 78.8 million customer records, which can be sold to middlemen on the dark web at $50 apiece ($4 billion in total) and then resold by those middlemen to criminal groups and individuals at a standard price of $350 for each ID.

The criminals who purchase and use these stolen IDs only have the resources to purchase this valuable information in small bundles, usually no more than 2,000–10,000 IDs at a time. They quickly use them and resell them to other groups to reclaim their original investment. The stolen Anthem customer IDs originally placed on the dark web can be sold repeatedly over time, whether piecemeal or in bulk, for use in acquiring passports and credit cards and performing banking fraud.

Since the Anthem break-in is such a clear-cut example, we will step through the process in sequential sections, illustrating at each step the tools and techniques that were almost certainly employed. We begin with the reconnaissance phase, possibly the most important step. Then, we address the capture of an Anthem technician's identity and how, subsequently, a hacker gained entry by posing as that authorized system technician or system user.

We then discuss how the intruders scanned Anthem's networks, systems, servers, and databases; strategically placed malware at carefully selected locations in the system; performed the initial extraction of information, downloading it across the Internet to selected web locations; and then continued to withdraw from Anthem's systems.

Then, we examine the hackers' periodic reentry of the system to establish a persistent presence, test new variations of their malware, and eventually perform their intended actions. And finally, we examine the spread of the attack across the trusted connections to the rest of the health-care industry, and we speculate on the purposes of such a widespread presence.

Step 1: Reconnaissance

The first step in research is exploration: the discovery of the layout of the operation to be attacked. Nation-state hacking groups are distant and thus have two sources. First, there is an array of social-media sites to be searched for Anthem-based employees including LinkedIn, Facebook, and many others, which provide employee-identifying information and activity descriptions as well as employment information, telephone numbers, and most of all, e-mail addresses—which are all-important to the hackers.

However, the specific identities that the hackers wish to acquire are those with special access privileges. Once these are acquired, a quick entry, placement, and download can be efficiently conducted without detection. This indicates that the best target was the technicians that support Anthem's computer applications, systems, and data centers.

How does one best discover these addresses? The simplest approach is to hire someone to gain employment in (or at least gain entry to) Anthem buildings and acquire an Anthem telephone book. All companies have these for easy discovery of internal telephone, mail, and location information. Even organization charts are frequently provided as an additional benefit. Where this information is not provided in book form, there is generally an easily accessible computerized file of such information available online to most employees. This file or book is valuable for understanding who is who in the company, where they are located, and in what organization they reside. Most important to the hackers is accessibility to entry-level employees, as well as contract employees who might be also be accessed.

Step 2: Picking the Right Target and Spear Phishing Them

The goal of the hacker is to "become" the target technician. To this end, they want to observe all the keystrokes that the technician initiates, the technician's keyed-in password and identification information, the systems that the technician can access, and the locations of applications, services, and databases across the Anthem site. The hacker seeks all the passwords and special-access information that the technician normally uses to gain entry to these systems.

Two basic techniques are employed to acquire the targeted technician's credentials, access the systems that he or she can access, and further access information and passwords. Those techniques are *spear phishing* and the use of attractive *waterholes*.

Spear Phishing

With spear phishing, the attacker sends an e-mail to the identified technician with a clickable URL identified for response. An example might be an e-mail purportedly from a supervisor asking for next week's schedule for the technician or the unit, the application patches, or some routine process. The technician clicks on the URL, which triggers the downloading of a keystroke-logging software, quite frequently the software package ScanBox, and sends a benign message to the supervisor, which is usually ignored. From then on, the hackers see everything the technician sees and everything the technician types, including passwords, IDs, system numbers, and database names and locations.

Waterholes

The other approach used to capture credentials is to create an attractive nuisance: a waterhole. In the animal world, instead of chasing prey, the smart predators hang around waterholes and wait for their prey to come to them. Similarly, malware can be placed on a website that contains information that the technician might find useful. Then, that site is advertised to the technician, and the technician may connect and find useful information that contains a link to the hidden ScanBox key logging software; this link causes it to be downloaded, installed, and executed on the technician's computer. From then on, every keystroke that the technician makes and every screen displayed on the technician's screen are transmitted to the hackers. This allows the hackers to see the credentials, passwords, and IDs that the technician uses; all the systems, networks, applications, and databases that the technician is accessing; where they are all located; and what is required to access them.

Step 3: Initial System Entry

If the technician works an 8 am–5 pm shift, the attacker will usually enter on the least active shift, usually between midnight and 5 am. And if the attacker is in China, that time is comfortably in the afternoon for them.

The purpose of this initial entry is to place special undetectable software on principal systems, with Trojan. Derusbi and backdoor L-traps being the most commonly placed malware. Usually, these are encrypted so that they are unlikely to match the signatures of malware for which the scanners and monitors will be looking during their searches. Triggers can also be placed in the software of application systems or even in the operating systems (with Linux, UNIX, and Windows being most vulnerable) and database management systems, such as Oracle, that the target enterprise might employ.

The next step is to traverse the connecting network to create a map of the location on the internal Anthem network where the systems are located, determine what other sites exist, and find out how they might each be accessed. Then, the user and system password files are located and transmitted to the hacking group, either directly to China or to an intermediate site on the dark web.

Cleanup is the last step. Since all traffic against any system and its database is logged on a log tape/data set, a before, after, and transaction detail is created for each access. The attacker must employ specialized software to read these log tapes, clean them of any evidence, and restore their timing and appearance as they were before the entry occurred. Frequently, malware might also be placed in that log system for future use to ensure anonymity.

Next Steps to Establish an Undetectable Anonymous Persistent Presence

RSA research published an in-depth report on a commercial virtual private network (VPN), originating in China, which is called the Terracotta VPN. Frequently, the hackers will employ their special Terracotta VPN to enter the target site so they look like regular off-site users accessing the systems. Others continue to enter using the stolen technician's ID credentials and password.

Password Decryption Process and Equipment

Once the password files are downloaded, they must be decrypted. Although the files contain thousands of user passwords, the attackers only need to decrypt an initial working set, so brute-force techniques are employed. Although they can use many tools, a currently popular approach is to employ one of Jamey Gosley's decryption machines, which use a massively parallel processing approach. Four machines, each with a main processor and a distributed set of up to 48 advanced graphic processors (AGPs), are placed in an array. A modified version of the graphic software VLC is then used to distribute groups of the passwords to each AGP. They begin in parallel a trial-and-error process to try to decrypt these passwords and compare the results with a file of commonly known and frequently used passwords.

When a match is found, the hackers now have a vehicle for authorized entry. After they have found a useful set, they can then take their time breaking the rest of the encrypted passwords. Time is on their side. Meanwhile, the customer identification files are downloaded. Unfortunately, these files, similarly to all files used by the Anthem application systems, are not encrypted. Only files transmitted outside the Anthem network are encrypted for transmission, the assumption being that that is where they are most vulnerable. However, the hackers are now insiders with knowledge about these encryptions and their associated keys, so even the transmitted files are now vulnerable.

Testbed

On subsequent entries, usually monthly, the hackers place a series of software components that will persistently and undetectably hide in the Anthem systems. The hackers then periodically examine the hidden software to see if it has been detected and removed. Over time, they will place variations of the malware in the system to experiment with what is detectable by the scanners and monitors, and to determine what still remains undetectable. This is an ongoing experimental process with the victim providing the testbed for discovering and trying out new variations of the attackers' malware.

Final Steps

The hackers traverse the trusted connecting networks to other insurance companies' systems, hospital systems, medical provider systems, pharmaceutical company systems, and pharmacies. Undetectable persistent infection of those systems is the initial intent, facilitating later malicious processing.

The customer ID information is then sold in small batches (2,000–10,000) on the dark web. The purchasers have recently been small criminal gangs in South Florida and the Bahamas. They have bought clusters of IDs for universities and companies in small towns, usually in the Midwest and Central Plains states, where they will be less evident to the understaffed, undereducated, and slow-moving Federal Bureau of Investigation (FBI) technicians and investigators. For example, the FBI has one such individual, recently hired from college, as their single investigator.

The gang might pay 10,000 * $300 for a set. Those IDs representing the top third of the highest earners will go to a team of hired temporary clerks. They will type in customer information on an imitation 1040 Internal Revenue Service (IRS) form using a common system such as TurboTax, make up $20,000 worth of deductions, and file for a return under $10,000, usually around $9,000.

Another set of individuals acquires debit cards, telephone cards, and temporary bank accounts that can be used to allow the fraudulent filings to be paid to the IRS, usually with the imitated Anthem customer's real address identified. Then the address is changed to a South Florida temporary site where it can be accessed.

Within one month, the purchase of the 10,000 IDs, filing of false 1040s, and payment reception have been completed; the gang is disbursed, frequently with no knowledge of the gang leader, who receives the bulk of the money. It is months later before the IRS uncovers the fraud, and months more before the FBI may become involved. By then, the gang is long gone and the information has been sold to Californian, Russian, Ukrainian, and Eastern European gangs for their purposes. Figure 2.1 portrays that sequence of events.

Beyond selecting a path that will make their access anonymous, attackers will edit and reverse or "clean" the logs after they have performed their desired activities on the compromised

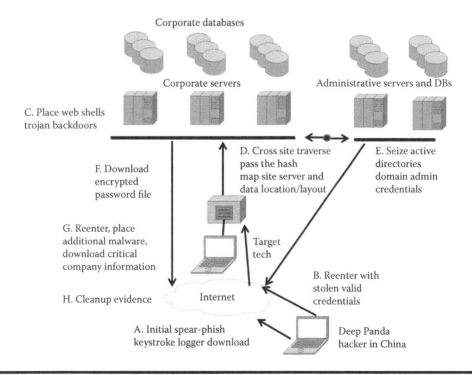

Figure 2.1   The steps in the Anthem break-in.

information system. Initially, these modifications are brief, since they are only downloading a few critical files that contain passwords. On the second round of attack, once useful passwords have been cracked, the hackers will reenter the system and diversify their attack openings through the installation of Trojans, web shells, timers, and more keystroke loggers. After each pass, the logs, warnings, and notification of changes are overwritten, hidden, or deleted in order to prevent legitimate administrators and users from detecting their presence.

Tools Used by Hackers to Acquire Valid Entry Credentials and Tools Used by Security Personnel to Detect Activity and Malware and Protect the Stored Data

Tool 1: Initial Spear-Phishing Entry Leading to the ScanBox Keystroke Logger

The most common method of stealing sensitive information and authentication credentials in order to traverse the portals to an enterprise's network is with a keystroke grabber. These programs are secretly installed on target computers to record or log the keys struck on a keyboard by the user on the affected device. This malware is used to obtain sensitive data such as login information to further infiltrate a system or network. There are numerous keylogging methods, ranging from hardware- and software-based approaches, which we shall briefly describe in the following section, to the most popular keystroke-logging software—ScanBox (Figure 2.2).

Among these varied types of keystroke loggers are

1. *Software-based keyloggers*: Software-based keyloggers are computer programs designed to work on a target computer's specific software. There are a number of varied keylogger software categories.

Figure 2.2 Keystroke logging and stealing as the user types.

2. *Hypervisor-based keyloggers*: Modern virtualized computing employs a hypervisor module upon which a number of operating systems can sit, each running their own set of applications. If that hypervisor becomes infected with malware, keylogger software can theoretically reside in that malware-infected hypervisor environment, running underneath the operating system. The keylogger is difficult to detect and essentially becomes a virtual machine in its own right, operating independently.

3. *Kernel-based keyloggers*: Malware, once inserted on a machine, can obtain root access in order to hide itself in the operating system and begin intercepting keystrokes that pass through the kernel module that interfaces with the machine hardware. Keyloggers such as these (which reside at the kernel level) are quite difficult to detect, especially by scanning applications that do not themselves have root access. They are frequently implemented as rootkits that subvert the operating system kernel and thus gain unauthorized access to the hardware, making them very powerful. A keylogger using this method can act as a keyboard device driver, for example, and thus gain access to any information typed on the keyboard as it goes to the operating system.

4. *API-based keyloggers*: These application programming interface (API) keyloggers hook keyboard APIs inside a running application. The keylogger registers for keystroke events as if it was a normal piece of the application instead of malware. The keylogger receives an event each time the user presses or releases a key. The keylogger simply records it, and the malware transmits the logged information to the hackers.

5. *Form grabbing–based keyloggers*: Form grabbing–based keyloggers log web-form submissions by recording the web-browsing history on submit events. These happen when the user finishes filling in a form and submits it, usually by clicking a button or hitting enter. This records form data before it is passed over the Internet.

6. *Memory injection–based (MitB) keyloggers*: Memory injection (MitB)–based keyloggers alter memory tables associated with the browser and other system functions to perform their logging. By patching memory tables or injecting directly into memory, this technique can be used by malware authors who are looking to bypass Windows user account control (UAC). Non-Windows systems have their own similar protection mechanisms that need to be thwarted somehow by the keylogger.

7. *Remote access software keyloggers*: These are local software keyloggers with an added feature that allows access to the locally recorded data from a remote location. Remote communication may be achieved using one of the following methods:
   a. Data is uploaded to a website, database, or FTP server.
   b. Data is periodically e-mailed to a predefined e-mail address.
   c. Data is wirelessly transmitted by means of an attached hardware system.
   d. The software enables a remote login to the local machine from the Internet or the local network, allowing data logs stored on the target machine to be accessed.

      Most of these processes are not stopped by Hypertext Transfer Protocol secure (HTTPS) encryption because that only protects data in transit between computers, whereas this is a threat within your own computer—directly connected to the keyboard.

8. *Hardware-based keyloggers*: Hardware-based keyloggers do not depend on any software being installed, as they exist at a hardware level in a computer system.

9. *Firmware-based keyloggers*: This basic input/output system (BIOS)-level firmware that handles keyboard events can be modified to record these events as they are processed. Physical and/or root-level access to the machine is required, and the logging software loaded into the BIOS has to be tailored to the specific hardware that it will be running on (Figure 2.3).

Figure 2.3 Firmware-based keylogger.

KeyGrabber   (Wi Fi)   KeyGrabber   KeyGrabber

Figure 2.4 Hardware keylogger examples.

10. *Keyboard hardware*: Hardware keyloggers are used for keystroke logging by means of a hardware circuit that is attached somewhere in between the computer keyboard and the computer, typically in-line with the keyboard's cable connector. There are also USB connector–based hardware keyloggers. More stealthy implementations can be installed or built into standard keyboards, so no device is visible on the external cable. Both types log all keyboard activity to their internal memory, which can subsequently be accessed, for example, by typing in a secret key sequence. A hardware keylogger has an advantage over a software solution: It is not dependent on being installed on the target computer's operating system and therefore will not interfere with any program running on the target machine or be detected by any software. However, its physical presence may be detected if, for example, it is installed outside the case as an in-line device between the computer and the keyboard. Some of these implementations have the ability to be controlled and monitored remotely by means of wireless communication (Figure 2.4).

11. *Wireless keyboard sniffers*: These passive sniffers collect packets of data being transferred from a wireless keyboard and its receiver. As encryption may be used to secure the wireless communications between the two devices, this may need to be cracked beforehand if the transmissions are to be read.

12. *Keyboard overlays*: Criminals have been known to use keyboard overlays on ATMs to capture people's personal identification numbers (PINs). Each keypress is registered by the keyboard of the ATM as well as by the keypad that the criminal has placed over it. The device is designed to look like an integrated part of the machine so that bank customers are unaware of its presence.

13. *Acoustic keyloggers*: Acoustic cryptanalysis can be used to monitor the sound created by someone typing on a computer. Each key on the keyboard makes a subtly different acoustic signature when struck. It is then possible to identify which keystroke signature relates to which keyboard character via statistical methods such as frequency analysis. The repetition frequency of similar acoustic keystroke signatures, the timings between different keyboard strokes, and other context information such as the probable language in which the user is writing are used in this analysis to map sounds to letters. For this method, a fairly long recording (1000 or more keystrokes) is required so that a big enough sample is collected.

14. *Electromagnetic emissions*: It is possible to capture the electromagnetic emissions of a wired keyboard from up to 20 m (66 ft.) away, without being physically wired to it. In 2009, Swiss researchers tested 11 different USB, PS/2, and laptop keyboards in a semianechoic chamber and found them all vulnerable, primarily because of the prohibitive cost of adding shielding during manufacture. The researchers used a wideband receiver to tune into the specific frequency of the emissions radiated from the keyboards.

15. *Smartphone sensors*: Researchers have demonstrated that it is possible to capture the keystrokes of nearby computer keyboards using only the commodity accelerometer found in smartphones. The attack is made possible by placing a smartphone near a keyboard on the same desk. The smartphone's accelerometer can then detect the vibrations created by typing on the keyboard and translate this raw accelerometer signal into readable sentences with as much as 80% accuracy. The technique involves working through probability by detecting pairs of keystrokes rather than individual keys. It models "keyboard events" in pairs and then works out whether the pair of keys pressed is on the left or the right side of the keyboard and whether they are close together or far apart on the QWERTY keyboard. Once it has worked this out, it compares the results with a preloaded dictionary in which each word has been broken down in the same way. Similar techniques have also been shown to be effective in capturing keystrokes on touchscreen keyboards, and in some cases in combination with a gyroscope (Figure 2.5).

16. *ScanBox*: ScanBox, a particularly malicious keystroke grabbing program, performs the keylogging of users when they visit a compromised website without requiring malware to be deployed, and it can collect a great deal of information that can be used to design future attacks.

    Depending on the browser used, ScanBox would deploy reconnaissance software, code for detecting Flash, SharePoint, Adobe PDF Reader, and Java. Some of them, including the JavaScript keylogger, are launched on any of the major browsers on the market (Internet Explorer, Mozilla Firefox, Google Chrome, and Safari).

There are now several alterations to the ScanBox code base, including new modules and changes to avoid signature-based detection, as well as extra techniques to try to identify whether those being scanned are real machines or researchers.

A motivation for selectively loading plug-ins is likely to be to prevent crashes or any errors appearing (which may alert the owner of the compromised site) when the page is loaded, as some of the plug-ins are only compatible with specific browsers. Selectively loading plug-ins has the added bonus of slightly reducing researchers' access to the attacker's code. Developers are continuing to update and test variants of the framework, including new server-side code being tested by budding hackers.

Keystroke loggers are a particularly dangerous security threat because users typically don't realize they're even there. As increasing amounts of personal, corporate, and financial data is

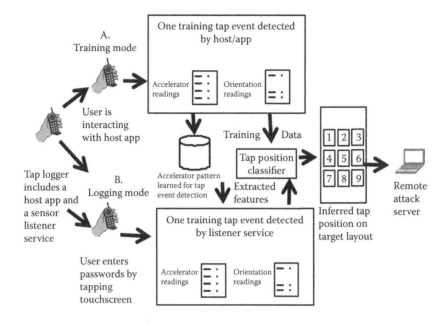

Figure 2.5   Smartphone keylogging sensor.

logged and saved on devices, it is vital to understand the risks at both the software and the hardware level. Even the most secure user-authentication system is vulnerable if the passwords are sniffed directly from the keyboard.

Tool 2: Setting Up an Anonymous Path Using Tor

The attacking team intends their source location, as well as the path and sequence of routers their traffic flows through, to be untraceable by either victims, police, FBI, Interpol, governments, or institutions. To set up such paths and hide their traffic, not only from these parties but also from the routing entities used along their path to the victim, the attackers employ a variety of tools, sites, and methods. Using these, they create an anonymous path from the attackers to the victim and an anonymous return path back to those attackers. Over those anonymous return paths flow the information stolen in their current attack venture. Among the tools and techniques employed in creating these anonymous paths are

Tor/onion routing: The Tor protocol was written by the U.S. Navy research laboratory. Tor directs Internet traffic through a subnetwork of the World Wide Web of the public Internet, termed the *dark* or *deep web*. This network is composed of sites hosting anonymous routers that are managed and set up by activists or volunteers. These sites and the services they offer are reached using an "onion" address—a pseudo address that is part of a special top-level domain and is hidden from the Internet's domain name system. Users of such services frequently use Foxfire 4.3 as their browser to access such services.

Among the services offered is anonymous routing employing the Tor protocol. This allows the creation of a network of virtual tunnels, which are used to hide websites from each other and outsiders. They are forward creating networks and hidden backward paths (Figure 2.6).

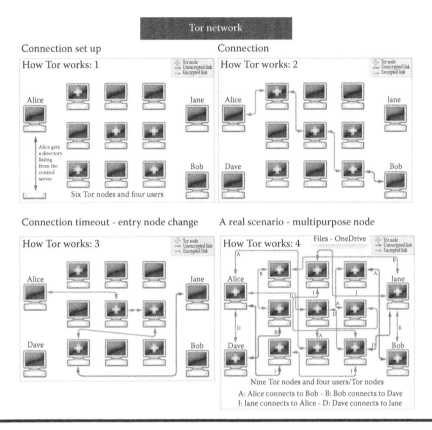

Figure 2.6 How the Tor network works (https://www.torproject.org/).

On this anonymous subset of the web, anonymous attackers need to know the available routers and their capacities, have access to the routers, and have the ability to select a subset of a few routers with which they can set up a hidden, anonymous path to a target; and a similar hidden, anonymous return path. They pick a set of between three and five routers to create a path, never using the same path twice. They set up each path so that no single point along the way can look backward and see where traffic is generated from, nor its ultimate destination. Once a path through this network is established, and they can access the target site, submit chosen initial malware, and then download information back through that path to the original site in such a way that it can't be tracked; the attackers can then reenter the target site to insinuate further malware and retrieve additional information.

An example of such an anonymous route through a set of three possible routing sites on the dark web is one where the path might be from Shanghai, China (where the location of Dark Panda has been identified), through an anonymous router in Hong Kong, to similar ones in Moscow and Amsterdam, and then on to the target site of one of Anthem's proprietary and/or cloud-based data centers (Figure 2.7).

There are two types of Tor packets: control and relay packets. Figure 2.8 shows a control Tor packet.

The Tor control process sets up the anonymous path. The initial control packets are sent out from the source site's anonymous edge router to an initial anonymous router on the dark web. This establishes a control link, and an acknowledgment is received that the link has been successfully

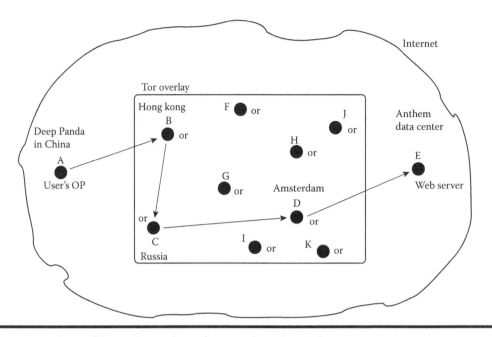

Figure 2.7   A possible routing path used to attack Anthem's data center.

2 bytes	1 bytes	509 bytes	
Circuit ID	Command	Data	512 bytes total

Figure 2.8   Tor control packet.

2 bytes	1 bytes	2 bytes	6 bytes	2 bytes	1 bytes	498 bytes	
Circuit ID	Relay	Stream ID	Digest	Length	Command	Data	512 bytes total

Figure 2.9   Tor relay packet.

created. Another control packet is then sent from the first link along to the second link, followed by a further acknowledgment. The process continues in this manner from the second to the third link and so forth. The links along the anonymous path are thus established by the Tor control process with Tor control packets, one link at a time, along the anonymous path.

When the whole end-to-end path has been created, the attackers send relay packets containing their malware, code, and software to the destination target site to establish an anonymous and persistent presence in that corporation's system. They then access files and return them along the anonymous path back to the attacker's chosen website. Figure 2.9 shows the structure of the relay Tor packet.

This relay packet forwards the attacker's Internet Protocol (IP) packets along the established anonymous paths to the target's site and returns extracted information along the anonymous path back to the original site. So, relay packets are used in this way to deliver the malware to the target site and retrieve stolen valuable information files from that target along the anonymous path to the attacker's hidden destination site. And this process begins downloading an entire stream of packets—not just one small record at a time.

There are specialized Tor browsers that help attackers discover useful relay sites that can be used for constructing their Tor network, but many just use Foxfire 4.3 for exploring sites on the dark web. The use of the more specialized Tor browsers, however, prevents somebody watching your Internet connections and learning the sites you visit and prevents the sites you visit from learning your physical location. Furthermore, they enable a potential attacker to access sites that are blocked from and by standard browsers.

The main point of the Tor network is to mask a user's location and Internet usage from people whom they suspect might be viewing their traffic activities. Using Tor does not make you completely invisible, but it certainly does make it more difficult to trace an end user's Internet activity. The main principle and purpose of Tor is to protect users' personal privacy and freedom and ensure their right to privacy. This is achieved to a significant degree by Tor through their relays, which prevent their Internet activities from being monitored, and the protocol offers a significant set of facilities for nation-states, hackers, and criminal gangs to perform destructive and unlawful activities cloaked by the Tor anonymous routing system.

In *onion wrapping*, the source of the data sends the onion-wrapped message or information to Router A, which adds an outer layer of route addressing and may perform internal packet encryption. That site learns nothing about the enclosed packet—only where to send it next. Router A sends the onion-wrapped packet to Router B, which adds another onion wrapper before sending it on to Router C, which transmits the original message to its destination (Figure 2.10).

The information return process follows a similar pattern, whereby each router along the way can only see the next address along the way, with the previous router, the source, and the ultimate destination cloaked from view.

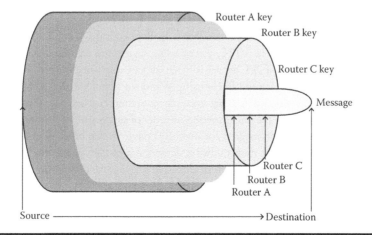

Figure 2.10   Onion-wrapping the Tor packets.

Tool 3: CrowdStrike Identified Hacker Clusters, China Chopper Web-Shell Controller

CrowdStrike's Identified Hacking Clusters

CrowdStrike, the well-known network security firm, has identified a more extensive group of hacking clusters. Malware is responsible for only 40% of breaches, and external attackers are increasingly leveraging malware-free intrusion approaches to blend in and "fly under the radar" by assuming insider credentials within victim organizations. The nature of the game now is persistence and gaining long-term access to the enterprise. The chances of ultimate discovery and effective remediation diminish greatly when no external binaries are brought into the environment and no unusual outbound command and control (C&C) traffic is taking place.

The idea behind a malware-free intrusion is very simple—malware, even if it's unknown to antivirus, is still very noisy. The presence of unknown and previously unseen binaries running in your environment, making file and registry changes to your system, and calling out to the network—these are all things that can be observed and will eventually trigger suspicion on the part of a proactive security operations center (SOC) analyst or incident responder. So, if you're an attacker who is trying to stay undetected for as long as possible, what do you do?

The obvious answer is that you break in without using malware, emulating legitimate insiders. Insider detection has always been one of the hardest problems to solve in cyber security because the attacker, by definition, looks like someone who is supposed to be inside your network and is doing things that are largely legitimate and expected. Thus, wherever the adversaries can emulate this behavior, they are quite successful in achieving their objective of stealth.

Malware-Free Intrusion Process

A large defense contractor hired CrowdStrike services after struggling for months to remediate an intrusion from a sophisticated nation-state affiliated actor. The adversary kept coming back, and the client could not identify the point of entry, despite having numerous host and network forensics and whitelisting as well as indicator of compromise (IOC) scanning malware detection tools. The explicit mission was to identify the C&C channels that the adversary was using to get inside the environment. In the end, it turned out that the question they were asking—that is, which C&C servers were being compromised—was the wrong one. Once the services team deployed next-generation end-point technology across their servers and desktops to profile and identify all adversary activity, it was determined that the adversary had compromised their two-factor authentication system, had stolen the seed values, and was coming in through the VPN system using legitimate credentials and generated two-factor token values. There were no C&C server IOCs to detect, and once the adversary was inside the network, they were able to move around freely using Windows system administration tools, without the actual use of malware. This critical gap between current enterprise defense strategy and the evolution in adversary tactics is responsible for a growing number of successful intrusions, as well as the fact that a typical breach remains undiscovered for over 200 days. In response, organizations now need to adapt their strategy and augment their malware detection and IOC scanning tools with solutions that can hunt for, detect, and ultimately prevent intrusive activity even when no malware is present.

How CrowdStrike Describes How Malware-Free Attackers Operate

CrowdStrike describes the attacking components and tools commonly employed as "malware-free intrusion tradecraft" and a set of procedures they follow using these tools and techniques.

Malware-free intrusion tradecraft: Actors affiliated with the Chinese nation-state, such as Deep Panda and Hurricane Panda, have been observed using the following tradecraft. Such compromise can be achieved via

1. Structured Query Language (SQL) is a simplified programming language for querying information stored in relational databases.
2. Web Distributed Authoring and Versioning (WebDAV) is an extension of the Hypertext Transfer Protocol (HTTP) that allows clients to perform remote Web content authoring operations.
3. Attacks against Linux web servers have recently been detected.
4. The use of the Bash vulnerability known as ShellShock.
5. That allows actors to install a web shell on the server, with China Chopper being the most common tool of choice. The reason it's so popular is that it is almost elegant in its simplicity. The web shell consists of a tiny text file (often as little as 24 bytes in size) that contains little more than an "eval( )" statement, which allows the attacker to execute processes on the web server. That script can be easily obfuscated to evade signature and IOC scanning technologies.
6. The intrusion begins with the compromise of an external-facing web server, often a Windows IIS server.

China Chopper Web Shell Controller

On the attackers' site, a controller application is executed that allows them to upload or download files and provides access to a virtual terminal from which they can execute commands.

Through the installed web shell, the attacker uploads a credential theft tool to steal Windows passwords and hashes and on occasion upload "Kerberos Golden Tickets," which can provide the attackers with persistent access to the network for as long as they deem necessary.

Technically, such a credential theft tool should be considered malware, but it is malware that traditional antimalware defenses do not identify and deal with, since there have been a continuous stream of repackaged and rewritten versions of these credential theft tools that can escape all signature and IOC-based detections; moreover, new mutant variations are constantly being made available and deployed.

Once appropriate credentials have been acquired, the attacker continues laterally across the internal corporate network using Windows Management Instrumentation (WMI) commands or Remote Desktop Protocol (RDP) sessions, just as a Windows administrator might employ, and creates scheduled tasks with Powershell scripts to maintain a persistent presence in the system. RDP is a proprietary protocol developed by Microsoft, which provides a user with a graphical interface to connect to another computer over a network connection. The user employs RDP client software for this purpose, while the other computer must run RDP server software. WMI is the Microsoft implementation of Web-Based Enterprise Management (WBEM), which is an industry initiative to develop a standard technology for accessing management information in an enterprise environment.

Also frequently observed is the use of the "sticky keys" trick for maintaining malware-free persistence on a victim network. With the "sticky keys" trick, the attacker modifies the registry on a target's system server using WMI to set a "cmd.exe" as a debugger for tools such as sethc. exe of StickyKeys and osk.exe to allow an on-screen keyboard. To *reset* a forgotten administrator password, there are a well-known, oft-published set of steps to follow after first rebooting from

Windows and accessing the command prompt and then using the drive letter of the partition where Windows is installed and typing a set of simple commands.

Once that is completed, an attacker can remotely use RDP to enter a compromised server, press the StickyKeys or on-screen keyboard hotkeys, and instantly trigger a command prompt running with system-level privileges, without even being required to login to that remote compromised server. Even if passwords are eventually reset across the victim's environment, the attacker still maintains persistent access unless the victim goes through the process of cleaning up all the registry entries on that server and across the victim's entire network.

Types of Common Monitoring Software Employed

Understanding the difficulty in avoiding spear phishing and the associated valid-credential capture 100% of the time, modern enterprises assume that they have already been penetrated and employ a set of monitoring software that looks for the signatures of malware and abnormal activity on their systems. Such abnormality may show as

1. Normal activity occurring at the wrong time of day
2. Normal activity coming from a wrong source
3. Activity occurring abnormally between systems
4. Presence of abnormal activity or abnormal software

Looking for Derusbi Parsing Software

Among these abnormal software items are frequently found one of various forms of Derusbi parsing malware, of which the two most popular are

1. derusbi_server.lua, a parser for Derusbi handshakes
2. derusbi_varient.parser, a parser for Derusbi variant beaconing

The Trojan.Derusbi software avoids detection by using its own proprietary handshakes with pseudorandomly calculated and assigned values, which are dynamically calculated at run-time and then used with the handshake execution. This is hard to detect as abnormal.

1. *Employing security analytic parsers*: We can detect these Trojan handshakes and new emerging variations of them. The parsers generate metadata under the names:
   a. derusbi_handshake
   b. derusbi_varient
2. *Imported security feeds*: Security feeds are also imported into security analytic routines to detect hacker activity. Feeds identify any machines on the network that may be communicating with maliciously placed IP addresses or URLs that have been linked with Shell Crew previously identified domains or IP addresses. *Shell Crew* is the term applied by the security firm RSA to those groups, frequently associated with nation states, that attempt to invade and insert persistently resident malware in the systems of companies they have invaded. The following feeds with generated metadata named are malware:
   a. derusbi_domain_march2015
   b. derusbi_ip_march2015

RSA's ECAT Scanning Software

RSA's Enterprise Compromise Assessment Tool (ECAT) scanning software is an end-point threat detection and response solution that automates the detection of anomalies; identifies programs that have been modified; exposes targeted, advanced malware; and highlights suspicious activity. ECAT is particularly effective at identifying what is classified as "signature-less malware," which does not have the appearance of malware but must be identified by its behavior patterns. Malicious executable software can be identified as RSA's ECAT scans across thousands of machines to identify malicious programs and especially identifies all that are configured to run automatically at startup, which might include, among valid software, malware that is triggered to run at startup. ECAT is an end point threat detection and response solution that exposes targeted, advanced malware, highlights suspicious activity for investigation, and instantly determines the scope of a compromise to help security teams stop advanced threats faster. ECAT's unique behavioral-based detection identifies unknown, zero-day malware and compromises that other tools don't see.

ECAT incorporates an intelligent risk–level scoring system, which prioritizes suspicious endpoint activity while leveraging dynamic data-trained (through automatic machine) learning as it systematically performs its scans and focuses the analyst on real threats in the early stages.

ECAT Steps

1. First, ECAT creates a "normal activity" file of what normal activity in the systems looks like. This includes, but is not limited to, who regularly accesses what files, the time of day and day of the week this occurs, and what activities are undertaken. Then ECAT creates a file of the material that is normally transferred outside the system, including what file, by whom, at what time of day/day of the week, in what form, and to what designated destination.
2. ECAT then looks at all outbound traffic and both the content being sent and its destinations. ECAT detects the creation of a suspicious outbound connection by comparing the source of files being created for transmission with normal traffic and the destinations they will be sent to with traditional destinations. Any differences from the norm are tagged. The time of day and day of the week that such activity occurs are also compared with the times and days of normal activity.
3. ECAT then sends an "alert" message to system security technicians of the creation of a suspicious outbound connection, including the files and the abnormal destinations.
4. Finally, ECAT sends a view of the files being sent over the outbound connection to the system security technicians.

Yara's Operation

Hackers employ tools such as the open software VirusTotal to test whether variations of the Trojan family of code can be detected until they find one that is currently undetected. The hackers continue to make small changes to the Trojan code until they find a variant that is not currently detected by any of the popular antivirus software.

There are two operational approaches when malware is detected: blocking and observational steps.

1. Blocking: The traditional approach is to block all abnormal activity as soon as it is detected. However, this also notifies the attacker that detection has occurred.

2. Observational: An alternative is to let the outbound transmission occur and set up observational software to attempt to observe the pattern of such activity and the path to the destination that the attacker employs to retrieve the stolen files. Tor Anonymity Wrapping can defeat this observational process step.

3. Honey pots: Frequently, the security personnel will then set up an attractive system and files, termed a *honey pot*, where seemingly valid internal information appears, and then watch, wait, and track activity. Results are then shared with the FBI, appropriate security firms, and other industry organizations.

QUESTIONS

1. The goal of a hacker is to become the target technician to observe all the keystrokes. What are the two basic techniques that a hacker uses to do this?
2. What is a scanning software that detects suspicious outbound connection?
3. This server helps give hackers free rein to attack and invade web servers.
4. Using Windows Management Instrumentation (WMI) extensions to the Windows Driver Model to set a cmd.exe, what is a trick a hacker uses and how do they do it?
5. How does the Tor protocol work?
6. Describe the two types of Tor packets that hackers use to attack their target.
7. Tor messages are encapsulated in layers of encryption. This is analogous to a vegetable. What is this process called?

Chapter 3

Anonymous Persistent Threats

A number of security firms have issued detailed reports on groups of attackers who intend not only to "hack" into the website of a company's data systems, but also to establish a persistent beachhead in those systems so that it can use that company's information; connect to other company systems through "trusted," less secure connections; and establish a long-term site where they can test out new versions of their malware and update it when it is discovered to have been detected. Among these identified persistent threat groups are the following.

Rivest–Shamir–Adleman (RSA) Identified Shell Crew

The Shell Crew are a set of hacking groups, frequently closely aligned with nation-states (China and Russia), who have particularly well-educated and extremely highly skilled technicians who continue to experiment and test new versions of malware and break-in approaches and then cross communicate their discoveries with other hacking communities.

Among the most prominent groups identified by RSA that address common adversaries and have targeted common client infrastructure and assets are

- Deep Panda
- WebMasters
- KungFU Kittens
- SportsFans
- Pink Panther
- Equation Group
- Master APT nation-state group

The Shell Crew groups utilize the following tactics and techniques:

- Prevalent use of web shells to maintain low-level persistence despite determined remediation efforts
- Altering or poisoning existing legitimate web pages maintained by an organization

- Occasional use of web application framework exploits to achieve initial entry versus standard spearfishing attacks
- Lateral movement and compromise of digital code signing certificate infrastructure
- Abuse of code signing infrastructure to validly sign custom backdoor malware
- Exploiting systems using different SETHC.exe methods accessible via Remote Desktop Protocol (RDP)
- Long history of Internet Protocol/Domain Name Server (IP/DNS) telemetry, allowing for historical research and link analysis
- Placement of malicious proxy tools introduced into the environment on Windows server–based proxies to bypass proxy logging
- Extensive use of time/date stamping of malicious files to hinder forensic analysis
- Use of malware leveraging compromised credentials to bypass authentication Windows New Technology Local Area Network Manager (NTLM) proxies (proxy aware)

The Shell Crew's initial penetration, subsequent placement of malware, and establishment of a hidden beachhead in a target system follows the pattern detected in the recent 2014–2015 Anthem break-in. Figure 3.1 shows the anatomy of a Shell Crew website application penetration that is believed to have been employed by the attackers.

The tools employed by the Shell Crew hackers—in addition to the initial spear phishing and ScanBox keylogging used to acquire a technician's passwords and a map of the data system and its servers, application systems, and data files—are

1. Implant web shells
2. Modify System.Web.DLL file

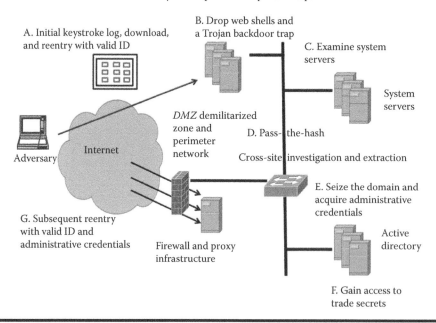

Figure 3.1 Shell Crew web attack process.

3. Insert variations of Trojan.Derusbi malware routines
4. Insert "Sticky Keys" backdoor routines—particularly Seth RDP backdoor routines
5. Insert modified handshake packets (for authentication steps)
6. Modify registry files and insert RDP backdoor routines
7. Insert malicious files
8. Insert an initial Trojan.Derusbi and then try out new variations
9. Insert NotePad—malicious command lines and file details
10. Insert credential loggers
    a. Hash dumping routines
    b. Keystroke-logging routines (SmartBox)
    c. MSGINA, a corruption of msgina.dll—a module loaded by Winlogon to implement the authentication policy. The file performs all user identification and authentication interactions.
    d. Hooking authentication function

Kaspersky Lab Has Identified a Recent Attack Group That Identifies Its Tools as Careto: The Mask

The Mask is an advanced threat actor that has been involved in cyberespionage operations since at least 2007. What makes The Mask special is the complexity of the toolset used by the attackers. This includes an extremely sophisticated piece of malware, a rootkit, a bootkit, Mac OS X and Linux versions, and possibly versions for Android and iPad/iPhone (iOS).

The Mask also uses a customized attack against older Kaspersky Lab products in order to successfully hide in the system. This puts it above Duqu in terms of sophistication, making The Mask one of the most advanced threats at the current time. This and several other factors lead us to believe that this could be a state-sponsored operation.

The initial attack begins with spear-phishing. A technician receives a valid-appearing email which, when opened, connects him to an infected website. That infected website surreptitiously downloads a keystroke-logging program to his device and may also download national news information or even a YouTube video in order to hide that malicious download. Some known exploit websites are "linkconf.net," "redirserver.net," and "swupdt.com." Furthermore, valid certificates are frequently employed from real or fake companies–quite frequently from TecSystem of Bulgaria, which appears to be a real company with real certificates, but which have been stolen and misused by hackers.

Careto is the official name of the hacking group also known as The Mask, which is a translation from the Spanish (mask = "ugly mug"). More generally, it is a type of icon in the shape of a face that shows emotions and expressions like a human face.

The main targets of Careto fall into the following categories:

■ Government institutions
■ Diplomatic offices and embassies
■ Energy, oil, and gas companies
■ Research institutions
■ Private equity firms
■ Activists

Backdoor components of Careto:

■ Windows backdoor components rootkit and bootkit for 32- and 64-bit versions
  – Two CAB files: shrink32.dll and shrink64.dll
  – Three executable files packed along with CAB files
    • dinner.jpg
    • waiter.jpg
    • chef.jpg
■ Max OS X: rootkit and bootkit
■ Linux: rootkit and bootkit
■ IPad: rootkit and bootkit

Mask implants:

■ Intercept network traffic
■ Capture keystrokes
■ Analyze Wi-Fi traffic
■ Capture PGP keys
■ Screen capture
■ Monitor all file operations
■ Fetch info from Nokia and other cell devices

Dark Web

A program named "Recorded Future" scrapes everything posted on Pastebin and other "paste" websites—the sites on the dark web where plaintext can be posted anonymously. Pastebin is a popular example of such a place to find torrents and hacking data dumps, and, in December 2014, it was the site where links to the leaked files from the Sony hack ended up. It's also a fantastic place to find links to other dark web sites. The company also monitors Twitter and forums all around the normal Internet for links to the dark web.

QUESTIONS
1. What are three techniques that the Shell Crew uses for hacking?
2. Explain: What is "The Mask"?
3. How is The Mask different from any other advance persistent attack?
4. What are three main targets of The Mask?

Chapter 4

Creating Secure Code

First Principle of Code Protection: Code Isolation and Confinement

In today's Internet-driven world, we often find ourselves running untrusted code on our devices. This code is contained in programs, applications, extensions, plug-ins, and codecs for media players, which we have become accustomed to naively trusting and downloading. However, malware creators take advantage of unknowing users who download or use infected code. Such infected code can be directed toward a variety of devices including our computers, tablets, and smartphones. Hackers may hide their malware code in any component where they see an opportunity to catch unaware users. Specialized codecs for media are examples of components that are frequently used to conceal code. Other examples include pdf viewers and frequently used applications such as Microsoft Outlook. Legacy routines such as UNIX's Sendmail, which was exposed in the famous book *Under the Cuckoo's Nest*, have continually been targeted by hackers for decades. Furthermore, honeypots, which are advertised Internet websites from which users frequently retrieve what appear to be useful applications or information, can contain hidden malware that downloads along with the intended software.

As a standard process, when users recognize that an application may be running untrusted code, they should immediately kill that application. Users should also run virus scanners to check for and delete any infected files and malware on a regular basis.

In an ideal situation, modules and applications running on the same operating system (OS) should be built to function separately from each other in order to preserve their integrity and to protect the system's software. This principle is that, if system applications are run together, any security threat that affects one part of the system can easily spread and affect all the other applications and system areas as they operate in that shared area of the computer. However, the more they are separated, the more difficult it becomes for untrusted code and malware to cause extensive damage. Hence, the principle of confinement—the process of separating applications from each other and from systems components—ensures that misbehaving applications are not able to harm the rest of the applications and systems software of the overall system.

Code Isolation Techniques

Code isolation and confinement techniques are employed as a means to limit potential cross infection of code, force any damage to stay within an isolated area, and to protect against cross-area contamination. And within the isolation area, medialization and isolation methods are employed to minimize the spread between modules within the enclosed isolation unit. These isolation techniques make it more difficult for malware to spread or transmit their effects between modules in an isolation unit by limiting their interaction and information exchange and then completely blocking any spread across the chasm to separate isolation confinement areas to infect the isolated "good-code" protected modules.

There are four commonly employed confinement approaches designed to mitigate the effects of untrusted code and possible malware upon our isolated and protected production code. Among these are:

1. *Physical confinement*: The most primitive of these confinement methods is physical separation. The idea of this process is to design hardware that is only partially integrated. In essence, there should be physical air space between one piece of equipment and another. The same would apply for the separation of networks, if possible, with physical space between them. Physical confinement methods provide some definite advantages. If one device is attacked, other devices or networks that are separated physically will remain unharmed. However, this confinement method has some key drawbacks. It is difficult to operate a data center when all its components are physically isolated from one another. The user terminals and PCs that access the computer systems can be physically isolated from those systems, but many of the applications and routines that run on the system need to interact with each other, making it nearly impossible to preserve this physical isolation. Physical confinement is illustrated in Figure 4.1.

2. *Virtual confinement*: The second approach involves the creation of "virtual" machines as a method of confinement. This is typically employed in data centers where one computer will run many different applications. Under virtual-machine approaches, the confinement occurs within each device as applications are isolated to specific OSs and then multiple OSs are hosted on one computer, each OS running its own set of applications. For example, application A runs on Windows 10 while application B runs on Linux, with both OSs running on the same device. These OSs do not communicate with each other in any manner. This confinement method safeguards those applications running over one OS from those running over another. Furthermore, it safeguards one OS itself from anything affecting

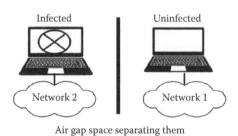

Figure 4.1   Separating machines by physically placing them on separate networks.

the other. However, the drawback is that such an arrangement is difficult to manage. An example of virtual confinement is shown in Figure 4.2.

3. *Operating system confinement*: As a third method of program code confinement, restrictions are imposed on OSs themselves by affecting the process by which these OSs may talk to each other. An intermediary system is employed to facilitate communication between the two different OSs as a means to enforce confinement while enabling communication. The intermediary OS performs the task of first locating the two communicating OSs and then using a standard system call to communicate information from one OS to the other. Based on the criteria identified by a set of parameters within the system call, the intermediary device can be used to isolate infected or untrusted code located in the originating OS by choosing not to enable communication between OSs if any of the parameters appear suspicious.

4. *The isolation of threads*: A fourth method of confinement is to isolate threads of code. Within the same address space, one address thread should be made to run in parallel to another providing software fault isolation (SFI). As the threads are isolated from each other, they don't share the information they carry from one specific source. Instead, they treat their operation on that information as separate and independent, even though it may originate from the same source, and the separated threads don't exchange their independently computed results.

Returning to the analysis of system calls, the Open Systems Interconnection (OSI) seven-layer model exemplifies the use of this process. The seven-layer model's encapsulation process, under which each successive layer adds a header to the previous encapsulation packet or frame, utilizes a system of such system calls. The software at each layer communicates in an addressed data packet to the next layer by calling the OS and requesting that the OS pass that addressed packet on to the next layer's software. It is important to point out that the applications and the software implementing each layer of the model (e.g., Transmission Control Protocol [TCP] at level 4, Internet Protocol [IP] at level 3, and Ethernet at level 2) don't know where in the computer each successive layer is located. Only the OS knows, and the OS is in charge of maintaining and using this location information. Therefore, system calls to the OS are used to relay information between each layer of the model. System calls occur as each layer of the seven-layer model needs to pass information to the next layer (e.g., TCP to Ethernet). This system call process, carried out by passing location information through and by means of the OS, is a means of facilitating confinement and protection.

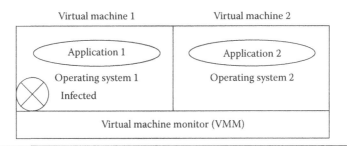

Figure 4.2 Applications in separate partitions of one computer, each with their own OS.

Implementation of the Four Code-Confinement Methods

The emerging and more popular approach for code-confinement implementation is to employ a reference monitor. However, there are also specific monitoring and code jailing (isolation) routines and methods that are remnant components of specific older OSs.

Reference Monitors

The primary key to implementing confinement techniques is increasingly to employ a reference monitor. A reference monitor is a separate program that observes the chosen and implemented isolation method and regularly checks to ensure that that chosen technique is properly functioning in its mission of isolating modules of code from each other and results in isolating malware from good code. In one possible implementation, a reference monitor might be placed between a program and an OS so that it can track the data flow between these areas. Reference monitors are small with little overhead. But in order for them to be effective and efficient, they need to be updated regularly so that they are able to detect the latest security threats. On the other hand, hackers can't easily install Trojans and backdoors that can kill or damage these reference monitors.

OS Chroots

There are certain kinds of routines provided with OSs. Many OSs were built on the design of the original UNIX OS. In doing so, designers adopted a lot of the same operations and processes used to separate areas in the original UNIX OS and incorporated them in modern OSs. An operation in an OS can change the root directory so that, once modified, it can be used to create restrictions in the environment. One such operation is called a *Chroot*, which is an operation that changes what appears as the root directory for current running processes and their children. A running process appears to be running from a certain directory, but it can be modified so that it looks like it's coming from an entirely different area. In essence, Chroots allow users to create modified environments known as Chroot "jails"; a program that is run inside this area cannot access files outside of the designated environment—they are locked into a narrow jail operating area. The programs are allowed to run inside this restricted environment, but their interaction with applications and facilities outside the jail area is limited. Chroot operations are typically used for guest accounts or FTP (file transport) sites. However, it's important to remember that simple Chroot jails do not limit network access, which is a source of infection.

OS Jail Routines

Another routine is called a Jailkit. Jailkits are utility programs that are used in UNIX environments. Any kind of program that users want to run is placed inside a Jailkit environment, which restricts their network access and interaction with other programs and applications on the protected device. This environment is more restricted than a simple Chroot jail. It particularly affects Java and C++ object-based programs since such programs are frequently used to trigger routines in other areas of the targeted device or other networks.

There are ways in which untrusted code or malware can escape from jail. Essentially, this may occur when attacking programs open a temporary guest account and are then allowed to run as "guests." However, jails should only be executed by a root routine.

There are multiple ways to escape jail from a root routine:

■ Create a device that permits rogue programs or code to access raw data on a disk
■ Send signals but not IP packets to a non-Chroot process, requesting an action
■ Allow systems to trigger a reboot of the system but prevent running of additional programs or code
■ Bind a Chroot process to specific ports or sockets depending on their purpose and goal

FreeBSD Jail

Another type of operation and confinement area is the FreeBSD jail. It is stronger than a traditional Chroot jail and its purpose is to confine stronger mechanisms than those handled by Chroot by binding sockets with specified IP addresses and authorized ports. It allows applications to communicate with other processes and programs located inside the jail. When a FreeBSD jail is being used, the root is limited so that it cannot load kernel modules, which are the core module used by the OS and its supported applications to communicate with the computer hardware. Only the kernel module talks to the hardware. For other modules to communicate with the hardware, they must communicate through the OS's kernel module. Thus, the kernel is a subroutine of the OS that enables programs hosted by an OS to talk to the hardware and for the hardware to talk to the OS and its supported applications.

One of the problems with the UNIX jail approach is that only specific types of programs can run effectively in jail-restricted environments. For example, web servers can run in jail, and audio, video, and media routines can also be jailed and run effectively. However, programs and applications that we use often and continuously, such as web browsers and mail clients, do not run effectively in jail environments. This is a serious drawback given how frequently we all search the web and send and receive e-mail messages.

Both Chroot and jail routines as well as service calls to the OS have disadvantages, the biggest of which for Chroot and jail routines is that these operations tend to have coarse inflexible policies. They operate on the basis of an "all or nothing" access policy and thus are not suitable for applications that are routinely used by the general user, particularly for web browsing. Furthermore, unless a specialized procedure is used, Chroot and jails are not good at preventing malicious applications from accessing the network or communicating with other machines, and they don't prevent malware or untrusted code from trying to crash the host OS. The common employment of system calls to communicate through the OS as well as to invoke OS routine has been a standard for decades, but this method also has flaws. Service-call routines also need to have developed their own special protection processes to prevent possible damage from malware that addresses them specifically. Furthermore, every system call must be included in the monitoring process, which requires large amounts of processing resources due to the frequency with which these processes are invoked; and every suspicious call that is discovered needs to be tracked, blocked, and unauthorized. Unfortunately, every solution to one problem brings its own disadvantages, which require their own solutions.

Linux's Ptrace Monitor and Systrace Routines

For the Linux OS, Ptrace is a commonly used routine. With UNIX and Linux (which is derived from UNIX), Ptrace acts as a monitor to intercept calls and verify the calls' authenticity and safety. If a particular program fails to pass the monitor parameters, Ptrace attempts to destroy the message's source while maintaining as protected all states, system directories, and user IDs.

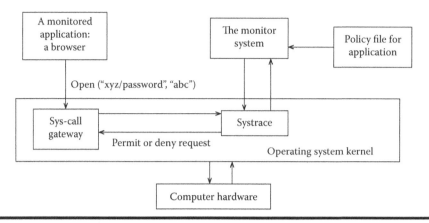

Figure 4.3   Monitor system reviewing all browser requests.

Monitors such as Ptrace are thus continuously deciding if code is safe, employing policies concerning this monitoring routine that must be stringent and inflexible.

Another computer security utility, Systrace, limits each application's access through a set of system-call policies. Systrace runs on Mac OS X, Linux, and most UNIX-like systems. In particular, Systrace supports 64-bit Linux versions. Systrace concentrates on situations wherein an application wants to open a call to the OS. Systrace monitors intercept these calls, apply the corresponding policy, and then proceed to allow or block the request. Similarly to Ptrace, Systrace follows an "all or nothing" standard. Only monitored system calls ever go to the OS for execution in the implementation of this isolation technique. If the call is not monitored, it does not get processed. Figure 4.3 illustrates the Systrace process sequence.

Employing Applications Such as Ostia or NACI

A more modern monitoring approach involves using applications such as Ostia, which use a delegation architecture. Under Ostia monitoring, a program might submit an "open call" rather than a standard systems call to the OS. Ostia would disallow that call and the associated transmission and would terminate the calling application. To support its monitoring mission, Ostia employs a policy file that details all appropriate activity and blocks and then terminates whatever is not allowed in the policy file. Unfortunately, defining and outlining the set of correct policies is a difficult process, and the allowed activity may change over time as new situations, new programs, and new updates to the OS are installed.

National Agency Check Inquiries (NACI) is another modern monitoring system. It is the minimum level of investigation required of federal employees as a condition of employment with the federal government. NACI also restricts a program's ability to perform system calls based on a precise allowance policy file system. It typically does so in Intel x86 devices, which compose the large array of servers deployed in modern cloud data centers.

Isolation of Virtual Machines

Modern cloud computing starts the process of virtualizing each computer, network, and data storage in the data center and even the desktops that access the systems in that center. With

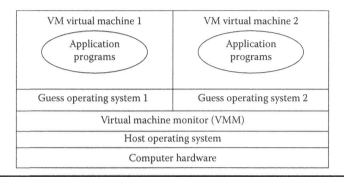

Figure 4.4   Virtual machine separation and isolation architecture.

virtualized computing, thousands of large-server PCs (usually with x86 processors) perform the processing functions for the systems in a distributed fashion spread over an array of such processors. In these virtualized environments, the design begins with an underlying OS (called a *hypervisor*) as the core enabler and a set of guest OSs running on top of the hypervisor, each running their own set of application programs and isolated from each other. These guest OSs tend to be Linux, Mac OS X, or MS Windows.

Computer Virtualization

The virtualization of a computer is a process whereby multiple OSs can run simultaneously as guest OSs on top of an overall computer OS—the hypervisor, also termed the *virtual machine monitor* (VMM). Each guest OS (virtual OS) can then support a specific set of applications in isolation from other guest (virtual) OSs, each with their own applications. Each virtual/guest OS and its applications operate independently from each other, and their programs are isolated and protected from another virtual/guest OS's applications. It is the hypervisor's job to enable each guest OS and its applications; to allow them to pass information to the computer hardware, if appropriate; and to block intercommunication between guest operating systems unless strict policy rules are met. Figure 4.4 illustrates the concept of virtual machine isolation.

Keep in mind that there may be up to 1000 x86-based computers in a data center, and these isolation techniques are meant to ensure that infections can't spread from one OS and its applications to another across one and then 1000 machines. VMMs (hypervisors), accompanied by other OS routines (Chroots, jails, etc.) protect the crossing point between OSs, both local and across the complete center. The hypervisor, acting as the overall computer OS and VMM, isolates each guest OS from each other, continuously observes all possible attempted cross interactions, and only allows those that meet its preestablished policy restrictions.

Threats to Computer Virtualization

As with any isolation method, there are specific elements to be aware of. Covert (hidden) channels represent a threat to the isolation of two guest OSs by enabling unintended communication between these OSs and their components. Advances in technology have enabled monitors to catch and prohibit or deny guest OSs to use covert channels for cross-OS communication. However, other systems such as antivirus programs may be affected by covert channels. Given that antivirus systems have to be protected so that they can detect malware and untrusted code, it becomes important that they be able to detect activity at the root kernel, which is the part of the OS that talks to the hardware. Ensuring that the intrusion detection system (IDS) runs as part of the VMM/hypervisor is critical. This enables the monitor to detect untrusted code and malware as it attempts to communicate to the hardware (and in particular to the network) and to other applications under other guest OSs. Running the IDS with the VMM is the first step of a security process. The IDS operates as a virus signal detector that looks for certain kinds of suspect code and malware, which it identifies by their behavior patterns. The second security step requires the VMM to compute a hash or user app code and then to compare the potential threat's hash code with the IDS's generated hash. If the potential threat doesn't match and is thus unknown, the VMM proceeds to kill the suspect program. A third security step involves ensuring the integrity of the guest OS's kernel through trial system calls. Once again, discrepancies between the system call issued and the stored data will cause the VMM to take action against the presumed threat. Finally, a virus signature detector may be deployed to run a basic virus signature detector scan on each of the guest OSs and their hosted application programs.

Subverting VM Isolation

The standard name given to VMMs is the *hypervisor*, which operates not only as an over-system monitor of activity but as an overall OS supporting a set of guest OSs. When policy restrictions allow, the hypervisor enables communications between OSs and between guest OSs and hardware, while monitoring all such activity. Subversion of the hypervisor is a dangerous problem. If a virus can gain access to and invade the hypervisor, this threat can affect not only a particular computer but potentially all the computers in the data center and all users connected to that data center. And such malware can hide in the hypervisor and trigger damage immediately or be triggered to cause considerable damage at a later date.

VM-Based Malware

VM-based malware is malware that specifically targets hypervisors. Because of the vulnerability of the complete processing center to such malware, newer malware tends to be constructed to try new methods of penetrating a hypervisor's defenses. The nature of this problem is one of constant change and creation. New threats and viruses are being created and distributed so frequently that Microsoft delivers a security bulletin detailing new emerging threats on a monthly basis. New virus-detector components in antivirus software play an important role in detecting the new mutations of viruses that are specifically targeting and attacking hypervisors and other protection and security tools.

Software Fault Isolation

Many types of software exist that can easily be corrupted and thus pose a security threat, and these are particularly a problem due to their vast deployment and usage. Among these are codecs; these support and enable specific media players, which need and will have a specific codec to execute the media files. Device drivers, such as USB connectors and other external devices that are plugged into computers, can also easily be corrupted. Additionally, automated downloads create risk as they trigger actions on devices automatically. Other types of threats include common but unsafe

Code segment 1	Data segment 1	Code segment 2	Data segment 2	- - - - - - - - - -
Application 1		Application 2		Application n

Figure 4.5 Sections of application code and the data each uses in its execution process.

instructions. Java JMP instructions, load instructions, and cross domain calls are all particularly risky as they represent a particular target for concealed threats.

Given this volatile computing environment, it is extremely important to isolate software through the SFI process. This involves carrying out segment matching by running special routines to recognize secure segments of code. Insurance routines and variable address sandboxing techniques are used in combination with segment matching to ensure proper isolation. However, complete isolation is inappropriate for data processing, and there are other existing vulnerabilities to this technique. For example, shared memory issues represent a threat between two attempted memory-sharing programs, which should be prohibited from sharing common virtual memory. Performance monitoring routines, where detected 4% slowdowns might be an indicator that an extra set of code is operating on the machine, can provide hints to the existence and execution of untrusted code. However, SFI routines have their own limitations, many of which extend to the x86 Intel-based machine implementation that populates our cloud data center computer environments.

Figure 4.5 shows how the SFI process partitions memory into segments.

QUESTIONS
1. Explain why one performs the code isolation technique.
2. What are four confinement methods?
3. Out of the four methods, which one is most important and why?
4. Describe three OS routines and explain what they all have in common.
5. Are there any disadvantages?

Chapter 5

Providing a Secure Architecture

Hacking and the deployment of an appropriate security architecture are at the forefront of every company's attention. As many companies are experiencing their systems being hacked, security architectures can be put in place to minimize the severity of such attacks. The process begins with attempting to think like a hacker. This approach helps companies find vulnerabilities that they were not aware of and may not even have been able to envision.

Providing a Secure Architecture

There are four primary topics of secure architectures:

1. Isolation and least privilege
2. Access control concepts
3. Operating systems isolation
4. Browser isolation and least privilege

Within these topics, there are three main principles that help ensure a secure design:

1. Compartmentalization and isolation of data
2. Defense in depth by utilizing more than one security mechanism
3. Keeping the design simple yet effective

Isolation and Least Privilege

Privilege is an ability to access or modify a resource and to separate and limit the interaction between modules. Least privilege is the concept that a system module should only have the minimal privileges needed for its intended purposes and the entities it deals with, including people, processes, and devices. People should be assigned the fewest privileges consistent with their assigned

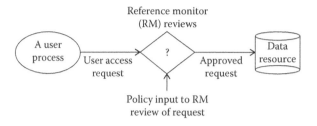

Figure 5.1   Reference monitor review of user data requests.

		File 1	File 2	File 3	File n
			Accessible files		
	User 1	Read	Write		Write
Users	User 2	Write	Write	Write	Write
	User 3				
	User 4	Read	Write	Read	Write
	User n				

Figure 5.2   Permissions to read or write to/from specific files.

duties and functions. For example, designing a restrictive "need-to-know" approach indicates zero access by default and then provides security privileges as required.

An example of these is the *principle of least privilege*. This means that systems should only have the minimal amount of privileges required to complete the designated tasks. Granting too much system access to a miniscule task could be catastrophic if that task and eventually the entire system were compromised. For example, Sendmail was a utility within UNIX that had notorious vulnerabilities that could grant a hacker access to critical information by overflowing system buffers and then executing hacker software to compromise the entire system.

Access control is another key concept of secure system architecture. To access the system, a user must pass through a reference monitor before the user is granted access to secure files. This process is depicted in Figure 5.1.

However, this is not the only access control that is implemented within a secure architecture. Each resource that can be accessed can also have access controls associated with them, including read, write, and execute privileges, each depending on the level of access that is granted to a specific user. An example of this is illustrated in Figure 5.2.

Access Control Concepts

Access control is an approach to restricting system access only to authorized users. The system knows who the user is, and their identity is authenticated by name, password, or further identification credentials. Any user's access request or process is passed through a reference monitor acting as a gatekeeper and must be validated before the user or the process is granted access. There are two types of implementation concepts to accomplish this task—access control lists (ACLs) and access capabilities. ACLs associate a list with each object and the reference monitor checks the user/group against the list after the user or process has first been authenticated. First, authentication must occur, and then access to certain files and systems must be separately granted through matching by means of the ACLs, which identify which of the many researches a particular user or process is allowed access to. Capabilities do not require reauthentication but rather are assigned by means of an unforgettable ticket, managed by either a random bit sequence on a ticket or by the operating system maintaining a ticket file.

In addition, role-based access control (RBAC) can be utilized for access control by assigning permissions to a set of users or groups to enable or restrict those users to perform specific roles or be assigned to specific resources. For example, roles can consist of individuals assigned to engineering, marketing, or projects and can be assigned to access specific resources such as servers 1, 2, 3, or a combination thereof.

Operating Systems

Operating systems also have the ability to provide security and control access by managing computer hardware and software resources. The operating system can assign permissions or access rights to specific users and groups of users by controlling the ability of those users to view or make changes to the contents of specific files and file systems.

UNIX access control systems have at least one user with the right to access (a granted privilege) any file of the system that is available to the root user and has the assigned special "root" ID, allowing one to bypass access control restrictions. In the UNIX file access control list, each file has an owner who has read, write, and execute permissions assigned by the root owner. Only this root owner can change permissions for the file. This is a flexible system and provides some protection for most users, but it can be too tempting to rely only on root privileges for security since there is no way to gain a root privilege without all root privileges being granted. Weaknesses with UNIX isolation and privileges can exist in the following:

- *Network-facing daemons*: These can expose root processes with network ports open to all remote parties.
- *Rootkits*: These allow system extension via dynamically loaded kernel modules.
- *Environment variables*: LIBPATH is a system variable on UNIX computer operating systems that is used in the runtime linking process, where it influences the search order for shared libraries at alternate locations. It is considered an environment variable similar to the variable LD LIBRARY PATH on IBM's AIX UNIX Operating Systems.
- *Shared resources*: Since any process can create files in/tmp directory, an untrusted process may create files that are used by arbitrary system processes.
- *Time-of-check-to-time-of-use (TOCTTOU)*: Typically, a root process uses a system call to determine if the initiating user has permission to access a particular file, for example, /tmp/X. After access is authorized and before the file is opened, the user may change the file/tmp/X to a symbolic link to a target file/etc/shadow.

Microsoft Windows access control is generally more flexible than UNIX and incorporates the additional concepts of tokens and security attributes. Windows uses security ID (SID) to replace user ID (UID) for users, groups, computers, domains, and domain members. Windows also uses tokens to verify security context, privileges, accounts, and groups, as well as a security reference monitor to examine the identity security context of a process or thread and to look for a user attempting to temporarily adopt the security context of a real, normally authorized user. Weaknesses with Windows isolation and privileges can exist in the following:

- Rootkits leveraging dynamically loaded kernel modules
- Windows registry: Global hierarchical database to store data for all programs
- Enabled by default: Full permissions and functionality enabled

Browser Isolation and Least Privilege

The web browser enforces its own internal policy. If the browser implementation is corrupted, this mechanism becomes unreliable, and websites are designed to rely on existing browser security policies. Browser design decisions require compatibility with many types of system. A browser is only as useful as the sites it can render, which make it difficult to enforce "clean slate" design approaches. In a browser with process isolation, the isolated processes may still be allowed limited but controlled interaction between processes. However, this is meant to occur only if the processes mutually accept collaboration over the shared, interprocess communication (IPC) channels such as shared memory local sockets or Internet sockets. With this scheme, most of the process's memory is isolated from other processes, except the variables/memory, where the process is allowing input from the collaborating processes.

Hacking Attacks

Another key aspect of security is obviously preventing hijacking attacks. There are three main approaches to deal with hijacking: first, detecting and fixing known bugs in applications and system software as soon as they are made available; then, where buffer overflows occur and some are legitimate, conceding the overflows but preventing associated code execution; and last, adding specific run-time code to detect overflow exploits that might occur.

Key to developing a secure architecture is having the ability to think like a hacker. To think like a hacker, it is important to understand the full spectrum of cyber criminals. There are state-sponsored cyber criminals (like the Chinese Deep Panda and Russian groups), political extremist cyber criminals (the hacker group Anonymous), cyber-criminal organizations (the Mexican mafia), criminal gangs that use stolen information such as those in South Florida and the Bahamas, and rogue cyber criminals (a "script kiddie"). By understanding the spectrum of the hacking community, organizations can better understand and anticipate the severity of a threat and attribute unwanted activity to one of these classifications based on the nature and severity of the threat.

There are a number of ways that a hacker can go about entering an unauthorized system. Exploratory research of the network must first be done so that the hacker can gain detailed information on the company they will be penetrating and its people. While this is the most important aspect of security, it is a key step that most organizations gloss over when it comes to cyber security. Companies provide technical barriers to entry into their computer environment but ignore their most vulnerable component—protecting passwords and access credentials. Stealing passwords and other access credentials are the most common means for hackers to gain access to into systems. The most common method, as described in the discussion in Chapter 2 on the Anthem break-in, are spear phishing, honeypots, and the downloading of keylogging routines to discover passwords and two-factor identification information and then to discover the complete layout of the company's information environment.

There are then a number of technical ways that hackers can crack a user's encrypted password, once acquired. Hackers currently use graphics processing units (GPUs) to calculate various character combinations in order to brute force the eventual cracking of a user's password and allow a complete download of a company's password file. GPUs are used in this situation due to their high rate of calculation speed when running a password-cracking algorithm.

Overall, designing secure systems must be at the forefront of a system administrator's mind. However, it also helps to think of how vulnerabilities within code can be patched by simply thinking like a hacker. Recognizing that passwords are still the biggest way that hackers gain access to systems allows system administrators to implement better password policies for their companies and to train all employees to be aware of the techniques that hackers use to trick employees into giving up their passwords and ID information.

In order to defend against hackers and potential attacks, it is important to first understand the process that hackers use when sizing up potential targets. There follows a brief summary of the steps taken by hackers before, during, and after an attack:

1. Perform reconnaissance
2. Identify appropriate targets with particularly useful passwords—systems technicians
3. Attract the victim using spear phishing, honeypots, and watering holes
4. Gain control
5. Exfiltrate data and conscript
6. Incorporate persistent presence enabling software with the target company's systems
7. Hide all evidence of the entry
8. Continue to use the company's systems as a testbed for new versions of the malware and entirely new malware
9. Use one company's resources to invade and commandeer interconnected companies
10. Get out and hide

Antivirus software can help save users between some of the later stages. It is not a save all, though, since antivirus software can only detect what it understands. Exploits such as Zero Day have been generally undetectable as a result of their having been entered by a trusted employee and embedded in critical command and control (C&C) systems by a trusted source. It is difficult to deter attacks that do not appear on attack radars in the first place. If it's not what you are looking for, it is just harder to discover and eliminate.

Spear Phishing and Behavioral Attacks

Spear phishing plays on the trust, behavior, and perception of targeted users. The most common attacking method is through e-mail. The metaphor of phishing is about luring a broad range of users into completing a specific action. This differs from spear phishing, which is targeted at a specific individual or a select group of individuals. Spear phishing behaves more like an intelligent spam and can defeat even the most advanced and skeptical of users. This method becomes most effective when the credibility of the situation is accurate and it is mixed with a technical wrapping, such as spoofing the e-mail domain of a trusted source and asking for a response to a common request—such as a request to open a form and fill in your annual goals, which you then forward to your supervisor. It happens all the time correctly and can happen once with a hacker.

Spoofing, Digital Misrepresentation, and Mobile Security

Many individuals have a false perception that since their mobile devices are simple to use, they are not subject to same dangerous situations that plague standard computing devices. What plagues smartphones and other mobile devices is that they are almost always transmitting information, and they are frequently and consistently connected. In 2012, over 1.6 million Americans had information taken from them through the use of their smartphone. Some companies have created remote wipe features as a method to prevent data from being used once it has been maliciously stolen.

QUESTIONS

1. List the four main topics of secure architectures.
2. How do you prevent hijacking attacks?
3. What is the most popular way for hackers to get into systems?
4. What are the key elements to providing a secure architecture?

Chapter 6

The Hacker Strategy: Expanded

Third-party software is the most vulnerable component in a system. For example, the iPhones released by Apple might have been fully penetration tested and checked out, but a single app installed after the user has access could circumvent the barriers set up by the manufacturer (Figure 6.1).

It is incorrect to describe "third parties" as simply additional apps that have been installed. Additional third parties could be an application programming interface (API) that was installed for a specific feature in an operating system (OS). Most of the time, this third party may not be in use and is merely lying dormant, waiting to accept input from a local app or from remote users. In many cases, attacks will start at a very simple low level, but the pinhole of vulnerability can then be continuously widened to allow more advanced and structured code to enter.

Lab Analysis and Learning Vulnerabilities

A short period of "binary analysis" will help individuals understand what healthy code looks like. In one week, an individual will be exposed to at least one new vulnerability, and in one month, he or she will have found a unique vulnerability that no one else has yet discovered. While automated tools exist to discover dangerous patterns in code, they often are subjected to false positives. Automated tools are still limited in their ability to truly understand the overall security goals that humans are best at interpreting.

Hacker Strategies

It is important for security personnel to attempt to think like a hacker in order to effectively find ways to offset the various approaches that hackers employ. Wherever possible, hackers start by manipulating people in order to gain unauthorized access, and they can then progress to entering target processes and inserting malicious code at strategic locations in order to achieve their set of goals. Increasingly, the goal of modern hackers, and especially those linked to nation-states, is

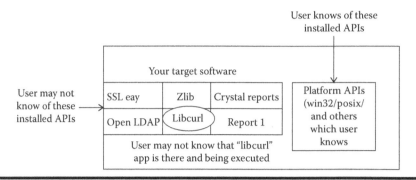

Figure 6.1 Third-party software—known installed apps and possibly unknown ones.

to establish a long-term persistent presence in a target's computer system. And only once this is accomplished do they proceed to extract information or take destructive action, either immediately or in a time-delayed fashion, within the target system.

There are several global locations where cyber adversaries are based and from which they can carry out their malicious deeds in such a way that they are undetectable. More recent and potentially more dangerous are those associated with or closely aligned with nation-states, such as those in China and Russia. Threats emanating from these state-sponsored cyber operations consist of cyber-warfare espionage, ideological and political extremism, profit-motivated criminal activities, or supplying other criminal organizations that are geared to use acquired data, particularly ID information, for criminal gain and influence. Recent usage by local criminal gangs in the United States has varied from credit card fraud and false Internal Revenue Service (IRS) filings to large-scale bank fraud. But such stolen information can filter down to street-level criminals or to individual hackers who use that stolen information for personal gain, vengeance, or simply to achieve some level of fame within the hacking community.

The steps a hacker takes to become successful begin with surveillance. Remote hackers need to carry out surveillance of the people, communication systems, organization charts, buildings, and the data process structure of a company in order to penetrate their target. The first action a hacker will take is to identify which targets suit their purposes. The target may be a company such as Anthem, JP Morgan Chase, Sony, or any other large American company. Alternatively, the hackers may target a third-party software vendor, many of which are particularly attractive to hackers since they then provide a vehicle to ride on into unsuspecting target sides. There are many behind-the-scenes applications that typical users may not even know are running and present an open opportunity to hackers. Once a vulnerable target is identified, the hacking process can begin.

Reconnaissance

Successful hackers are diligent and persistent researchers. They will first study potential targets in a non-intrusive way, collecting information from social media and websites and other available information to understand the behaviors and resources that a target will use. Common information sources and tools that hackers use to gather information are the target's corporate website, getting telephone contact and organization information from the website or from organizational telephone books. The hacker then might employ simple social engineering to gather information from target company employees or from the target's suppliers or customers. They will then examine the Facebook and LinkedIn pages of specific individuals, looking for information that they can use. As a result, hackers will create custom client protocol libraries, conduct manual security analysis, and begin looking for opportunities to gain authentication, utilize overflow techniques, and place backdoor traps and Trojan.Derusbi-like malware.

Attracting the Victim

An approach that hackers will utilize to attract their targets is to single them out based on their personal behaviors that the hackers have researched. As previously mentioned, spear-phishing e-mails are commonly used in efforts to trick the target into giving information. By tricking the victim into clicking on a link in an e-mail, this technique leads the victim to unintentionally download software, which is then used by the hacker to acquire the target's personal identification information and thus enabling the attacker to immediately gain authorized access to and interact with the victim's systems within minutes.

Another attack approach initiated by hackers is the use of watering holes. Hackers create an attractive website catering to the target's particular patterns of Internet access and behaviors. The hackers then wait for the victim to access the website and come to them. Hackers will infect a specific attractively identified component with an associated download and wait for the target to download the infected files; this allows the hacker to gain the information required to enter the target company's information systems as an "authorized" user—frequently a systems technician who has widespread access to the company's systems, software, OSs, and database management systems.

Gain Control

The strategy of the hacker is to get control of an initial victim so that they can acquire credentials, understand the layout of the complete data-processing environment, gain access into a specific system, install custom-made malicious software, gain administrator credentials to go deeper into a network, establish one or more backdoors, and communicate with and eventually infiltrate an overall command and control (C&C) server. The more current the updates and fixes to all the company's computer systems, the more difficult it is for the hackers to penetrate them once inside the target's data-processing networks. This is a good reason to keep your computers and programs current and backed up.

Exfiltrate Data and Conscript

Hackers withdraw intellectual property and/or your credentials from the C&C servers. They can draft your computer for later use in additional attacks such as a distributed denial of service (DDoS) in an attempt to make a machine or network resource unavailable to its intended users. The theft of intellectual property in the United States alone is measured in terabytes of data a year.

Overall: Cloak the Source

Universities are often a source that hackers will regularly penetrate to cloak their source and will route major attacks through them. Employees are prime targets for hackers to research and gain access into universities. Universities tend to be decentralized and are porous, creating perfect proxies.

Antivirus Protection

Antivirus protection is something that you need to have to detect attacks early on; however, antivirus programs tend only to be speed bumps to a determined hacker. Hackers can also use zero-day attacks, which are attacks that exploit a previously unknown vulnerability in a computer application and which no antivirus can detect.

Crack Passwords

Hackers can attempt to penetrate companies by stealing and obtaining corporate passwords. With passwords obtained, hackers can gain access to the personal computers of the employees, collect information, and install custom pieces of malware.

The Key

When hackers have been discovered within a company's systems, a key approach is to leave the hackers' activity alone and to track that activity. By doing this, a company can learn the attackers' methods and procedures, where they have installed malware, what that malware code looks like, and the code's creation signatures, so that they can later identify it and its possible variations and eventually prevent a return. And then, they can share their information with other companies and the Federal Bureau of Investigation (FBI).

Many companies then create a false but attractive subsystem within their network, which has fake but apparently real and useful information so that the hacker is attracted to access that false site—termed a *honeypot*. The company then keeps populating that honeypot with an increasing amount of attractive information, determining which seems of interest to the hacker. From this, the company's security personnel can create profiles of the hacker, their behavior, and their vulnerabilities, which will later prove valuable in creating monitoring tools.

The goal of a hacker is typically to harvest any points of information they can obtain. They will try to collect usernames and passwords, financial information, extortion potentials (useful for ransomware), identity hijacking, botnets, virtual goods. Botnets are a collection of infected computers that a botmaster triggers by command over the Internet to simultaneously send a flood of messages to a target site in order to overload it. This is a classic form of a DDoS attack. The "bots" are the infected computers.

Attack vectors may include

■ Spear-phishing e-mail messages
■ Phone calls that target you at home
■ USB sticks left lying around anywhere
■ Weak passwords, vulnerable machines
■ Drive-by downloads: the unintentional download of malware onto your computer which usually take advantage of a browser, application, or operating system security flaw
■ Coupon bars: web browser add-ins that analyze the websites your browser visits and may make that information available to hackers

As previously discussed, spear phishing is the most common way for hackers to attack their victims. In phishing, you (the victim) are the fish! Hackers will spear their targets with e-mails that request you to click on something that appears to be legit but provides the hackers with a vehicle to gain personal information and access to your system. All the hacker needs is one response from one victim to gain access to the targeted corporate victim. Anything can be spoofed and made to appear to be real. Phones can be spoofed to display a fake name. Wireless hotspots can be spoofed in public places.

The human is always the weakest link and the most attractive target for hacking. Hackers strike by studying the behavior of people and learning about their vulnerabilities. They strike from a distance. Third-party software is likely to be a target. Hackers create their own protocol libraries and use a set of tools to gain access. Vulnerable software may be software that the user does not even know is present on their system and is being actively executed.

Security efforts frequently involve basic binary analysis. Security experts need to be able to identify what good binary code looks like and what binary damage looks like, and they need to be able to find malware and malware damage as it exists in binary form on their computer systems. Best practice includes (1) looking at all the dynamic link libraries (DLLs, which provide a mechanism for sharing code and data) that are loaded with each application, (2) examining all exposed APIs and text strings, (3) performing a trace on all incoming packets to get a feel for the structure of the application, (4) looking for dangerous code patterns, and (5) conducting code-coverage reviews. Binary analysis can uncover potential vulnerabilities associated with basic data flow from the network, the use of bad APIs or simple backdoors traps and malware, exploitable bugs, and vulnerabilities that have not yet been discovered.

Special test programs can be employed for the purpose of placing a procedure call to application programs for the purpose of discovering coding errors and identifying security loopholes in that called software. These test programs can also discover similar exploitable loopholes in the operating system, the database software, and network software. This test process inputs massive amounts of random data, commonly termed fuzz, to the computer system in an attempt to make it crash and, in a trial and error fashion, discovers where there are errors in the software.

Hackers share and have access to the source code used by most OSs, database management systems, networking systems, and many popular applications, and they are constantly analyzing it for loopholes. Furthermore, they share what they have learned at popular websites on the dark web. Automated source-code analyzers designed to look for hacker modifications do not solve this problem and have a high false positive rate.

Defensive security approaches can be employed:

- Carrying out manual analysis (this tends to burn out programmers rather quickly, however)
- Employing programmers with special talent to design especially secure software
- Moving systems to a more secure platform and OS, and using vendor-supplied hardware and software systems that are certified to be secure

Another strategy is to continually research emergent hacker behavior. Hackers maintain a pipeline of activities and post their results on dark websites. Look for

- The protocols that are the most buggy
- The bug classes that are hard to scan
- The bugs that create themselves
- Currently deployed exploitation techniques

Zero-Days

Zero-day exploits are hacker obsessions. These are attempted by hackers on the day that the notice of the vulnerability is released to the public or even before. Sometimes, exploits are available even before the author is aware of a vulnerability or has developed corrected code. Zero-day attacks are a severe threat and are known as zero day because once the flaw is known, the programmer or developer has zero days to fix it. Modern zero-day attacks often combine multiple attack vectors and vulnerabilities into one exploit, making it difficult for forensic teams or intrusion detection and prevention systems (IDS/IPS) to identify a signature. Many of these are used only once on high-value targets. An average zero-day lifetime is around 348 days. However, a long-life zero-day exploit can exist for up to 3 years.

In the future of hacking, you can look for hackers to combine efforts using hacker teamwork. Additionally, you can look for more embedded system attacks and for far more interesting classifications of bugs and viruses.

Basic Control of Hijacking Attacks

An attacker's goal is to take over and have hidden ownership of a target machine, such as a web server, and to execute arbitrary code on that server by hijacking an application's control flow. One historical technique is a buffer overflow attack. Overflows are extremely common bugs in C/C++ programs executing on UNIX or Linus OSs; flaws are exploited when more data (containing malware code) is deliberately written to a block of memory, or buffer, than that buffer has actually been allocated to hold.

To exploit buffer overflows, the attackers need to know which central processing unit (CPU), OS, and code language is being used on the target machine. Buffers are blocks of memory allocated in the form of an array. When the size of an information field is not verified in terms of that provided by the OS, it is possible for a hacker to write or send an information field containing malware in the intended overflow, which will overflow the allocated buffer. If such an action takes place in a block of memory higher than that of the buffer return address, it is called a *buffer overrun*. An attacker will determine the return address in the memory stack by guessing the approximate stack state and inserting no operation (NOP) lines of code. The attacker then falls through the NOP lines of code to locate the return address or the malware code.

A similar problem exists when writing to a buffer within memory addresses below the allocated buffer. In this case, it is called a *buffer underflow*. Underflows occur much more rarely than overruns, but they do occasionally show up. A buffer overrun that injects code into a running process is referred to as an *exploitable buffer overrun*.

What you need to know to combat an attack is an understanding of C-language functions, the stack and the heap; and knowing how system calls (from the program to the OS) are made and executed. To find such an intended an overflow, you need to be able to run a web server on a local machine and issue malformed requests (such as requests ending in $$$$) to find overflow locations. If the web server crashes, one searches the core dump for $$$$ to determine the location of the overflow material.

More hacking opportunities exist:

■ Integer overflow: This is the condition that occurs when the result of an arithmetic operation exceeds the maximum size of the integer type used to store it.

- Format string bugs: Print functions and logging functions are common vulnerable functions where format string bugs occur and can allow the disclosure of information. Format string problems can also be used to execute arbitrary code.
- Dumping arbitrary memory: An exploit that can be used to print out a password file that could be manually picked up.

Platform Defenses

In order to protect their information, processing platform companies need to invest in building and purchasing a complete security tool set. Investing in tools such as StackGuard and LibSafe can enable companies to customize, protect, and defend against the efforts of hijacking. StackGuard and LibSafe are tools designed to prevent attackers from overwriting the return address and hijacking the control flow of a running program. The steps companies should take to take prevent hijacking attempts are as follows:

1. Fix bugs: Audit software with automated tools and, if necessary, rewrite software in a type safe language (such as JAVA, ML). This process is difficult for existing legacy code.
2. Concede overflow but prevent code execution.
3. Add run-time code to detect overflow exploits and halt the process when an overflow exploit is detected.
4. Data execution prevention (DEP): Prevent attack code execution by making stack and heap as non-executables.

Return-oriented programming, or ROP, is an advanced version of a stack-smashing attack. An adversary manipulates the call stack by taking advantage of a bug in the program, which is often a buffer overrun. A function that does not perform proper bounds checking before storing user-provided data into memory and accepts more input data than it can properly store indicates a buffer overrun.

If the data is being written onto the stack, the excess data may overflow the space allocated to the function's variables and overwrite the return address. This address will later be used by the function to redirect control flow back to the caller. If it has been overwritten, control flow will be diverted to the location specified by the new return address.

Address space layout randomization (ASLR) is a computer security technique involved in protecting systems from buffer overflow attacks and preventing shellcode from being successful. In order to prevent an attacker from reliably jumping to a particular exploited function in memory, ASLR randomly arranges the address space positions of key data areas in a process, including the base of the executable and the positions of the stack, heap, and libraries.

ASLR hinders some types of security attacks by making it more difficult for an attacker to predict target addresses and address space layout randomization based on the slim chance of an attacker guessing the locations of randomly placed areas.

Just-in-time (JIT) spraying is a class of computer security exploits that circumvent the protection ASLR and data execution prevention (DEP) offer by exploiting the behavior of the JIT compiler. It has been reported to have been used to penetrate security features in the PDF format and in Adobe's Flash technology.

By definition, a JIT produces code as its data. Since the purpose is to produce executable data, a JIT compiler is one of the few types of programs that cannot be run in a no-executable-data environment. Because of this, JIT compilers are normally exempt from data execution prevention. A JIT spray attack carries out heap spraying with the generated code. To protect against JIT spraying, the JIT code can be disabled or made less predictable for the attacker.

Run-Time Defenses

The first solution is to employ StackGuard, a simple compiler extension that limits the amount of damage that a buffer overflow attack can inflict on a program. StackGuard completes runtime tests for stack integrity by embedding a "canary" word next (prior) to the return address on the stack. Once this function is done, the new tear-down code verifies that the canary word is unmodified and intact prior to function return. If the integrity of the canary word is compromised, the program will terminate. StackGuard utilizes two types of canaries to defeat an attack. The first is a Random Canary, which is a 32-bit number chosen only at runtime. To corrupt that Random Canary number, an attacker needs to attempt a scan through the executable images of the code after the number has been computed and prior to the execution of the program. The second is a terminator canary made up of common termination symbols that prevent string functions from being copied into memory space. The weakness of StackGuard is that canaries do not provide full protection. Function parameters are not fully protected, frame pointers can be altered, and local variables can be controlled. ProPolice (from IBM) can be used to protect pointer args and local pointers from buffer overflow. Pointer args means "pointer argument," where the argument attached to the pointer tells the direction that the pointer is indicating should be followed. Additionally, PointGuard can provide heap protection and protect function pointers and setjmp buffers by encrypting them. Setjmp is a C language device to provide branching (jumps) control flow that deviates from the usual subroutine call and return sequence.

Canaries are an important defense tool, but they do not prevent all control hijacking attacks. Heap-based attacks, integer overflow, and exception handling attacks are still possible. Additional tools such as/SAFESH, a linker flag of safe exception handlers; and/SEHOP, a platform defense that inserts and then verifies dummy records, are also needed.

The second solution is to employ a program such as LibSafe (from Avaya Labs), which is a dynamically loaded library designed to intercept all function calls made to library functions known to be vulnerable. A substitute version of the corresponding function implements the original function in a way that ensures that any buffer overflows are contained within the current stack frame, which prevents attackers from overwriting the return address and hijacking the control flow of a running program. The true benefit of using LibSafe is to protect against future attacks on programs that are not yet known to be vulnerable. The performance overhead of LibSafe is negligible, it does not require changes to the OS, it works with existing binary programs, and it does not need access to the source code of defective programs, recompilation, or off-line processing of binaries.

Advanced Hijacking Attacks: Heap Spraying

In computer security, heap spraying is a technique used in exploits to facilitate arbitrary code execution. The part of the source code of an exploit that implements this technique is called a *heap spray*. In general, code that sprays the heap attempts to put a certain sequence of bytes at a predetermined location in the memory of a target process by having it allocate (large) blocks on the process's heap and fill the bytes in these blocks with the right values.

Heap sprays have been used occasionally in exploits since at least 2001, but the technique started to see widespread use in exploits for web browsers in the summer of 2005 after the release of several such exploits that used the technique against a wide range of bugs in Internet Explorer. The heap sprays used in all these exploits were very similar, which showed the versatility of the technique and its ease of use, without the need for major modifications between exploits. It proved simple enough to understand and use to allow novice hackers to quickly write reliable exploits for many types of vulnerabilities in web browsers and web-browser plug-ins. Many web browser exploits that use heap spraying consist only of a heap spray that is copy-pasted from a previous exploit, combined with a small piece of script or HTML that triggers the vulnerability.

Heap sprays for web browsers are commonly implemented in JavaScript, and they spray the heap by creating large strings. The most common technique used is to start with a string of one character and concatenate this with itself over and over. This way, the length of the string can grow exponentially up to the maximum length allowed by the scripting engine. Depending on how the browser implements strings, either American Standard Code for Information Exchange (ASCII) or Unicode characters can be used in the string. The heap spraying code makes copies of the long string with shellcode and stores these in an array, up to the point where enough memory has been sprayed to ensure that the exploit works.

The Final Solution to Hacking Attacks

The final protection is to employ a monitoring system, such as Rivest–Shamir–Adleman (RSA)'s ECAT Monitor, which has a large and growing file of malware signatures and behavior patterns; these are continually scanned for and trigger the planned-for response that the security team is organized to employ.

QUESTIONS

1. Hackers need to do what in order to penetrate their targets?
2. Provide two examples of how hackers attract the victim.
3. Explain what binary analysis is.
4. What makes a vulnerability a zero-day vulnerability?
5. How do hackers overwrite the return address?
6. What technique can you use to protect yourself from buffer overflow?
7. How many steps can companies take to prevent hijacking and what are they?

Chapter 7

Malware, Viruses, Worms, Bugs, and Botnets

Introduction

Malware, viruses, worms, and bugs have caused headaches for system administrators since the beginning of computer networking. In fact, one of the first known worms was detected as early as 1988 and spread via the Internet. There are different classifications of malware based on size. Whether dealing with large-scale attacks or even simple small attacks, it is important to detect the threat and act accordingly. The action taken will depend on which type of malware has infected the system. However, the way to detect this malware is primarily based on IDSs and data forensics.

Many types of malware are present in today's cyber space. The large-scale malware consists of worms and botnets (which can be created using worms). Worms have had some of the most devastating effects on computer networking because the code of a worm self-propagates and replicates across systems. Among the most famous examples of this are the Morris worm and the Code Red 1 and 2 worms. The Morris worm was one of the most famous because it was the first worm to be spread via the Internet to affect approximately 6000 machines. At the time (1988), this represented 10% of all computers connected to the Internet. This was achieved by exploiting vulnerabilities in UNIX sendmail, finger, and rsh/rexec, along with weak passwords. The error that transformed this code into an extensive denial-of-service attack was located within the spreading mechanism code. While this was a very large deal at the time, the Code Red 1 and 2 worms were much more intensive. These worms were descendants of the Morris worm and affected more than 500,000 servers. Clearly, this was one of the most catastrophic worms, causing almost $2.6 billion in damages.

Rootkits are also a very large problem within cyber space because they hide the presence of the intruder. Not only does this software hide the attacker's presence but it also provides a backdoor into the system so the hacker can acquire more information. While there are levels of different sophisticated rootkits, the ones that system administrators worry about the most are rootkits that modify the kernel itself. This is because they are extremely hard to detect once they have been implemented. Once the rootkit has been set up, an attacker can inject spyware into a system to gain further information on the users through the use of keylogging software. In some extreme cases, a hacker may utilize ransomware to "lockdown" a system until a payment has been made that will effectively decrypt the ransomware. The most recent example of this was the CryptoLocker ransomware, which encrypted drives until a Bitcoin payment had been made.

While malware, worms, rootkits, and other bugs will always occur, detecting them is absolutely critical to preserve the integrity of the data within a system. There are intrusion detection systems (IDSs) that consist of software that is specifically designed to monitor networks and system activities for policy violations and abnormalities. Once these abnormalities have been detected, the intrusion detection software will produce a report for the management station. While some IDSs will attempt to stop an intrusion attempt, not all are successful. For this reason, system administrators will employ the use of a honeypot. A honeypot is essentially a quarantine trap within a network. It is disguised as information that would be beneficial to a hacker; however, it is closely monitored for any intruders.

While there are many ways for malware, worms, rootkits, and other bugs to infect a system, properly secured architectures and IDSs are in place to help prevent, and minimize, the effects of this software on computer networking and host-based systems.

Large-scale malware comes in two separate types: worms and botnets. Worms are able to self-propagate, while a botnet is a series of machines that have been compromised and are under the control (command and control [C&C]) of an attacker. This work focuses on the definitions and categorization of common malicious file types and attacks. What's most interesting about these classifications is that no person is more or less vulnerable from a socioeconomic perspective. High-Profile, well-known, or high-income individuals may be targets of these attacks as often as low-income or other merely basic users of the Internet.

Botnets: Process and Components and History

Botnets are networks of infected processors that represent the aftereffects of infection with multiple forms of malicious applications. Botnets are a networked collection of machines that have been compromised by one of many methods, allowing a single C&C machine or a group of such control machines to send commands out to that network of infected machines, commanding them to perform a selected task in unison. Usually, the owner/operators of these infected machines have no indication that such a process is underway. Thus, a botnet is a distributed cluster of infected computers that unknowingly execute the commands of a malicious control computer. Such distributed botnets are a common approach for implementing distributed denial-of-service (DDoS) attacks. Furthermore, hackers may also rent out the access and control of these botnets to other hacking groups for them to conduct their own malicious intent. The power of these botnets can be measured by a few core variables—the number of machines in the botnet, their total processing power, their connected bandwidth, and the distribution of their geographic locations. All are critical parts in the success of a botnet's malicious performance. Furthermore, having access to potential machines for infection enhances the botnets' expansion and reinfection capabilities.

Viruses and Worms

In order to infect machines, multiple mediums or approaches exist to circumvent security measures put in place by end users. These types are not classified by the code itself but rather the approach used to infect. In many cases, multiple approaches are required to infect machines at a high level, so worms and viruses are not mutually exclusive to completing malicious goals. Worms, for example, do not require a host program; they exist on their own, carrying a payload of some basic backdoor components, and they replicate themselves on vulnerable machines as they are discovered. Worms go through four phases:

1. Probe
2. Explore
3. Replicate
4. Deliver payload

As the speed of computers and networks has increased, the rate at which a worm can spread has been enhanced. One of the most rapidly spread early worms was the "Code Red Worm," but that pales in comparison to the speed with which current state-of-the-art worms spread infection. Chapter 20 will discuss the sophistication and spread of the Stuxnet worm as compared with historical worms. However, the number of new emerging worms has begun to decline.

The reason for the drop in growth is that the United States took action in shifting some top-level network settings on which worms relied. When these were changed, it became more difficult for worms to adapt and continue replicating using the historically effective techniques. The newer Stuxnet worm relies on a technician bringing a worm in by means of a flash drive, rather than fighting through an array of network-defending software, scanners, and defenders. It is personally and manually, but unwittingly, carried around those defenses.

However, there are still worms that will attack the low-hanging fruit of unprotected sites on the Internet, first infecting the obviously unprotected machines before hitting machines with slightly better protection.

Worms typically contain a small amount of code in order to remain nimble as they traverse the Internet and eventually a corporation's large local area networks (LANs). An example of worm file size and compression is the "Slammer" worm, which infected 75,000 + machines within 10 minutes. It fit inside a single Universal Data Protocol (UDP) packet, which is connectionless in nature, making it the perfect transport protocol medium for worm replication. The UDP base of this worm had significant effects on the worm's growth abilities.

Worms are an extremely dangerous logical weapon that can directly deliver physical damage, as occurred with the Canadian Logic Bomb or the Stuxnet worm in Iran. But they can also be used for information espionage and for stealing or blocking revenue, as well as for creating their own form of denial of service. Once they are effectively deployed, they may linger within the public Internet for some time with occasional cross-site infection occurring. To fight the global spreading of worms, "white worms" have been designed to infect and clean exploited machines. However, this approach is unpredictable and may cause more harm than the damage they are trying to alleviate. The ethics of releasing disinfecting worms in an uncontrolled fashion across the Internet is highly questionable. Fighting fire with fire is not always the best solution.

A More Detailed Examination of Malware, Viruses, Trojans, and Bots/Botnets

Malware is a contraction of the words "malicious software." Malware is considered to be any software or file that is harmful to a computer or system. Malware incorporates viruses, worms, bugs, botnets, rootkits, and trapdoors, which can be difficult to discover and sometimes more difficult to eradicate once detected. This section will examine the most common malware, focusing on how various types of malware work and how best to approach blocking, detecting, avoiding, and removing them.

Worms

Worms comprise code that replicates by self-propagation and then spreads across systems by arranging to have the code immediately executed. The worm code that is executed can contain both the malware itself as well as the self-propagation and spread technology. It then uses the local computer network to spread itself locally, heavily relying on internal security failures to access target computers. It then seeks access to edge routers as a gateway out to the public Internet and the vast array of global sites that it can then spread to and infect.

Moreover, a worm does not need to attach itself to existing programs in order to perform its infection. The worm can act alone. And when a worm spreads across a network, it does not tend to change the systems on the computers it infects. A worm can stand alone as executable malware or it can infect other software by placing itself at the back-end of existing code and directly affecting that code as it executes or overlaying files that valid code uses as it executes. In the process of spreading from computer to computer, worms may use a significant amount of bandwidth, which helps in their discovery.

Worms typically carry a payload of the malware tasks to be performed, which can also include the delivery of additional trapdoors, Trojan horses, viruses, and so on. The worm is the messenger, digging its way into the system and then delivering the message, the malware payload, to the intended victim(s).

The four phases of a worm's operation are probing for vulnerabilities, exploiting those vulnerabilities to enter a selected site, performing the replication of copies of itself, and delivering the malicious payload.

Some Examples of Historical Worm Attacks

Morris Worm

Released in 1988, this was one of the first computer worms spread by means of an early form of the Internet, and it was certainly the first to gain vast media attention. It was written by graduate student Robert Tappan Morris of Cornell University (son of the famous security expert Robert Morris of the National Security Agency [NSA]). According to Morris, the worm was not written with the intent of doing damage but to gauge the size of the Internet. The result was that the worm infected approximately 6000 machines, which, at the time, represented about 10% of the Internet. It cost around $10 million in downtime and cleanup.

Code Red I and Code Red II Worms

Code Red I was the worm that attacked computers running Microsoft's IIS web servers on July 15, 2001. It was a direct descendant of Morris's worm, exploiting buffer overflow in Microsoft's IIS. It infected more than 500,000 servers, causing $2.6 billion in damage. Fortunately, Kenneth D. Eichmann figured out a way to block that worm. Code Red II, a similar worm to Code Red I, was released two weeks after its predecessor. Unlike Code Red I, Code Red II primarily focused on creating backdoors rather than attacking. While Microsoft had developed a security patch for this exploit, not everyone had installed that patch, allowing Code Red II to still be effective and continue spreading.

Nimda Worm

This was released on September 18, 2001. It was a worm that used several types of propagation techniques, making it the most widespread worm on the Internet within 22 minutes of initial infection. The name Nimda is the reverse of "admin," indicating it attempted to use administrator privileges.

SQL Slammer

The SQL Slammer was a worm that caused denial of service on selected Internet hosts and slowed down Internet traffic. It was spread on January 25, 2003, quickly infecting 75,000 computers within 10 minutes. This worm exploited Microsoft's Structured Query Language (SQL) server but did not actually use SQL as part of its infected processes.

Conficker Worm

This worm, also known as Downup, Kido, and Downadup, targeted Microsoft Windows operating systems, as well as performing dictionary attacks on administrator passwords in order to propagate itself and subsequently create botnets. Conficker was first detected in November 2008 and was difficult to defend against due to the combined set of multiple advanced malware techniques that it employed. Conficker eventually infected 9–15 million computers worldwide.

The Conficker worm exploits several vulnerabilities:

1. Protected from Conficker worm: Computers with strong passwords and secured, shared-folder, up-to-date antivirus software and security updates
2. Unprotected from Conficker worm: Network computers with weak passwords and outdated antivirus software and security updates
3. Unprotected from Conficker worm: Out-of-network computers with weak passwords and outdated antivirus software and security updates
4. Unprotected from Conficker worm: Computers with unsecured/open shared folders and outdated antivirus software and security updates

These vulnerabilities to the Conficker worm as submitted by a remote attacker are illustrated in Figure 7.1.

E-Mail Worms

These were passed as attachments to e-mail messages and could be particularly quick in their spread as broadcast e-mails to a large list of associates.

Love Bug Worm

Also known as the ILOVEYOU worm, the Love Bug worm spread through an e-mail message with the subject of the message being "ILOVEYOU," with an attachment of "LOVE-LETTER-FOR-YOU.txt.vbs." At the time, the vbs was hidden by default on Windows computers, leading victims to believe it was a normal text file. Opening the attachment activated the attached malicious visual basic script. The worm then damaged the local machine and sent a copy of itself to

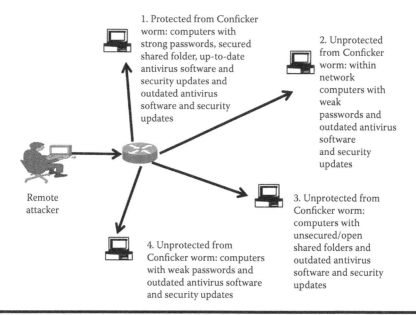

1. Protected from Conficker worm: computers with strong passwords, secured shared folder, up-to-date antivirus software and security updates and outdated antivirus software and security updates

2. Unprotected from Conficker worm: within network computers with weak passwords and outdated antivirus software and security updates

Remote attacker

3. Unprotected from Conficker worm: computers with unsecured/open shared folders and outdated antivirus software and security updates

4. Unprotected from Conficker worm: computers with weak passwords and outdated antivirus software and security updates

Figure 7.1 The array of protection from and vulnerabilities to the Conficker worm.

the addresses in that machine's Windows address book. The worm was released on May 3, 2000. Overall, the worm managed to cause $5.5–$10 million worth of damage.

MyDoom Worm

This worm was released on January 26, 2004, and it became the fastest spreading e-mail worm as of 2004, exceeding the Love Bug worm. There were two versions of MyDoom—Mydoom.A and Mydoom.B. Mydoom.A had two payloads, one to create a backdoor and the other to perform a denial of service. Mydoom.B had the same payloads, but in addition it blocked Microsoft's website and other popular antivirus websites. The denial-of-service attack was focused on the SCO Group Company.

Storm Worm and Storm Botnet

Identified on January 17, 2007, this worm's payload included code to create a backdoor Trojan horse that affected Microsoft operating systems. It spread itself using an e-mail with the subject of the e-mail concerning a weather disaster: "230 dead as storm batters Europe." By January 22, 2007, the Storm worm accounted for 8% of malware infections globally. By June 30, it had infected 1.7 million computers.

Viruses

A virus is self-replicating code that inserts itself into other computer programs, hard drives, and data files. Viruses utilize attachment approaches to attempt to avoid detection so that they can do their damage, replicate themselves, and spread to infect additional systems. The important aspect common to all viruses is that they are self-replicating program code and install themselves without a user's consent, either as attachments to existing programs or as stand-alone code. And they do not necessarily have to contain a malicious payload to be considered a virus.

Furthermore, viruses are opportunistic, meaning that their code will continue to seek out ways that will allow them to eventually execute. Typically, the viruses' execution is triggered by a user action, such as running an infected application or restarting the computer so that as part of the restart process, the infected code is executed. Similar to worms, viruses tend to have a malicious payload and a propagation methodology.

Virus Propagation

When a virus executes, it also looks for an opportunity to infect additional systems. As an example, a virus might look for a USB-attached flash/thumb drive to infect, so that when the thumb drive is placed in another system, the virus can spread (the Stuxnext worm approach). Another way a virus can spread is when a user sends an e-mail with a virus attached. The virus can alter an intended e-mail attachment and implant itself; this is usually done with a microset of code at the beginning of the original attachment, which, upon execution, branch around the good original code to the virus payload code placed at the end of the original code. To avoid detection, the infected attachment and the original code are compressed down to the original size of the intended attachment code. This virus approach is especially effective in infecting attachment types that are programs (such as Microsoft Word [macros] and PDFs with JavaScript), rather than simple Word documents and simple PDFs. A virus can also send out e-mail on its own with attachments of itself.

So the basic process is that when a virus infects a program or file, it first places a branch routine at the front of the original program and then places the virus payload code at the end of the original program. Upon execution, the entry code branches directly around the original code to the virus code attached at the end for its execution. The combined infected code is then compressed back down to the size of the original code in order to avoid detection. The entry code triggers the decompression of the code as well as the branch to the virus code at the end. Figure 7.2 illustrates this process.

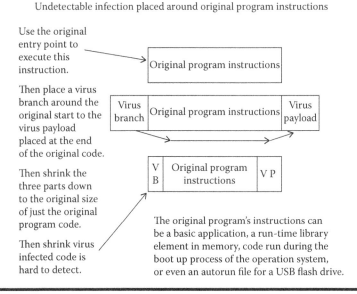

Figure 7.2   Virus wrapped around a program and then shrunk to original size.

Payload

Virus code can do anything that is desired. It can pop up messages, delete files, damage hardware, perform keylogging, encrypt your files and hold them for ransom, install potentially logic bombs that can detonate at a later date, and perform any type of deletion or further infiltration.

Detecting a Virus

Viruses do billions of dollars' worth of damage every year and as a result created the multibillion-dollar antivirus industry (AV). An antivirus runs a signature-based detection. It looks through bytes corresponding to the injected virus code. Once you find a virus, you can protect the computer and other computers by installing a recognizer for the virus. Antivirus companies compete on the basis of the number of signatures they possess.

If you were a virus writer and you realized that companies are finding your viruses and blocking that specific pattern, the ideal thing would be to change the virus or its appearance. Having to write a new virus takes a lot of time, so one solution would be to have the virus alter itself with propagation, making different-looking copies each time it spreads.

Polymorphic Code

Polymorphic code is code that uses a polymorphic engine to mutate while keeping the original algorithm intact. In other words, each time the code runs, the structure changes but the functions do not. Encryption is the most common method used to hide code. It is important to note that encryption alone is not polymorphism. To be considered polymorphic, the encryption and decryption must mutate with each copy of the code, allowing for varied versions while the functions remain the same. When the code runs, the virus decrypts itself to obtain the payload then execute it. Figures 7.3 and 7.4 illustrate an example of a byte that is infected with a virus and what polymorphic code would look like when encrypted and then decrypted.

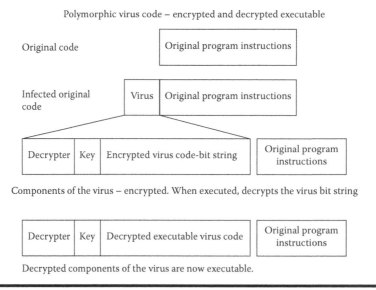

Figure 7.3 Polymorphic virus infection and decryption process.

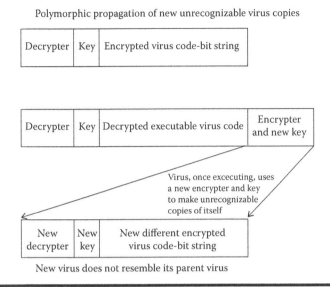

Polymorphic propagation of new unrecognizable virus copies

Figure 7.4 Polymorphic virus propagation of unrecognizable child viruses.

Polymorphic code was the first technique that became a serious threat to virus scanners. One idea to defend against it is to use narrow signatures that target the decryptor for the polymorphic code. There are a few problems with this countermeasure. For one, there is less code to compare, resulting in more false positives (i.e., code that is fine but is scanned as a threat); also, virus writers can spread the decryptor across the existing code, making it hard to find. A different approach is to analyze code to see if it decrypts. The problem with this strategy is that not all code that has decryption is malicious or unwanted. The other issue is that you have to let the malware decrypt in order to find it, but how long do you allow the malware to run before you stop it? As is the case most of the time, virus writers are two steps ahead of antivirus companies. To combat against these new tactics, virus writers came up with a new solution.

Metamorphic Code

Each time the virus propagates, it generates semantically different versions of itself. In other words, the virus rewrites itself completely each time it infects a new component of the system. When it runs, it produces a logically equivalent version of its own code with various interpretations. This child virus will perform the same task as the parent, but the binary representation will be different. Some ways of doing this include renumbering registers, changing the order of conditional code, reordering operations not dependent on one another, replacing one low-level algorithm with another, or removing some do-nothing padding and replacing it with different do-nothing padding. A metamorphic is extremely large and complex code.

When looking for metamorphic code, the virus scanner looks for its behavior rather than its structure. In other words, what is the outcome of this code? Is it malicious? There are two stages in searching for a virus:

1. Antivirus company analyzes new virus to find behavior signature.
2. Antivirus company software on the end system analyzes suspect code to test for signature match.

As usual, virus writers are two steps ahead. A virus writer can delay the analysis. One major weakness of this type of scan is that it has to find the behavior to find the virus, so if the virus writer can stall the program to not function during a scan, it can avoid being detected. Antivirus companies look for these tactics and skip over them. It is the ever ongoing battle in security.

When Malware Is Detected

Getting rid of malware may require restoring or repairing files. If the malware was executed on administrator privileges, it might be best to wipe the slate clean. Once you're infected, you never really know if you have gotten rid of all the malware on your computer. You will need to be careful about using backups because the virus may have infected your backups as well.

An example would be a forensic analysis showing that a virus introduced a backdoor in/bin/login executable. The cleanup procedure is rebuild/bin/login from source (Figure 7.5).

Once the compiler becomes infected, it is very difficult to correct that compiler. And if a backdoor trap has been created from that compiler infection, it is very difficult to detect it and, even if it is detected, to permanently remove it.

Botnets

A botnet is a collection of compromised machines under the control of an attacker or *botmaster*. Botnets are also known as zombie armies, and their name is a contraction of the words "robot" and "network." Botnets are typically used for denial-of-service attacks. As previously, the method of compromise or propagation is decoupled from the method of control or payload. Typically, a botnet will be spread using a worm, virus, or drive-by infection. The botnet itself is the payload of these tools. Once the target is infected, the bot will get in touch with the botnet C&C. The C&C is what the botmaster will use to send out commands to the various bots. There are a variety of

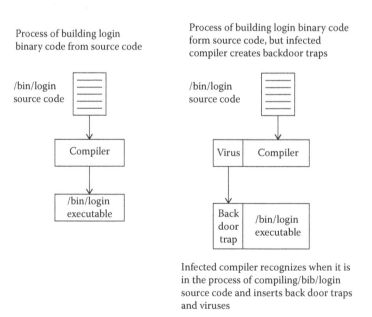

Figure 7.5   Introduction of a backdoor trap.

ways to create an architecture with C&C: a star topology, a hierarchical approach, a multiserver approach, and so on. When communicating with C&C, stealthy communication with encryption is used.

Star-Structured Botnets

The star topology centralizes the C&C to each bot. Each bot receives instructions directly from the C&C. The advantage is the direct communication with the bots, allowing for quick theft and directions. The disadvantage is that if the C&C is blocked or disabled, the bot is useless (Figure 7.6).

The multiserver approach is a logical extension of a star topology. Instead of having one server, multiple servers are used to give commands. Should a server fail or be removed, the others can take over the commands. Placing the servers geographically near the bots improves speed, and C&Cs hosted in multiple countries can avoid being completely shut down by law. The disadvantage of multiservers is that they take a lot of preparation and effort to build (Figure 7.7).

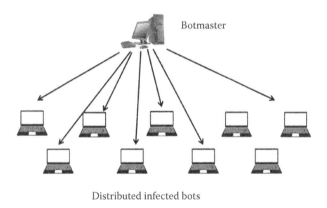

Figure 7.6 Star topology C&C botmaster to bot topology.

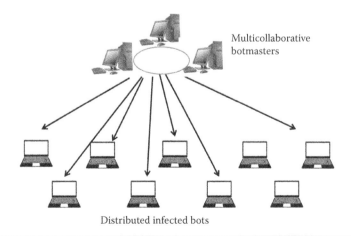

Figure 7.7 A collaborative C&C botmaster.

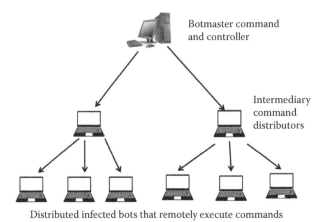

Botmaster command and controller

Intermediary command distributors

Distributed infected bots that remotely execute commands

Figure 7.8   Two-stage C&C of a distributed botnet.

Hierarchical Botnets

Instead of all the botnets replying to the C&C, some botnets can be put in charge of a cluster of botnets and distribute the commands on the botmaster's behalf. The problem, however, is that updated commands more often suffer latency issues, making it difficult for the botmaster to use his or her bots for real-time activity. With the hierarchical model, no single bot is aware of the entire botnet, which can make it difficult for security to find and measure its size. Botmasters can sell their individual bots or break them into further subcategories (Figure 7.8).

Defending from Botnets

The first approach, and the most obvious, is to prevent the initial bot infection. However, because the original bot machine infection precedes and is decoupled from the bots' participation in the botnet attacks, botnets are difficult to stop at both the infection stage and then later in the attack phase.

One approach is to locate and take down the C&C computer, the source of the botnet, and to defuse that C&C along with the botmaster. If you can find the C&C's IP address, you can have the associated Internet Service Provider (ISP) deny the botmaster's access. The problem, however, is that the botmaster can keep moving the master server, either by moving to a different domain or by rapidly altering the address associated with that name, a process termed *Fast Flux*. Botmasters can hide their servers and themselves in a hierarchy of multilayered, multiserver construction. Furthermore, botmasters can also pay their ISP to not shut them down. And there are ISP businesses that guarantee your website will never be shut down. An example of a "no shut down" ISP is GooHost.ru, a located in Russia.

Anonymity and Sneakiness

A difficult problem is dealing with those who know how to browse the Internet with anonymity by hiding their IP address using onion routing and anonymity websites, augmented by using other more sophisticated sneaky ways of communicating or computing.

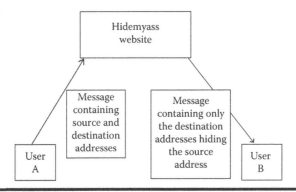

Figure 7.9 Hiding the sender's address in the delivered message.

There are a variety of options for achieving privacy through technical means, such as removing cookies (including flash cookies) or turning off JavaScript so that Google Analytics cannot track you. In order to hide an IP address, one approach is to trust a third party to perform that obfuscation process.

Hidemyass is one example of a third party that can hide your IP address for you. With Hidemyass, you set up an encrypted virtual private network (VPN) to the Hidemyass site. Then all of your traffic goes to them. An example would be if User A wants to send a message to User B while ensuring that a third party, User C, cannot determine that User A is communicating with User B (Figure 7.9).

Hidemyass will (1) accept messages encrypted for User B submitted by User A, (2) will extract User B's destination but hide User A's source address, and (3) will forward the message to User B. The problem with using a third party is that your Internet browsing performance may suffer, and of course it is a fairly pricey service, costing up to $200 a year. A further issue is that your identity can be uncovered by means of "rubber-hose cryptanalysis," which involves someone "beating" the encryption key Hidemyass employs by means of threat or extortion. In this case, hackers and crackers can attack Hidemyass until they release the desired information (Figure 7.10).

Another option is onion routing. As mentioned in previous chapters, this approach generalizes to an arbitrary number of intermediaries. In other words, servers volunteer to help keep you anonymous and are shuffled as you travel the Internet (Figure 7.11).

As long as any of the volunteering intermediaries are honest and trustworthy, no one can link User A with User B. Onion routing is not without its flaws and risks, however. It affects performance due to the message being bounced around. There is also the threat of rubber-hose cryptanalysis (again, beating the information out of one of your volunteers). The defense against this is to mix the servers in different countries, but this also takes a toll on performance. In the worst case, the attacker may operate all of the mixes or intermediaries. The defense against this is to have a large variety of servers, and today onion routing has around 2000 volunteer servers. The other form of attack involves the attacker watching Alice and Bob and noticing that when Alice sends out an e-mail, Bob gets one around the same time; the attacker is able to put two and two together. The defense against this is to pad messages and/or introduce significant delays. The Tor protocol, for example, pads messages, but that alone is not enough for absolute defense.

One last issue Tor can suffer is leakage. What if all of your HTTP/HTTPS traffic goes through Tor but the rest of your traffic does not (i.e., FTP). The server notices that your anonymous HTTP/HTTPS connection is the same as your FTP connection. This coincidence allows people to put two and two together and deduce that you are the same person. The general problem

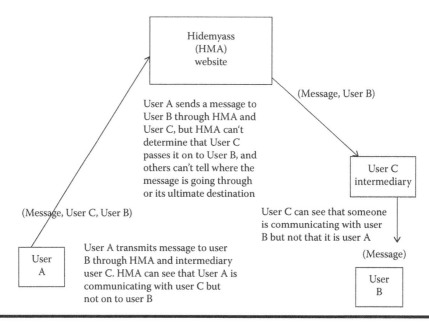

Figure 7.10 Transmitting through HMA and an intermediary.

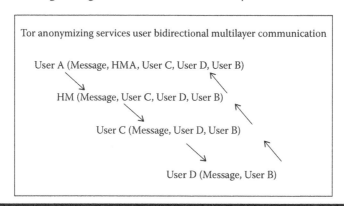

Figure 7.11 Tor anonymizing bidirectional communications.

with anonymity is that it is often put at risk when an adversary can correlate separate sources of information.

Sneakiness and Side-Channel Attacks

Steganography is the process of transmitting hidden messages using a known communication channel when used no one knows the message is there. This same principle applies to hiding extra hidden data inside known storage, for instance, hiding a potential worm inside an image file. The overall goal is to sneak communication past a reference monitor (a "warden"). This does not imply confidentiality; if the message is discovered, the malware is revealed, although you could potentially encrypt it. The advantage of steganography over cryptography alone is that the secret message does not attract attention to itself as an object of scrutiny.

Some examples of steganography can be traced back to tattooed heads of slaves. The story is told by Herodotus that in ancient Greece a man's head was tattooed with a secret message, and then his hair was grown out, hiding the message until he shaved. Some digital examples are least-significant bits of image pixels, or extra tags in HTML documents. All that is necessary for steganography to work is an agreement between the writer of the message and the reader of the message, along with the extra capacity to store the file.

How do you protect yourself from this? If the steganography is well designed and the monitor, or warden, can only watch passing traffic, it can be hard to detect. If, however, we permit the "warden" to modify communication, recode images, canconicalize HTML, or shave the head, then the warden can discover the hidden message.

Covert Channels

These are communications between two parties that use a hidden (secret) channel. The goal is to evade reference monitor inspection entirely. In this case, our "warden" is unaware that communication between Users A and B is possible. Just as in steganography, an agreement between sender and receiver must be established in advance for this to work. Here is an example of covert channels. Suppose (unprivileged) process Alice wants to send 128 bits of secret data to (unprivileged) process Bob. Process Alice cannot use pipes, sockets, signals, or shared memory, and she can only read files, not write them. Alice has a few options to get the information to Bob.

- Method #1: Alice can syslog her data, which B can read via/var/log/.
- Method #2: Alice can select 128 files in advance. Alice then opens the files for read only purposes that are marked with 1- bits, corresponding to the fact that they are secret. Bob recovers bit values by inspecting access times on files.
- Method #3: Alice can divide her file's running time up into 128 slots. The file either executes, or doesn't execute, in a given time slot depending on a corresponding secret bit being on or off. Bob's computer monitors Alice's CPU usage, observing the run-time slots used for her program execution.
- Method #4: Suppose Alice can run her file 128 times. Each time it either exits after 2 seconds (0 bit) or after 30 seconds (1 bit).
- Method #5: This list can go on for ever.

Security

The best way to secure against covert channels is, as with steganography, to identify the mechanisms. Some mechanisms can be very hard to remove—the duration of a program execution, for instance. The fundamental issue is the covert channel's capacity; it takes space to send the messages. Bits (or the bit rate) that the adversary can obtain by using it is one example. It is crucial for security to consider their threat model; the assumption is that the attacker wins, simply because we cannot effectively stop communication, especially if the communication is low rate.

Side Channels

A side-channel attack is any attack based on information gained from the physical implementation of a cryptosystem. For instance, timing information, power consumption, electromagnetic leaks, or sound can provide information and can be exploited to break into a system. Information can

```
/* This routine returns true if the password from the
* user, 'p', matches the correct master password. */

A001 check_password(char *r)
{
        static char *master_pw = "SecretPassword";
        int l;
        for(i=0; p[i] &&  master-pw[i]; ++i)
                if(p[i] ! = master-pw[i])
                        return false;
        /* Ensure both strings are the same length. */
        return p[i] == master-pw[i]
}
```

Figure 7.12   Code that checks a user's password.

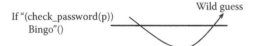

If "(check_password(p))
Bingo"()   Wild guess

Figure 7.13   Wild guessing of password.

```
If password doesn't start with, say, "W", then loop exits on first
iteration (i=0)
Then
For (i-0); p(i) && master_pw[i]; ++i)
        if(p[i]!= master_pw[i])
                return FALSE;

If the password doesn't start with, say "w", then loop proceeds to the
next iteration, generating a page fault, which the guesser can observe
and trigger the next guess. This proceeds until a correct first letter
occurs and then proceeds to the next letter /symbol of the password.
```

Figure 7.14   More on the password brute-force guessing process.

also come from higher-layer abstractions. This can be difficult to detect because the leaking elements might be deemed irrelevant information. Unlike steganography or covert channels, we do not assume a cooperating sender/receiver.

An example of code that checks a user's password is shown in Figures 7.12.

Suppose the attacker's code can call the "check_password" routine many times, but not millions of times, and the attacker cannot break or inspect the code. How could the attacker infer the master password using only side-channel information? Consider the layout of p in memory (Figure 7.13).

The code (Figure 7.13) checks the password, but what if the attacker wrote a loop to check each iteration? What would happen next is shown in Figure 7.14.

When there is a page fault indicating that the correct letter has not been found, the iterative process moves on to attempt the next guess in the sequence.

How do you stop this? One obvious method is to limit the amount of guesses a user can make. But there is a way around that. Suppose you didn't end the function each time you guessed? The code goes through each iteration and does not end the function until each iteration is guessed (Figure 7.15).

```
Bool check_password2(char {*p)
{
        static char *master_pw= "T0p$eCRET";
        int i;
        bool is_correct =TRUE;

        for (i=0; p[i] && master pw[I]; ++i)
                if(p[i] != master_ pw[i])
                        is_correct= FALSE;
        if(p[i] != master pw(i))
                is_correct =FALSE;
        return is_ correct;
}
```

Figure 7.15   Process of continuous guessing.

Side Channels in Web Surfing

Suppose Alice is surfing the web and all of her traffic is encrypted and running through an anony-mizer such as Hidemyass. Eve can observe the presence of Alice's packets and their size but cannot read their contents or determine their ultimate destination. How can Eve deduce that Alice is visiting Fox News? Because Eve knows the size and the amount of packets, she can compare them with Fox News's page information to see if there is a match.

Can we infer or deduce what terms User A is using to search? Can an attacker using System 1 scan the server of victim User V to see what services User V runs without User V being able to learn User A's IP address? Generally, he can't, since after all, how can User A receive the results of probes User A sends to User V unless those probes include User A's IP address for User V's replies?

Exploiting Side Channels for Stealth Scanning

Figure 7.16 is an IP header side channel.

The attacker makes requests to a web server and records the IDs used for those transmitted packets. The attacker keeps guessing and tries to time the correct guess with the victim. If the attacker succeeds, he or she will receive the same data that the victim requests (Figure 7.17).

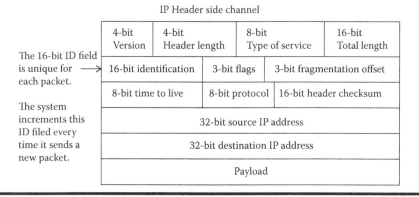

Figure 7.16   16-bit identification code incremented with each transmission.

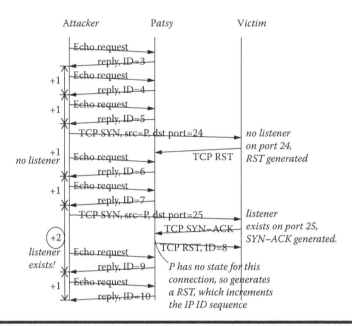

Figure 7.17 Complete sequence of requests and responses between attacker, patsy, victim.

UI Side-Channel Snooping

Suppose Ann, the attacker, works in a building across the street from Victor, the victim. Late one night, Ann can see Victor hard at work in his office but can't see his LCD display, just the glow off his face. How might Ann snoop on what Victor's display is showing? Solution: Cables from computer to screen and keyboards act as crude antennas. The cables broadcast weak radio frequency signals corresponding to data streams. They even include faint voltage fluctuations in the power lines (Figure 7.18).

Another way to snoop is based on the fact that keystrokes create sound. The audio components are unique per key. The timing reflects key sequencing, or touch-typing patterns. The attacker can listen in on a convenient microphone, such as a telephone, or can listen from a distance using a laser telescope. Next is an example of a checker routine for Linux servers provided by Coverity.

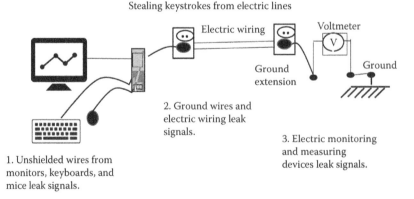

Figure 7.18 Electric lines leak signals.

Bugs

A software bug is a flaw, failure, error, or fault in a computer program or system. Bugs are made by developers who make a mistake in the code, such as a syntax error or an error in logic. Bugs can be exploited for malware, and it is important to find bugs in your system. This section will briefly look at different approaches to finding security bugs.

There are numerous bugging programs that check your code for security flaws. One company is Coverity, which is a leading provider of solutions for software quality and security testing. Figure 7.19 shows an example of debugging proprietary software from Coverity, which is "a Synopsys company." We will use Coverity to focus on how bugs work, how they are found, and how a company's service can be useful in helping you prevent bugs. Figure 7.19 shows the architecture of the Coverity Security Flaw Analysis platform.

Figure 7.20 is a list of bugs that can be detected by Coverity security software.

Most vulnerabilities and coding patterns are specific to the code base. Coverity offers a variety of "checkers" for your programming needs. The example they provide is for Linux. Issues that apply to the Linux kernel are unlikely to apply in application software. Figure 7.21 shows an example of a checker.

It is important to use checkers with your code to make sure you have no vulnerabilities.

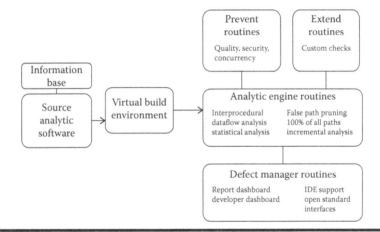

Figure 7.19   Architecture of the Coverity security flaw analysis platform.

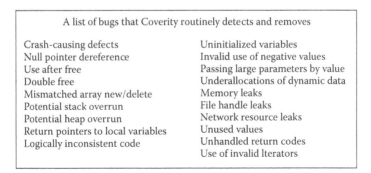

Figure 7.20   Bugs detected by the Coverity security package.

```
Coverity Linux Checker Routine

#include "extend .lang.h"

Start_Extend_Checker_Routine (no_assign, simple);

Analyze_Tree ()

{
        if (Match (Or (_=_) := 0 ), If (_=_) == 0))) ){
               Output_Error ("Within If.");
        }
}

End_ Extend_ Checker Routine();

Make_Main ( no_assign );
```

Figure 7.21   Coverity Linux checker routine.

Detecting Attacks and Removal Systems

Intrusion Detection Systems

An IDS is a device or software application that monitors network or system activities for malicious activities or policy violations and produces reports to a management station. These IDSs come in a variety of "flavors" and approach the goal of detecting suspicious traffic in different ways. There are network-based (NIDS) and host-based (HIDS) IDSs. Some systems may attempt to stop an intrusion attempt, but this is neither required nor expected of a monitoring system. Intrusion detection and prevention systems (IDPSs) are primarily focused on identifying possible incidents, logging information about them, and reporting attempts. In addition, organizations use IDPSs for other purposes, such as identifying problems with security policies, documenting existing threats, and deterring individuals from violating security policies. IDPSs have become a necessary addition to the security infrastructure of nearly every organization.

IDPSs typically record information related to observed events, notify security administrators of important observed events, and produce reports. Many IDPSs can also respond to a detected threat by attempting to prevent it from succeeding. They use several response techniques, which involve the IDPS stopping the attack itself, changing the security environment (e.g., reconfiguring a firewall), or changing the attack's content.

Host-Based and Network-Based Intrusion Detection Systems

To recap, there are two main types of IDSs: NIDS and HIDS.

Network-Based Intrusion Detection Systems

An NIDS is placed at a strategic point or points within the network to monitor traffic to and from all devices on the network. It performs an analysis of passing traffic on the entire subnet, works in a promiscuous mode, and matches the traffic that is passed on the subnets to the library of known attacks. New variants of attacks are thus not identifiable. Once an attack is identified or abnormal behavior is sensed, the alert can be sent to the administrator.

An example of using an NIDS would be installing it on the subnet where firewalls are located in order to see if someone is trying to break into the firewall. Ideally, one would scan all inbound and outbound traffic; however, doing so might create a bottleneck, which would impair the overall speed of the network. Two commonly used tools for NIDS are OPNET and NetSim.

Host-Based Intrusion Detection Systems

An HIDS runs on individual hosts or devices on the network. It monitors the inbound and outbound packets from the device only and will alert the user or administrator if suspicious activity is detected. It takes a snapshot of existing system files and matches it to the previous snapshot. If the critical systems files were modified or deleted, an alert is sent to the administrator to investigate. An example of HIDS usage can be seen in mission-critical machines, which are not expected to change their configurations.

Honeypot Traps out in the Network

A honeypot is a trap set to detect, to deflect, or in some manner to counteract attempts at unauthorized use of information systems. Generally, a honeypot consists of a computer, data, or network site that appears to be part of a network but is actually isolated and monitored, and which seems to contain information or a resource of value to attackers. This is similar to the process whereby police bait a criminal and then conduct ongoing undercover surveillance of that criminal and all their activities and contacts. Astar offers an integrated firewall, router, and honeypot service, which is popular among legal authorities and corporations; they deploy the service in their counteractivities against invaders as a way of turning the tables on these criminals and using those same hacking tools to trap and identify the hacking criminals by attracting them to holding and identification sites (Figure 7.22).

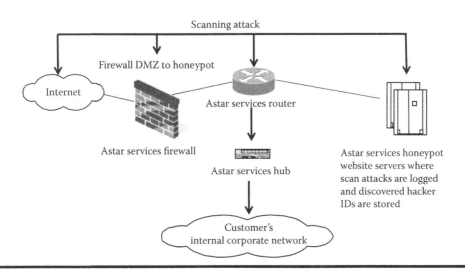

Figure 7.22   Using a honeypot to divert scanning attacks.

Passive and Reactive Systems

In a passive system, the IDS sensor detects a potential security breach, logs the information, and signals an alert on the console or owner. In a reactive system, also known as an *intrusion prevention system* (IPS), the IPS autoresponds to the suspicious activity by resetting the connection or by reprogramming the firewall to block network traffic from the suspected malicious source. The term *IDPS* is commonly used where this can happen automatically or at the command of an operator—systems that both "detect" (alert) and "prevent."

Statistical Anomaly and Signature-Based IDSs

All IDSs use one of two detection techniques:

1. Statistical anomaly–based IDS
   a. An IDS that is anomaly based will monitor network traffic and compare it with an established baseline. The baseline will identify what is "normal" for that network—what sort of bandwidth is generally used, what protocols are used, what ports and devices generally connect to each other—and will alert the administrator or user when traffic is detected that is anomalous to, or significantly different from, the baseline. The issue is that it may raise a false positive alarm for legitimate use of bandwidth if the baselines are not intelligently configured.
2. Signature-based IDS
   a. A signature-based IDS will monitor packets on the network and compare them with a database of signature or attributes from known malicious threats.

This is similar to the way most antivirus software detects malware. The issue is that there will be a lag between a new threat being discovered in the wild and the signature for detecting that threat being applied to your IDS. During that lag time, your IDS would be unable to detect the new threat.

Comparison with Firewalls

Though they both relate to network security, an IDS differs from a firewall in that a firewall looks outwardly for intrusions in order to stop them from happening. Firewalls limit access between networks to prevent intrusion rather than signaling an attack from inside the network. An IDS evaluates a suspected intrusion once it has taken place and signals an alarm. An IDS also watches for attacks that originate from within a system. This is traditionally achieved by examining network communications, identifying the heuristics and patterns (often known as signatures) of common computer attacks, and taking action to alert operators. A system that terminates connections is called an IPS and is another form of an application layer firewall.

Detection Evasion Techniques

Attackers use a number of techniques; the following are considered "simple" measures that can be taken to evade IDS:

1. Fragmentation
   a. By sending fragmented packets, the attacker will be under the radar and can easily bypass the detection system's ability to detect the attack signature.

2. Avoiding defaults
   a. The Transmission Control Protocol (TCP) port utilized by a protocol does not always provide an indication as to the protocol that is being transported. For example, an IDS may expect to detect a Trojan on port 12345. If an attacker has reconfigured it to use a different port, the IDS may not be able to detect the presence of the Trojan.
3. Coordinated, low-bandwidth attacks
   a. Coordinating a scan among numerous attackers (or agents) and allocating different ports or hosts to different attackers makes it difficult for the IDS to correlate the captured packets and deduce that a network scan is in progress.
4. Address spoofing or proxying
   a. Attackers can make it more difficult for security administrators to determine the source of the attack by using poorly secured or incorrectly configured proxy servers to bounce an attack. If the source is spoofed and bounced by a server, then it becomes very difficult for an IDS to detect the origin of the attack.
5. Pattern change evasion
   a. IDSs generally rely on "pattern matching" to detect an attack. By slightly changing the data used in the attack, it may be possible to evade detection. For example, an Internet Message Access Protocol (IMAP) server may be vulnerable to a buffer overflow, and the IDS is able to detect the attack signature of 10 common attack tools. By modifying the payload sent by the tool so that it does not resemble the data that the IDS expects, it may be possible to evade detection.

Here is a list of basic categories of IDS:

■ Anomaly-based intrusion system
■ Application protocol–based IDS (APIDS)
■ Artificial immune system
■ Autonomous agents for intrusion detection
■ Domain Name System (DNS) analytics
■ Host-based IDS (HIDS)
■ Intrusion prevention system (IPS)
■ Protocol-based IDS (PIDS)
■ Security management
■ Intrusion detection message exchange format (IDMEF)

Here is a list of some free IDSs:

■ ACARM-ng
■ AIDE
■ Bro NIDS
■ Fail2ban
■ OSSEC HIDS
■ Prelude Hybrid IDS
■ Samhain
■ Snort
■ Suricata

Forensics

A vital complement in detecting attacks is the process of figuring out what happened after a successful attack has occurred. This involves the creation of rich and extensive logs of all activity on a network and of application activity and each database access, read, extraction, and update. A set of tools for analyzing these logs is essential for teams to analyze and understand aberrant activities by the forensic team. This forensic process is one of looking for patterns in activity and comparing those patterns with both known and unusual activity. It also involves understanding the underlying structure of the corporate systems in place in order to detect unusual and possibly aberrant behavior or, data, activity or results.

Detecting Attacks and Attackers with Examples

Symmetric Cryptography

Symmetric cryptography assumes that all parties already share a secret key. For this type of cryptography to work correctly, the encryption algorithm must be publicly known and the use of a proprietary cipher is discouraged.

Use cases can either be single use or multiuse. Single-use keys are used only once to encrypt a single message. A new key is generated for every e-mail and there is no need for nonce (it is set to zero). Stream ciphers are an example of a single-use key. A multiuse key is used to encrypt many messages and requires either a unique or random nonce.

Block ciphers are the cryptography workhorse. This is a special cipher based on a deterministic algorithm operating on fixed-length groups of bits/blocks with an unvarying transformation that is specified in the symmetric key. These ciphers are important elementary components in the design of many cryptographic protocols and are widely used to implement encryption of bulk data.

The Problem of Detecting Attacks

Given a choice, we'd like our systems to be airtight-secure, but we often do not get that choice. The number one reason is because of cost, resulting in the messy alternative—to detect misuse rather than build a system that can't be misused. It is important to note that even with airtight security, it is still important to detect for misuse. Misuse might be more about your company's policy than security. A system has many dimensions to secure, and it's difficult to decide where to monitor, how to detect problems, how accurate those detections are, and what attackers can do to elude detection.

Directory Traversal

Suppose you've been hired to provide computer security for a company. They offer web-based services via backend programs invoked via this URL: http://company.com/amazeme.exe?profile=info/luser.txt.

Due to the installed base issues, you can't alter backend components such as amazeme.exe. One form of attack you're worried about is information leakage via directory traversal. For instance, an attacker could type GET/amazeme.exe?profile=./././../../etc/passwd.

What Is Another Method to Detect This Attack?

Beyond IDS, as mentioned in the previous section, one method you could try to implement is run scripts that analyze log files generated by web servers. One significant advantage of this method is that it is cheap, as web servers generally have logging facilities built into them. It also does not have issues with %-escapes or encrypted HTTPS. The issues come with filename tricks, and the fact that this method cannot actually block attacks and prevent them from occurring. The detection is also delayed, and if the attack is a compromise, then malware might be able to alter the logs before they are analyzed.

Another method is to monitor the system call activity of backend processes—other words, to look for attempts to access to the/etc/passwd. The advantages of this method are that it involves no issues with HTTP complexities, may avoid issues with filename tricks, and only generates an alert if an attack has succeeded. The issues are that you might have to analyze a large amount of data, other processes may make legitimate access causing false positives, or you would prefer detection alert for all attempts.

An Alternate Paradigm

Up until now, we have suggested simply detecting attacks as they come. But what if you launched attacks on yourself? Vulnerability scanning is a tool that allows you to probe your own systems with a wide range of attacks and to fix any that succeed. The advantages are that it is proactive and prevents future misuse, and it can ignore IDS alarms you know can't succeed. The downsides are that it can take a lot of work, it is not helpful for systems you cannot modify, and it can be potentially dangerous for disruptive attacks. In practice, this approach is prudent and widely used today.

Detection Accuracy

There are two types of detector errors:

1. False positive: alerting about a problem when in fact there is no problem.
2. False negative: failing to alert about a problem when in fact there is a problem.

Detector accuracy is often assessed in terms of the rates at which these occur. Is it possible to build a detector with perfect detection? The answer is yes, you can have a detector with no false negatives. However, you will pay in false positives. The ideal detector achieves an effective balance between false positives and false negatives. Which is it better to lean toward? It depends on the cost of each type of error. For example, a false positive might lead to paging a duty officer and consuming an hour of their time, while a false negative might lead to a $10K cleaning up and a compromised system because of what was missed. It also critically depends on the rate at which attacks occur on your environment.

Suppose our detector has a false positive rate of 0.1% and a false negative rate of 2% (not bad!). Our servers receive 1000 URLs/day and five of them are attacks.

■ Expected # of false positives each day = 0.1% * 995 = 1
■ Expected # false negatives each day = 2% * 5 = 0.1 (less than a week)

That's pretty good! But what if our traffic volume increased to 10,000,000 URLs/day and five of them are attacks?

■ Expected # of false positives each day = 10,000

Nothing changed with our detector; just the environment changed. Accuracy grows more difficult when the base rate of activity we want to detect is quite low.

Detecting Successful Attacks

Suppose we're more worried about a version of the attack that modifies/etc/passwd rather than retrieves it. Say the following code is used:

■ GET/amazeme.exe?profile=/passwd&newcolor=w00t:nIT9q23cjwVs:0:0:/:/bin/bash

How can we detect if this attack was successful? Maybe amazeme.exe generates specific output if a file is modified; if so, look for that. If not, then the NIDS/web-server instrumentation or log monitor all have difficulty in telling if the attack succeeded.

Another approach is a periodic process that looks for changes to sensitive files and creates flags for the operator. This program is not based on file modification time, as a program can simply change that. Instead, compare with a database oh SHA256 hashes. The problem is what if malware compromised the kernel, which can alter the hashes and/or the content returned when reading a given file? One fix for this is not to store hashes on a local system but instead to send over the Internet elsewhere. Another suggestion is to separate all read-only media from the computer booting process and the operating system kernel.

Detection versus Blocking

If we can detect attacks, how about blocking them? This is a lot trickier than it sounds. It is not a possibility for retrospective analysis (e.g., a nightly job that looks for logs). It can also be quite hard for a detector that's not in the data path. For instance, how can a NIDS that passively monitors traffic block attacks? You could change the firewall rules dynamically and forge RST packets. RST is a reset packet used in a TCP reset attack. The TCP header contains a bit known as the "reset" (RST) flag, which when turned on stops the packet flow. RST can be deployed validly or as a step in a hacker's TCP reset attack. Of course, there is a never-ending race regarding what the attacker does before the block. Another issue is that false positives get expensive. You do not just use up an operator but also begin damaging production activity. Fortunately, today's technologies pretty much all offer blocking or IPSs.

Styles of Detection

Signature Based

Suppose we can use the characteristics of malware to find more of it (Figure 7.23).

What's good about this approach is that its conceptually simple, takes care of known attacks, and makes it easy to share signatures and build up libraries. What is dangerous about it is that you

```
Styles of detection: signature-based detection

Look for activity that matches a similar known
attack that has already occurred.


An example:
Alert tcp $EXTERNAL_NET any-> $HOME_NET
   139 flow:to_server, established
Content:"leb2f Sfeb 4a5e 89fb 893e 89f2l"
msg: "EXPLOIT x86 linux samba overflow"
reference:bugtraq, 1816
Reference:cve, CVE-1999-0811
Classtype: attempted-admin


Can be at different semantic layers:
IP/TCP header fields, packet payload, or URLs
```

Figure 7.23   Signature-based detection, a routine example.

can become blind to novel attacks or miss variants of known attacks. Also, simpler versions tend to look at low-level syntax rather than at the semantics, which can lead to weak power. In other words, it misses variants or generates a lot of false positives.

Vulnerability Signatures

The idea here is to focus on known problems rather than known attacks. Figure 7.24 is an example.

Like the signature-based method, this approach is simple, takes care of known attacks, and makes it easy to share and build a library of such problems. In addition, it can detect variants of known attacks and is much more concise than per-attack signatures. The issues are that it cannot detect novel attacks, and signatures can be hard to write or express. In other words, you have to explain to a computer how the attack works; it's not enough to simply observe that it worked.

```
Vulnerability signatures
Don't try matching with known attacks, match on known
problems.
Example:
Alert top $EXTERNAL_NETany ->$HTTP SERVERS 80
Uricontent: ".ida?; nocase; dsize; > 239: flags: A+
Mag: "Web-lIS ISAPI .ida attempt"
Reference:bugtrap, 1816
Reference:cve,CAN-2000-0071
Classtype: attempted_admin

This above is a match for URLs that invoke *ida?, have 239 bytes of payload,
and have ACK (acknowledgment) set and maybe some others set as well.

This example detects any* attempt to exploit a particular buffer overflow in
IIS web Servers.

This is used by the "Code Red" worm.
* Note: The signature shown is not quite complete. Detection must be made
on only a partial signature.
```

Figure 7.24   Match on known problems rather than signatures.

Anomaly Based

This idea is based on the concept that attacks look peculiar. The high-level approach involves developing a model of normal behavior (based on analyzing historical logs) and flagging activity that deviates from it. For Instance, a processing routine looks at the distribution of characters in URL parameters and learns that some are rare and do not occur repeatedly. The big benefit is the potential detection of a wide range of attacks, including the novel ones. It is not a foolproof method, however. It can still fail to detect known and novel attacks if they do not look peculiar. Also, what happens if your history includes the attacks? Base rate fallacy is particularly acute: If the prevalence of attacks is low, then you are going to see benign outliers more often.

Specification-Based Detection

Instead of focusing on behavior, focus on what is allowed. For instance, in FooCorp we decide that all URL parameters sent to foocorp.com servers must have at most one "/" in them. If a URL has more than one "/", then it should be flagged. What is good about this approach is that it can detect novel attacks and has low false positives. The problem is that this method is expensive. It takes a lot of labor to derive specifications and keep them up to date as things change.

Behavioral Detection

In this approach, we do not look for attacks but for evidence of compromise. In other words, inspect all outgoing web traffic that transmits content for any part of that content that matches names contained in password files. Also look at the sequence of system calls and flag any that, after undergoing prior analysis of a given program, indicates that it does not normally indicate system calls. What's good about this approach is it can detect a wide range of novel attacks, it has low false positives, and it can be cheap to implement. The problem with this approach is that you can discover you have a problem with no opportunity to prevent it.

The Problem of Evasion

For any detection approach, it is important to consider how an adversary might (try to) elude it. It is important to note that, even if an approach is evadable, it is still important to run it, as it can catch most of the unwanted traffic—unless, of course, it is easy to evade. Some evasions reflect an incomplete analysis, for instance, hex escapes or "../////..//../" alias. In principle, we can deal with these if we take extra care in our implementation.

Some evasions exploit deviation from the spec. For instance, double-escapes for SQL injection:

- %25%32%37 =>%27=>

Some can exploit fundamental ambiguities. The problem grows as the monitoring viewpoint is increasingly removed from ultimate end points. This problem can be particularly acute for network monitoring. For instance, consider detecting occurrences of the string "root" inside a network connection. If we get a copy of each packet, how difficult can it be? (Figure 7.25).

Detecting text such as, for example, "root"

The Method is to scan each packet for "r," "o," 'o," and "t"
We might also employ filters in this comparison such as Boyer-Moore,
Aho-Corasick, or Bloom filters.

However, problems in such a scan may occur such when TCP doesn't account for
and preserve text boundaries,

Such as ------------ro   in packet 1 and   ot------------- in packet 2

We can set up our search to continue our search across packet boundaries to find
a match.

But beyond TCP issues, IP itself doesn't guarantee delivery of packets in order,
making cross-packet searching more difficult.

Figure 7.25   Detecting specific text.

How do we fix out-of-order packet delivery for matching purposes searching for problems? We need to reassemble the entire TCP byte stream. We need to match sequence numbers and buffer packets with later data (above a sequence "hole"). The problem is that this potentially requires a lot of storage maintenance of state, plus the attacker can cause us to exhaust state by sending lots of data above a sequence hole. Even TCP reassembly may not be sufficient (Figure 7.26).

How can we address this more complex issue? One idea is to alert the administrator upon seeing a retransmission inconsistency, as it most likely reflects someone with malicious intent. However, this approach does not work. TCP retransmissions broken in this fashion occur in live traffic. Another idea is that if NIDS sees a connection, it should be killed. This idea works in this case, since the benign instance is already fatally broken. But for other evasions, such actions have collateral damage. A third idea is to rewrite traffic to remove all ambiguities.

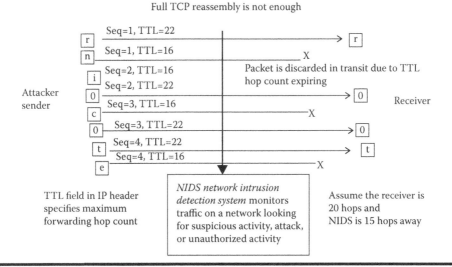

Figure 7.26   Even TCP reassembly may not be sufficient.

QUESTIONS

1. This method is used to "bait" people who attempt to penetrate other people's computer systems. What is it?
2. How does a botnet spread?
3. Explain the difference between how worms and viruses are spread and give an example of each.
4. Identify two techniques that protect viruses from virus scanners and explain the purpose of each.
5. These systems are computer network security systems used to protect systems from viruses, malware, and spyware. This system _____ only located on servers and routers. This system _____ located on every host machine.

Chapter 8

Cryptography and the RSA Algorithm

Cryptography is the practice of applying encryption techniques to ensure secure communication in the presence of third parties (whom we will consider adversaries). Generally, cryptography is about constructing and analyzing protocols that block adversaries, protect data confidentiality and data integrity, and provide authentication for the sender and the message. Modern cryptography is at the intersection of mathematics, computer science, and electrical engineering. Common applications of cryptography include the encryption of information on ATM cards, the encryption of computer passwords, and the process of encryption and the employment of keys for transmission and the conduct of electronic commerce.

Prior to the modern age, cryptography was generally synonymous only with encryption, which is the conversion of information from a readable state to untranslatable content that is unreadable by the unauthorized. The originator of an encrypted message shares the decoding technique for the transmission with the intended recipients. Since World War I and the advent of the computer, the methods used to carry out cryptology have become increasingly complex, and the application has become widespread and necessary.

Modern cryptography is heavily based on mathematical theory and computer science practice; cryptographic algorithms are designed around assumptions of computational hardness, making them difficult to break. It is theoretically possible to break such a system, but in practice, it is infeasible. These schemes are therefore termed *computationally secure*. Improvements in integer factorization algorithms and faster computing technology require these solutions to be continually adapted.

The history of cryptography is a long and storied one that includes contributions by luminaries such as Pierre de Fermat, Leonhard Euler, Johann Carl Friedrich Gauss, Alan Turing, and Claude Shannon.

Cryptography has two main goals: to secure communication and to protect files.

The employment of cryptography is a very important aspect of providing for the security of information, both as it is transported as well as when it is stored in encrypted form. Cryptography is centered around the process of creating algorithms to encrypt messages and stored data in such a way that they are hard to decipher (crack), based on estimates of the time it would take for an adversary to decrypt (crack) that material. However, as the computational power of computers has increased, allowing for both brute-force trial-and-error techniques as well as the application of sophisticated encryption-breaking algorithms, a series of adaptations to popular cryptography algorithms have been required for them to remain secure. Among these types of encryption are symmetric encryption, asymmetric encryption, and hashing.

Symmetric-key encryption (also called *private-key encryption*) is the process of scrambling information with a single key shared by both the sender and the receiver. The encrypted information is extremely difficult for someone to read without decrypting the data using the original key or a key made by the same algorithm with which it was originally encrypted. If the shared encryption key is disclosed, all communications between the sender and receiver are compromised.

Symmetric-key encryption assumes that all parties already share a secret key. For this type of cryptography to work correctly, the encryption algorithm must be publicly known, and the use of a proprietary cipher is discouraged.

Use cases can either be single use or multiuse. Single-use keys are used only once to encrypt a single message. A new key is generated for every e-mail and there is no need for nonce (it is set to zero). Stream ciphers are an example of a single-use key. A multiuse key is used to encrypt many messages and requires either a unique or random nonce.

Block ciphers are the cryptography workhorse. These are special ciphers that are based on a deterministic algorithm and operate on fixed-length groups of bits/blocks with an unvarying transformation that is specified in the symmetric key. These ciphers are important elementary components in the design of many cryptographic protocols and are widely used to implement the encryption of bulk data.

Some symmetric block cipher algorithms are Data Encryption Standard (DES), 3-DES, Advanced Encryption Standard (AES), Electronic Codebook (ECB), and Cipher Block Chaining (CBC). The simplest of the encryption modes is the Electronic Codebook (ECB) mode. The message is divided into blocks, and each block is encrypted separately. In CBC mode, each block of plaintext is computed with the previous ciphertext block before being encrypted. This way, each ciphertext block depends on all plaintext blocks processed up to that point. To make each message unique, an initialization vector must be used in the first block.

Data Encryption Standard and Advanced Encryption Standard

DES is an old version of encryption. There is an inherent weakness in DES that allows the encryption to be broken using certain methods of attack. DES uses a much smaller 56-bit encryption that has a maximum of 256 combinations. This is easy for a computer to break with a brute-force attack.

AES can use a 128-, 192-, or 256-bit encryption key with 2^{128}, 2^{129}, or 2^{256} combinations. This, coupled with the fact that the system has no other weaknesses, means that AES is considered relatively unbreakable (Figure 8.1).

In Figure 8.1, the symmetric key is a string of randomized data that is used in the process of encrypting the data. This process is normally used to secure computer storage drives, with a good example being the encryption used with MAC OS X's FireVault drives. However, this symmetric approach is not the most secure method, since the key used for encryption and decryption needs to be protected. Otherwise, the encrypted data will be compromised.

Asymmetric encryption is another more complicated form of encryption. The concept of public-key schemes (implemented in the first practical asymmetric scheme) was for key distribution only.

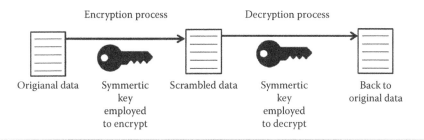

Figure 8.1   The symmetric-key encryption process.

This process was published in 1977 by Diffie and Hellman. This approach scrambles data during transmission by utilizing a public key during the encryption of the data, while a separate private key is utilized during the decryption process. The principle distinction between asymmetric and symmetric encryption is that the former uses one key while the latter uses a public key to encrypt and a different private key to decrypt (a two-key process). A very popular form of asymmetric encryption is the Rivest–Shamir–Adleman (RSA) algorithm, named for its three inventors, which is illustrated in Figure 8.2.

RSA encryption is designed to be very difficult to crack. In fact, Martin Gardner stated that he would give $100 dollars to the first person to break the cipher text based on a 129-digit product of primes that was based on RSA cryptography. However, as computing power grew, so did peoples' knowledge of how to break RSA encryption. One of the most famous ways to break RSA encryption is by utilizing a man-in-the-middle attack. What this does is to send your public key to an untrusted computer when you intend it to be sent to a trusted computer. The untrusted computer can then use that public key to decrypt the data that was supposed to be decrypted by the other intended, trusted machine within the network.

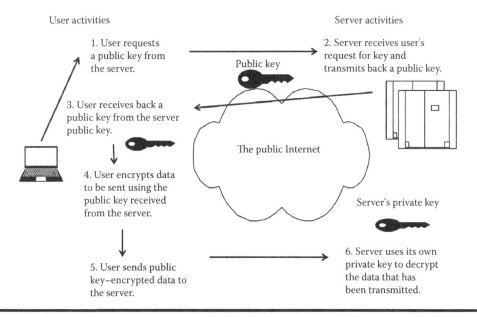

Figure 8.2   The RSA asymmetric encryption process.

The RSA algorithm relies on the difficulty of factoring large composite numbers. The largest factored RSA number thus far is RSA-200, which is 663 bits in length. The RSA algorithm generally uses integers of 1024 bits.

RSA employs a radically different public-key system in which two keys are used: a public and a private key.

Anyone who knows the public key can encrypt messages or verify signatures, but they cannot decrypt messages or create signatures.

It works by the clever use of number theory where problems that are easy to compute in one direction, such as encrypting material, are difficult to compute in a reverse direction, such as unencrypting that information to reverse the encryption process. Note that public-key schemes are neither more secure than private-key schemes (security depends on the key size for both), nor do they replace private-key schemes (they are too slow to do so). Rather, they complement them.

This algorithm was developed to address two key issues:

1. Distributing the two keys: How to have secure communications in general without having to trust a separate key distribution coordinator with your key
2. Using digital signatures: How to verify a message comes intact from the claimed sender

With RSA, each party—the sender and the receiver—has a pair of keys. If you know only the public key, you can encrypt but not decrypt the message. Those who encrypt messages or verify signatures cannot decrypt messages or create signatures.

The second key in the pair, a private key, is known only to the recipient and is used to decrypt messages and sign (create) signatures.

For the process to work, you choose two large prime numbers, say p and q.

An RSA number n is a number such that $n = p \times q$ where p and q are distinct, large prime integers (by large, we typically mean at least 512–2048 bits), and n is the product of these two large prime numbers.

Then compute $n = p \times q$ and $\varphi = (p - 1)(q - 1)$.

Then choose another prime number e, which is relatively prime to φ.

Then compute d from φ and e such that $e^*d \bmod \varphi = 1$.

The public key depends upon n and e. There must be no numbers that divide neatly into e and into $(p - 1)(q - 1)$, except for 1. That makes $e = a$ prime number.

The private key depends on p, q, and φ (e), and it is used to compute the private key d.

Obviously a simple process!

Hashing is another form of cryptography that is used to encrypt passwords. Hashing takes your password and transforms it into a string of data. Two main properties are associated with hashed data. The first is that the same data will always produce the same hash, and the second is that it is impossible to reverse the hashed data back to the original data without a hash key. As one can see, encryption and cryptography are very important when dealing with information security (IS) because they help ensure that the right data is being sent to the right person in a safe way.

Encryption and code has been in existence for hundreds of years. The hiding of information in plain sight for the desired audience is the most purposeful usage of encryption. How can information be broadcast to many individuals, but only the correct individuals understand what to do with the information? These concepts cover the overall use case for encryption and cryptography. Radio technology was the first example of the need for some sort of encryption for sensitive information transmitted. In World War I, there was no way to digitally encrypt communications, so all information that was broadcast for military logistics could be intercepted by the enemy and used against the transmitting party. To combat this challenge, encryption had to be implemented.

The famous Alan Turing was the inventor of the computing machine and most importantly for cryptography, many of its algorithms. This invention sparked an interest in automated or digital signal encryption, which much of the world relies on today. Alan Turing wrote a paper in 1936, "On Computable Numbers with an Application," that is considered the first description of a computing machine with loadable programs and loadable data. The first complete computer he built following that paper was the ACE computer, which he designed and built in 1948 at Manchester University in England. He previously built a special-purpose computing machine at Bletchley Park to decode the German Enigma code encryption machines. In 1950, he wrote the paper "Computing Machinery and Intelligence," which defined the Turing Test for whether an artificial process could be determined to be intelligent.

Public Keys

The development of public keys relies on a few very basic equations. The premise is that a "public key" can be provided in plain sight, but the private key of an individual is held private. The most common algorithm to use this concept is the previously mentioned RSA algorithm, which employs public and private keys. Securing the running of code relies on trust between two entities. One example of this is the digital certificates that are evaluated before lower-level code, such as drivers, are installed on a machine. Such "certificates" have been encoded with a public/private-key structure.

Modern Approaches for Breaking Encryption

The breaking of modern encryption began in the 1990s once regular usage occurred by higher profile companies and government entities. One method to break RSA-129 encryption was the "factorization" of messages sent using this standard. It took 8 months using this method with over 600 volunteers from more than 20 countries to decode a simple string—"The Magic Words Are Squeamish Ossifrage." This ability, from a computational perspective, has been drastically improved as Moore's law moves forward. The overall point is that once an encryption algorithm is released to the public, individuals immediately begin the process of deconstructing these algorithms. Encryption is a temporary possibility; it can ultimately always be broken given enough interest, time, and resources in the hands of capable individuals. Another modern encryption type is the previously mentioned AES. This was invented in 1997 and is still regularly used today. Most important in this method is to understand the "block size," which is what speeds or slows the process. The lower the "variable key size," the faster a computer will be able to decrypt—or, from a security perspective, break—the encryption. The larger the block size, the more difficult it is for the encryption to be broken.

Current Cryptography Concepts

The most recent point of interest and advancement in the data-processing world is the use of quantum computers. These machines use concepts drawn from physics to perform computing operations. These operations can also be used to perform the encryption and decryption of data.

Quantum computing provides room beyond the binary structure we are used to (in which 1 means on and 0 means off). Using quantum computing, there are any number of substates available to these values, meaning it is capable of doing far more parallel operations.

More Cryptography, Private-Key, Public-Key Encryption, RSA Algorithm Details

Offset codebook (OCB) mode was designed to provide both authentication and privacy. It is essentially a scheme for integrating a method authentication code (MAC) into the operation of a block cipher. In this way, OCB mode avoids the need to use two systems: a MAC for authentication and encryption for privacy. This results in lower computational cost compared with using separate encryption and authentication functions.

There are three versions of OCB: OCB1, OCB2, and OCB3. OCB1 was published in 2001. OCB2 improves on OCB1 by allowing associated data to be included with the message—that is, data that is not encrypted but should be authenticated—and a new method for generating a sequence of offsets. OCB2 was first published in 2003, originally named *authenticated encryption mode* or *advanced encryption mode* (AEM). OCB3, published in 2011, changed again the way offsets are computed and introduced minor performance improvements.

OCB mode is listed as an optional method in the IEEE 802.11 wireless security standard as an alternative to counter with CBC-MAC (CCM). OCB2 is standardized in ISO/IEC 19772:2009 and OCB3 in RFC 7253.

Initialization vectors: This vector is a fixed-size input to a cryptographic primitive that is typically required to be random or pseudorandom. The randomization is critical for encryption schemes to achieve semantic security (a property wherein repeated usage of the scheme under the same key does not allow an attacker to infer relationships between segments of the encrypted messages).

Data integrity: A MAC is a short piece of information used to authenticate a message and to provide integrity and authenticity assurances on that message. Integrity assurances detect accidental and intentional message changes, while authenticity assurances affirm the message's origins. A MAC algorithm accepts a secret key and an arbitrary-length message to be authenticated and then outputs a MAC (which is also sometimes known as a tag). This code protects the message's integrity and authenticity by allowing verifiers (who also possess the secret key) to detect any changes to the message content.

Keyed-hash MAC (HMAC) is a specific construction for calculating a MAC involving a cryptographic hash function in combination with a secret cryptographic key. Like a standard MAC, it can also be used to verify data integrity and message authentication simultaneously. The cryptographic strength of the HMAC depends on the cryptographic strength of the underlying hash function, the size of its hash output, and the size and quality of the key.

The Merkle–Damgard (MD) construction or hash function is a method of building collision-resistant cryptographic hash functions from collision-resistant one-way compression functions. This function applies an MD-compliant padding function to create an output whose size is a multiple of a fixed number (usually 512 or 1024); this is done because functions cannot handle inputs of arbitrary size. The hash function then breaks the result into blocks of fixed size and processes them one at a time with the compression function, each time combining a block of the input with the output of the previous round.

Public-key cryptography, also known as *asymmetric cryptography*, is a class of cryptographic protocols based on algorithms that require two separate keys, one of which is secret (or private) and one of which is public. Although different, the two parts of this key pair are mathematically linked. The public key is used to encrypt plaintext or to verify a digital signature, whereas the private key is used for the opposite operation, in these examples to decrypt cipher text or to create a digital signature. The term *asymmetric* stems from the use of different keys to perform these opposite functions, each the inverse of the other—as contrasted with conventional (*symmetric*) cryptography, which relies on the same key to perform both.

Public-key algorithms are based on mathematical problems that currently admit no efficient solution and are inherent in certain integer factorization, discrete logarithm, and elliptic curve relationships. It is computationally easy for a user to generate a public- and private-key pair and to use it for encryption and decryption. The strength lies in the "impossibility" (computational impracticality) of a properly generated private key being determined from its corresponding public key. Thus, the public key may be published without compromising security. Security depends only on keeping the private key private. Public-key algorithms, unlike symmetric-key algorithms, do not require a secure channel for the initial exchange of one or more secret keys between the parties.

Because of the computational complexity of asymmetrical encryption, it is typically used only to transfer a symmetrical encryption key by which the message (and usually the entire conversation) is encrypted. The symmetrical encryption/decryption is based on simpler algorithms and is much faster.

Message authentication involves hashing the message to produce a digest and encrypting the digest with the private key to produce a digital signature. Thereafter, anyone can verify this signature by (1) computing the hash of the message, (2) decrypting the signature with the signer's public key, and (3) comparing the computed digest with the decrypted digest. Equality between the digests confirms that the message is unmodified since it was signed and that the signer, and no one else, intentionally performed the signature operation—assuming the signer's private key has remained secret to the signer.

Public-key algorithms are fundamental security ingredients in cryptosystems, applications, and protocols. They underpin various Internet standards, such as Transport Layer Security (TLS), Secure/Multipurpose Internet Mail Extensions (S/MIME), Pretty Good Privacy (PGP), and GNU Privacy Guard (GPG). Some public-key algorithms provide key distribution and secrecy, some provide digital signatures, and some provide both (e.g., RSA).

Public-key cryptography finds application in, among others, the IT security discipline of IS. IS is concerned with all aspects of protecting electronic information assets against security threats. Public-key cryptography is used as a method of ensuring the confidentiality, authenticity, and non-reputability of electronic communications and data storage.

A digital signature is a mathematical scheme for demonstrating the authenticity of a digital message or document. A valid digital signature gives a recipient reason to believe that the message was created by a known sender, that the sender cannot deny having sent the message (authentication and non-repudiation), and that the message was not altered in transit (integrity). Digital signatures are commonly used for software distribution and financial transactions and in other cases where it is important to detect forgery or tampering.

A *public-key infrastructure* (PKI) is a set of hardware, software, people, policies, and procedures needed to create, manage, distribute, use, store, and revoke digital certificates and manage public-key encryption. The purpose of a PKI is to facilitate the secure electronic transfer of information for a range of network activities such as e-commerce, Internet banking, and confidential e-mail. It is required for activities in which simple passwords are an inadequate authentication method and more rigorous proof is required to confirm the identity of the parties involved in the communication and to validate the information being transferred.

A PKI is an arrangement that binds public keys with respective user identities by means of a certificate authority (CA). The user identity must be unique within each CA domain. The third-party validation authority (VA) can provide this information on behalf of the CA. The binding is established through the registration and issuance process. Depending on the assurance level of the binding, this may be carried out by software at a CA or under human supervision. The PKI role that assures this binding is called the registration authority (RA). The RA is responsible for accepting requests for digital certificates and for authenticating the person or organization making the request.

QUESTIONS

1. This is the cornerstone of modern electronic security technology used to protect valuable information. What is it?
2. What is the difference between cryptography and encryption?
3. This is the workhorse of cryptography. What is it?
4. Computer encryption systems belong in one of two categories: symmetric-key encryption and public-key encryption. Explain each and which one is more secure.
5. When would you use hashing?

Chapter 9

Browser Security and Cross-Site Scripting

Browser security is an important topic in information security because a large portion of the population uses computers, primarily for browsing the Internet. A simple lack of browser security knowledge plagues many Internet users who fall victim to constant pop-ups, adware, spyware, and other forms of malware downloaded from the Internet. There are a variety of attacks that can occur based on the vulnerabilities within various Internet browsers, which include exploiting JavaScript, Structured Query Language (SQL) injection, and cross-site scripting. Frequently, these browsers are not aware of the breaches when they occur and may often display a "fake safe" connection. For instance, if a user visited a site that was hosting malicious code and that exploited the vulnerabilities of the host's particular web browser, the website could run processes that were not originally intended by that accessing host. Once the hacker has gained access to the host's system, he or she can inject more malicious code into the host's browser, applications, and even the host's operating system, causing even further damage.

Cross-site scripting is a vulnerability found within web applications. Since the severity of these vulnerabilities can range from a simple annoyance to a significant security risk, it is important to get an understanding of cross-site scripting. Essentially, this occurs when malicious code (normally JavaScript) is inserted within the target's code. Famous cross-site scripting attacks have occurred on Twitter, Facebook, YouTube, and many other websites. An example would be having a hacker load malicious JavaScript, the purpose of which is to collect a website visitor's personal information and then send it to the hacker's secret server for private information collection. A breakdown of cross-site scripting is shown in further detail in Figure 9.1.

In addition to the growing cross-site scripting problem, SQL injection is creating similar problems. When an attacker infects a data-driven application with a malicious string of SQL commands, which are then executed, this is termed an *SQL-injection attack*. This can cause a server to dump private information that was contained in its database to the attacker's private server for personal collection. Retail websites are common targets for SQL injections due to the nature of the information that they store: personal information, credit-card numbers, street addresses, and so on.

However, these are only a few examples of web-browser security that must be addressed. In fact, Google stated in 2007 that they found Trojan malware on 300,000 web pages, along with adware

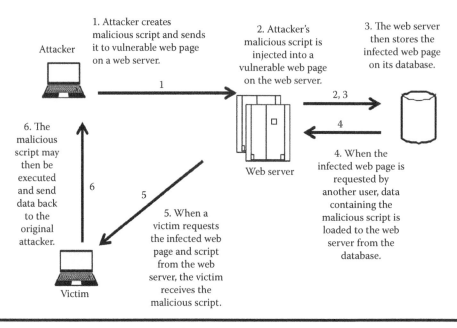

Figure 9.1   Cross-site scripting attack through a web server to an unwitting victim.

on another 18,000 pages. Some of these may be as simple as pasting malicious code to be rendered as a picture by the host's computer. Another example is disguising malicious code to redirect users to an unsafe site using advertisements. Once the client clicks the "advertisement," their personal information can be sent off to a third-party server for collection, eventually to be sold on the dark web.

Web-browser security is a growing problem within the information security sector. In fact, it is growing due to the increased use of third-party application programming interfaces (APIs), third-party extensions, and third-party libraries. Web developers utilizing these extensions may not even recognize that they are personally injecting bad code into their source code that can be seen by the hackers creating the malicious code.

Once of the most critical applications to computer usage is the web browser. It is becoming more commonly the most killer app in existence in the personal computing world. Increased processing responsibilities have been shifted to the "cloud" or away from the local machine to run specific applications. Programs such as "Google Apps" are an example of what can be done through a web browser. Because of this, the web browser is the most targeted area of user behavior, as it's the most common way to access outside resources from the Internet.

Three Web Threat Models

Attackers will often target the weakest layer to get them into a system, but nearly all vulnerable and important information will be taken from the upper levels—the layers that humans are most likely to deal with. Three threat models exist when attacking a system that uses some sort of hook to the web browser platforms.

1. Web attacker: The user's browser is compromised by visiting an infected site, and the malicious user can launch code through the trusted website.

2. Network attacker: The attacker can attack the wireless communications locally or nearby and then inject its own directions into the packets (such as Domain Name System [DNS] poisoning).
3. Malware attacker: The attacker is able to escape the sandbox of the browser (its isolation mechanisms) and launch code within the operating system itself.

Most notably, a web-based attack can lead to a malware attack once security has been breached. The first stop for browser security begins with the Hypertext Transfer Protocol (HTTP) response and user input. Users' behavior is the most targeted and weakest portion of computer system usage. Web browsers at their core are applications written to render code in a graphic format that can easily be interacted with by the user. This means that much of what's running behind the browser is unannounced to the user. Security checks are built into browsers to prevent the running of malicious codes, but missing an update for even a day might leave a browser vulnerable enough.

Web-Page Content

Many web browsers have a built-in indicator that displays when the website is operating in a fully secure mode. Many individuals will look past this and quickly hit "accept" when warnings pop up on the screen. One such warning is the loading of Hypertext Transfer Protocol secure (HTTPS) and HTTP together. If unsecure or non-HTTP(S) content is loaded, the potential arises for an outside party to place the browser at risk. Not all browsers can detect this "mixed" content; Safari is one of the browsers that do not use this capability. Figure 9.2 shows an example of one of these warnings.

What is most difficult to address in controlling the loading of content are the basics of the HTTP. By design, HTTP is a stateless protocol, much like how Universal Datagram Protocol (UDP) works in comparison to the Transmission Control Protocol/Internet Protocol (TCP/IP). Small data files that are temporarily stored with the browser are called *cookie* files. These files provide a browser with the opportunity to add state to the browsing session. Cookies permit seamless browsing, customized settings, and login capabilities for individual users, making them a target for attackers.

Code Isolation

One of the strategies for mitigating the security challenges of web browsing is to isolate the environment inside which code is run. By creating these isolated, sandboxed environments in which the code runs, the experience becomes much safer but is often just as seamless in terms of the user experience. To isolate code, restricting the interaction between "unique origins" is important. For

Figure 9.2   Warning of both secure and non-secure items.

example, if an image was loaded from one source on a page and another image is from a different source, isolating these by origin will ensure that the content is not aware of other content being loaded; its access to receiving input from other areas of the browser/screen would be cut off.

The greatest challenge with isolating code becomes the amount of resources it takes to create a sandbox for each individual area of code.

Browser Security Model

A browser exploit is a form of malicious code that takes advantage of a flaw or vulnerability in an operating system or piece of software with the intent of breaching browser security to alter a user's browser settings without their knowledge. Malicious code may exploit ActiveX, HTML, images, Java, JavaScript, and other web technologies and cause the browser to run arbitrary code. According to the 2015 vulnerability review by Secunia, 1035 vulnerabilities were discovered in the top five browsers. This is a 42% increase affecting Google Chrome, Mozilla Firefox, Internet Explorer, Opera, and Safari.

The goal of web security is to ensure that users can safely browse the web and support secure web applications. Users should be able to visit a variety of websites without having information stolen or having one site compromise the session of another site. Additionally, applications delivered over the web should have the same security properties we require for stand-alone applications.

There are three types of web threat that are living and persistent in the web today. The first is a web attacker that is seeking to take control of a victim. These attackers are seeking to obtain secure sockets layer (SSL)/transport layer security (TLS) certificates and take control of the victims' Facebook, apps, and so on. The second is the network attacker. This type of attacker is typically a passive wireless eavesdropper and is active in evil routing or DNS poisoning. The third is a malware attacker. A malware attacker attempts to escape browser isolation mechanisms and to run separately under the control of the operating system. Browsers may contain exploitable bugs and often enable remote code execution by websites. However, even if browsers were bug free, many vulnerabilities would still exist on the web. A Google study in 2007 found Trojans on 300,000 web pages (URLs) and adware on 18,000 web pages (URLs).

Hypertext Transfer Protocol

HTTP functions as a request-response protocol in the client–server computing model. A web browser, for example, may be the client, and an application running on a computer hosting a website may be the server. The client submits a HTTP request message to the server. The server, which provides resources such as HTML files and other content or performs other functions on behalf of the client, returns a response message to the client. The response contains completion status information about the request and may also contain requested content in its message body.

A uniform resource locator (URL) (also called a *web address*) is a global identifier of network-retrievable documents and a reference to a resource that specifies the location of the resource on a computer network and a mechanism for retrieving it.

Rendering Content

In the basic browser execution model, each browser window or frame loads content; renders it by processing HTML and scripts to display pages that may involve images, subframes, and so on; and then responds to the events.

The Document Object Model (DOM) is a cross-platform and language-independent convention object-oriented interface used to read and write documents in hypertext markup language (HTML), Extensible Hypertext Markup Language (XHTML), and Extensible Markup Language (XML). The nodes of every document are organized in a tree structure, called the *DOM tree*. Objects in the DOM tree may be addressed and manipulated by using methods on the objects. These include Browser Object Model (BOM) such as window, document, frames, history, location, and navigator (type and version of browser). The public interface of a DOM is specified in its API.

Image tags can also present security issues. It is important to remember that a web page can send information to any site and that the tag includes a whole *separate file* into your web page.

Port scanning is one of the most popular reconnaissance techniques that attackers use to discover services they can break into. Essentially, a port scan consists of sending a message to each port, one at a time. The kind of response received indicates whether the port is used and can therefore be probed further for weakness. JavaScript port scanning behind a firewall can request images from internal IP addresses, use timeout/on error to determine success/failure, and fingerprint web apps using known image names.

Remote scripting is a technology that allows scripts and programs that are running inside a browser to exchange information with a server without reloading the page. The local scripts can invoke scripts on the remote side and process the returned information, maintaining bidirectional communication with the browser (until the user closes or quits). Remote procedure call (RPC) can be done silently in JavaScript, passing and receiving arguments to server.html in query string.

Isolation

Web content comes from many sources, not all of which are equally trustworthy. Trusted and untrusted content are in close proximity (frames, tabs, sequential visits). It is important to separate various forms of content so that untrusted content cannot corrupt or misuse trusted content. For example, attackers can use the Guninski attack by buying advertisements and then using them to attack good pages. Modern browsers implement same-origin policy (SOP). The general idea is to separate content with different trust levels into different frames and then restrict communication between frames. One frame can access content in another frame only if they both came from the same origin, such as protocol, domain name, and port (in some browsers).

By itself, the SOP is too restrictive; there are times when it is useful for frames with different origins to communicate in various ways. This is the basis for domain relaxation. Consider www.facebook.com, facebook.com, and chat.facebook.com. If two frames each set the document. domain to the same value, then they can communicate, thereby making the documents appear to have the same origin and enabling each document to read properties of the other.

The second technique for relaxing the SOP is standardized under the name cross-origin resource sharing (CORS). This standard extends HTTP with a new origin request header and a new access-control-allow-origin (ACAO) response header. It allows servers to use a header to explicitly list origins that may request a file or to use a wildcard and allow a file to be requested by any site. Browsers such as Firefox 3.5, Safari 4, and Internet Explorer 10 use this header to allow the cross-origin HTTP requests with a "XMLHttpRequest" that would otherwise have been forbidden by the SOP.

Another new technique, cross-document messaging, allows a script from one page to pass textual messages to a script on another page regardless of the script origins. Calling the "postMessage ( )" method on a Window object asynchronously fires an "onmessage" event in that window, triggering any user-defined event handlers. A script in one page still cannot directly access methods or variables in the other page, but the scripts can communicate safely through this message-passing technique.

Security User Interface

When a HTTPS website references insecure (HTTP) resources, this is called *mixed content*. Browsers prevent a HTTPS website from loading most insecure resources, such as fonts, scripts, and so on. Migrating an existing website from HTTP to HTTPS means identifying and fixing or replacing mixed content.

Mixed content comes in two varieties:

1. *Active mixed content* includes resources that can greatly change the behavior of a website, such as JavaScript, CSS, fonts, and iframes. Browsers refuse to load active mixed content, which often results in affected pages being completely unstyled or broken. Browsers treat these very aggressively because of the consequences if they were compromised. For example, a single compromised JavaScript file compromises the entire website, regardless of how other resources are loaded.
2. *Passive mixed content* includes resources whose impact on the page's overall behavior is more minimal, such as images, audio, and video. Browsers will load passive mixed content but will typically change the HTTPS indicator.

Cookies

Cookies are a general mechanism that can be used by server-side connections (such as CGI scripts) to both store and retrieve information on the client side of the connection. The addition of a simple, persistent, client-side state significantly extends the capabilities of web-based client–server applications. A typical browser will retain at most 20 cookies per site at 3 KB per cookie.

Authentication cookies are the most common method used by web servers to determine whether the user is logged in or not and which account they are logged in with. Without such a mechanism, the site would not know whether to send a page containing sensitive information or require the user to authenticate themselves by logging in. The security of an authentication cookie generally depends on the security of the issuing website and the user's web browser and on whether the cookie data is encrypted. Security vulnerabilities may allow a cookie's data to be read by a hacker, used to gain access to user data, or used to gain access (with the user's credentials) to the website to which the cookie belongs.

Many websites use cookies for personalization based on the user's preferences. Users select their preferences by entering them in a web form and submitting the form to the server. The server encodes the preferences in a cookie and sends the cookie back to the browser. This way, every time the user accesses a page on the website, the server can personalize the page according to the user preferences.

Third-party cookies, however, belong to domains that are different from the one shown in the address bar. These sorts of cookies typically appear when web pages feature content, such as banner advertisements, from external websites. This opens up the potential for tracking the user's browsing history and is often used by advertisers in an effort to serve relevant advertisements to each user.

A secure or HttpOnly cookie's attributes do not have associated values. Rather, the presence of just their attribute names indicates that their behaviors should be enabled. The secure attribute is meant to keep cookie communication limited to encrypted transmission, directing browsers to use cookies only via secure or encrypted connections. However, if a web server sets a cookie with a secure attribute from a non-secure connection, the cookie can still be intercepted when it is sent to the user by man-in-the-middle attacks. Therefore, for maximum security, cookies with the secure attribute should only be sent over a secure connection. The HttpOnly attribute provides confidentiality against a network attacker by directing browsers not to expose cookies through channels other than HTTP (and HTTPS) requests. Cookies with this attribute are not accessible via non-HTTP methods such as calls via JavaScript.

Frame Busting

Frame busting is a technique used by web applications to prevent their web pages from being displayed within a frame. The goal of frame busting is to prevent a web page from loading in a frame. A frame is a subdivision of a web-browser window and can act like a smaller window. It is usually deployed to prevent a frame from an external website being loaded from within a frameset without permission, often as part of clickjacking attack.

Browser Code Isolation

Modern websites today are quite complex. They contain code that originates in many sources and may be combined in a number of different ways. Modern websites consist of pages of code, ad code, extensions, and third-party libraries and APIs. Many of these websites process very sensitive information collected by insurance companies, advertising companies, and various branches of state and national government. Information such as financial data associated with online banking, tax filing, shopping, and budgeting; health data containing genomics and prescription information; and personal data such as e-mail, messaging, affiliations, and photography may be stored and processed in remote websites.

So, the question is, how do we isolate code from different sources and still protect sensitive information in the browser, still ensuring integrity and allowing required functionality and flexibility? Protection can be achieved by utilizing some of the following structuring mechanisms to reinforce browser security.

Web Worker

A web worker is a JavaScript that runs in the background, independently of other scripts, without affecting the performance of the page. It can be used to isolate separate threads of code execution in a browser operation. The concept is to restrict interaction between logical compartments on the server and restrict particular network requests and responses. A web worker works by allowing for concurrent execution of the browser threads along with one or more JavaScript threads running in the background. The browser, which follows a single thread of execution, will have to wait on JavaScript programs to finish executing before proceeding; this might take a significant amount of extra time, which the programmer might prefer to hide from the user. The web worker thus allows the browser to continue its normal operation while running JavaScript in the background.

Sandbox

A sandbox is used to restrict frame actions. A sandbox allows websites to load with unique origin but with limited privileges. It is used as a security mechanism for separating running programs into separate "sandboxes" or distinct logical areas of memory. It is often used to execute untested code or untrusted programs from unverified third parties, suppliers, untrusted users, and untrusted websites. A sandbox typically provides a tightly controlled set of resources for guest programs to run, such as scratch space on disk and memory. Usually disallowed or heavily restricted with a sandbox are network access, the ability to inspect the host system, and the ability to read from any specified set of input devices.

Cross-Origin Resource Sharing

Cross-origin resource sharing (CORS) relaxes same-origin restrictions. CORS explicitly allows certain resources to be readable regardless of their site of origin (cross-origin). This mechanism allows restricted resources (e.g., fonts, JavaScript, etc.) on a web page to be requested from another domain outside the domain from which the resource originated. A web page may then freely embed images, stylesheets, scripts, iframes, and videos, as well as some plug-in content (such as Adobe Flash), from any other domain. However, embedded web fonts and AJAX (XMLHttpRequest) requests have traditionally been limited to accessing the same domain as the parent web page (as per the same-origin security policy).

Content Security Policy

The goal of content security policy (CSP) is to prevent damage from cross-site scripting (XSS). XSS attacks bypass the SOP by tricking a site into delivering malicious code along with the intended/ requested content. CSP restricts resource loading to a whitelist, which instructs the user's browser to only execute or render resources from specific sources. CSP provides a standard HTTP header that allows website owners to declare which are approved sources of content that browsers should be allowed to load on that page. Any other source is blocked from loading to that requested page.

QUESTIONS
1. What are three actors that a cross-site scripting attack needs?
2. What is the purpose of a sandbox?
3. What are the advantages and disadvantage of port scanning?
4. How do you protect yourself from clickjacking?

Chapter 10

Banking Security, Zeus, and SpyEye

As online banking becomes more prevalent globally, it is of the utmost importance to demonstrate the security measures in place around online banking. By examining what is currently of concern to banks in the area of online security, coupled with where the banking industry is headed, flaws in banking information security become increasingly prominent. Currently, banks are concerned with denial-of-service (DoS) attacks, online fraud, both Zeus and SpyEye Trojans, and a wide array of mobile banking threats.

DoS attacks are happening more frequently to banks, recently occurring at Wells Fargo, Citigroup, JPMorgan Chase, and Bank of America. During a DoS attack, hackers establish a series of meaningless connections to the bank's website, connections that are meant to overwhelm the bank's servers. Once the servers become overwhelmed and crash or freeze, they are rendered inaccessible until the banks fix them. To help curb this problem, the banks have been working with their bandwidth providers to help weed out malicious traffic prior to that traffic arriving at the bank's servers. Recently, however, hackers have become more sophisticated in their approach to denial-of-service attacks. And they have utilized more powerful machines to attack the secure communication protocols that banks and their customers use to communicate transactions with one another. A common type of DoS attack begins with the principle attacker establishing a DoS attack master device. Then, the attacker infects hundreds of user computers, which are widely distributed across the country and increasingly across the globe. Then, the principal attacker sends an instruction to each of the commandeered user computers to begin accessing a target bank's servers, such that they overwhelm the edge routers and switches and bring the servers to a standstill. This process can be activated repeatedly. And these attacks can be architected as waves: The East Coast PCs can start, then the midwestern ones can begin, then the West Coast ones begin, and then those in South East Asia begin. As the bank's security personnel deal with one set of transmissions, another one begins, and waves of transactions keep rolling in from across the globe. The web of commandeered user computers are called a *botnet* and sometimes a zombie network, since the user is not aware of what his or her PC is performing as part of this zombie botnet. An example of such a DoS attack architecture can be seen in Figure 10.1. The DoS attacking agents are widely spread geographically, e.g., California, Texas, Illinois, Florida, New York, and maybe

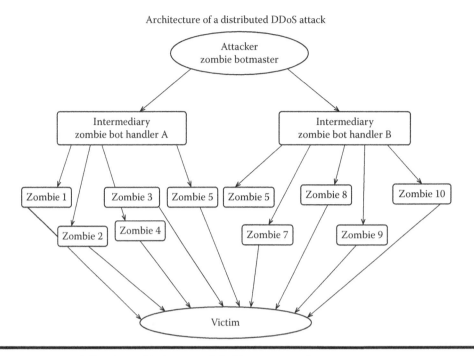

Figure 10.1 A multilevel zombie bot attack led by a remote botmaster.

Maine. Thus, they present a distributed DoS (DDoS) attack, since the bots are distributed and all simultaneously attempt a DoS attack.

While DDoS attacks are a growing problem, fraud has always been of prime concern within the banking industry as whole; it presents a huge risk, and the online banking format means that this is now especially the case. Two recent cases of online fraud spawned from two Trojan viruses known as *Zeus* and *SpyEye*. The Zeus Trojan is a package that is designed to run on versions of Microsoft's Windows operating system. This virus was able to steal banking information by implementing a keystroke logger within each commandeered host computer's web browser, along with a form-grabbing utility that would take personal and banking information. This Trojan was spread through downloads and e-mail phishing scams that installed the Trojan on the host's computer. Once the eastern European hackers had the information, they would wire thousands of dollars to fake accounts. In total, Zeus was responsible for the theft of more than $70 million from people all over the globe. In 2010, SpyEye, another form of Trojan malware, surpassed Zeus as the most dangerous banking Trojan. SpyEye is considered a "man-in-the-browser" technique that allows criminals to impersonate the customer to the bank and impersonate the banks to the customer with almost undetectable perfection. This makes protection from SpyEye a very difficult problem.

The future of online banking threats increasing arises from "man-in-the-mobile" threats. In these circumstances, hackers rely on the growing trend of performing mobile banking on smartphones and tablets. This is especially problematic for online banking and other services utilizing one-time short message service (SMS) or "texting" for authentication of devices. Figure 10.2 illustrates an example of how a traditional man-in-the-middle (MitM) attack is performed, wherein the attacker inserts himself in the middle of a mobile banking transaction between a mobile user and the bank, and even between two mobile users who are processing a transaction between themselves involving a common bank.

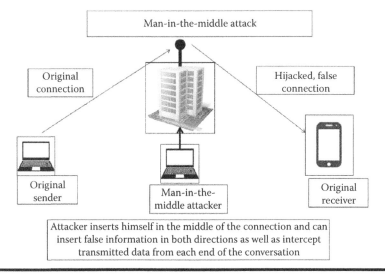

Figure 10.2   The structure of a man-in-the-middle (MitM) attack.

Furthermore, hackers can also gain control of a customer's mobile device or a user's browser and not merely imitate the user but also actually be the user sending the false transaction from the user's device, therefore facing a lesser chance of detection.

Modern hacking is often motivated by potential fiscal returns from the use or sale of data obtained in a malicious attack. Therefore, banks, with their large array of financial data and customer information as well as knowledge of the complete network interconnecting the banking system across the globe, are a primary target for hackers. The financial industry carries a significant security burden as a result of the data that their servers maintain. Customers of a bank or credit union have rather high identification and access standards set by how an individual customer's finances are managed. As these user groups request access by means of their mobile devices, which are integrated with software features such as Mint.com, users and financial institutions alike are widening the attack options for potential attackers.

Fraud Process

Part of launching an attack that provides significant returns for the attacker is to understand to whom to sell information, how to leverage and liquidate it, and how to remain as anonymous as possible while coordinating these risks. Attackers cannot simply use banking and financial information to pull money directly into their accounts; this would be a traceable and reversible operation. Instead, they must use a variety of transitional processes or vectors to cleanse the money. These accountability cleansers are called *money mules* and may be a purely digital or physical fraudulent company used by hackers. The "mule" then takes a percentage or fee for risking themselves in the cleansing process.

Risk Management Process for Banks

It is a fact that all online banks of significant size or holdings will be attacked. This means it is not a question of "if" they will be attacked but instead "what, when, where." The answer is not to

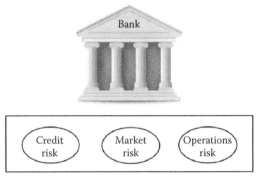

Risk associated with the customers, employees, systems,
and company processes of a bank subject to attack, fraud,
misrepresentation, and disruption of banking activities.

Figure 10.3   Risks for banks and customers from bank attacks and fraud.

shut down the bank, but instead to manage the risk that is presented by operating in this industry. All banks take on a varying amount risk with every decision that is made at every employee level. In fact, the most common methods by which banks lose valuable customer information are not a computational-based attack vector. Social engineering is a method of "attacking" humans from a behavioral perspective, understanding their context and how to make them at ease with releasing potentially damaging information. Figure 10.3 lists three general areas of risk—credit, market, and operations risks.

The area of operations risk contains a wide range of vulnerabilities, from the processes that employees use to do their job to the systems they use to input customer data. The goal is to mitigate these risks using training techniques, with topics ranging from all aspects of a social perspective where individuals might be vulnerable, to the very specific aspect of ensuring that all modifications, updates, and patches to software and hardware are routinely applied in a timely fashion.

Zeus and SpyEye Attacks

The two specific attacks previously mentioned, Zeus and SpyEye, have had profound effects on international banking services. While primarily attacking European banking, some U.S.-based banks have also been affected by both forms. Each is a MitM form of attack beginning with the use of keystroke logging or form-grabbing techniques to acquire credentials. After passwords have been acquired to obtain authorized access, they lock the user's machine after installing "CryptoLocker Ransomware," which is a form of "scare-ware." This software forces users to input their credit card information with the promise that they will be able to begin use their machines again after they have been unfrozen.

While using online banking software, SpyEye and Zeus have the ability to hijack or steal the session "cookies" that are used to maintain state data and security between sessions. A compromised system can have this secure session data hijacked and transferred to a remote host. That host is then able to perform operations under the user's stolen account. In 2012, IOActive, Inc. performed an advanced analysis of the SpyEye and Zeus malware, revealing the depth of the software's capabilities, and it published an open report of its analysis. Computers infected with either

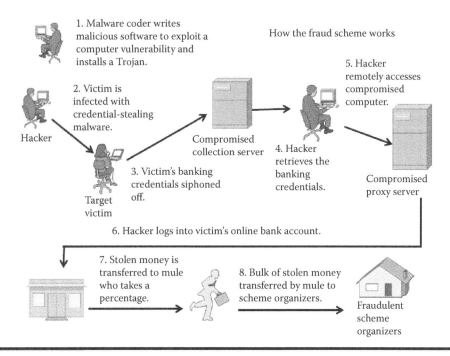

1. Malware coder writes malicious software to exploit a computer vulnerability and installs a Trojan.

How the fraud scheme works

5. Hacker remotely accesses compromised computer.

2. Victim is infected with credential-stealing malware.

Hacker

Compromised collection server

4. Hacker retrieves the banking credentials.

3. Victim's banking credentials siphoned off.

Target victim

Compromised proxy server

6. Hacker logs into victim's online bank account.

7. Stolen money is transferred to mule who takes a percentage.

8. Bulk of stolen money transferred by mule to scheme organizers.

Fraudulent scheme organizers

Figure 10.4 A schematic layout of how bank fraud works.

of these become part of a botnet from which commands can be remotely executed. From such botnets, malware is often broadcast to variety of demographics and targets with the hope that the compromised security of a less valuable system may lead to the compromise of higher-level and higher-value systems. Figure 10.4 portrays the sequence by which bank fraud frequently occurs.

Bank fraud tends to occur in the following steps. First, a malware coder writes malicious software to exploit computer vulnerability and installs a Trojan. Once the victim's computer is infected with credential-stealing malware, the victim's banking credentials are siphoned. The hacker retrieves the credentials, gaining complete control of the computer and the ability to remotely access and direct the compromised computer. The hacker then logs into the victim's online bank account, transfers money to a "mule," and then transfers the money from the mule to the criminal organizers of the operation, which may be an individual but frequently is some fraudulent company.

Both the owners of infected machines and the financial institutions are victims of this fraudulent action. The money mules transfer stolen money for criminals, while shaving a small percentage for themselves and shielding the original attacker and the criminal organization that is the ultimate recipient of the stolen funds. Financial criminals can be separate individuals or collections of malware coders, malware exploiters, and mule organizations.

Analyzing, assessing, and then protecting via information gained from the risk management process and information security measures invoked are factors that determine how competitive and successful a bank will be in the future.

A sequence of major financial security events from 1999 to 2011 is arrayed in Figure 10.5.

This culminated in a series of DoS attacks in 2011 on financial institutions, government branches, international police agencies, and news organizations throughout the globe, as illustrated in Figure 10.6.

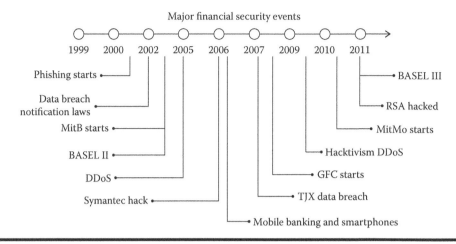

Figure 10.5 Major financial security events from 1999 to 2011.

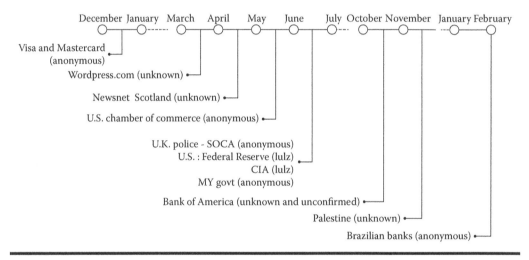

Figure 10.6 Major denial-of-service attacks in the year 2011.

Online Fraud and the Impacts of Zeus and SpyEye Attacks

Zeus (and its alternate forms ZeuS or Zbot) is a Trojan horse computer malware that runs on versions of both Microsoft Windows and the Apple Mac OS X operating systems. While these attacks can be used to carry out many malicious and criminal tasks, they are most often used to steal banking information by means of man-in-the-browser keystroke logging and form grabbing. Furthermore, they are also used to install the CryptoLocker ransomware. Zeus attacks tend to be focused on spreading mainly through drive-by downloads and phishing schemes. First identified in July 2007, when it was used to steal information from the U.S. Department of Transportation, Zeus became more widespread in March of 2009. And then in June 2009, the security company Prevx discovered that Zeus had compromised over 74,000 FTP accounts on the websites of such companies as Bank of America, Monster.com, ABC, Oracle, Play.com, Cisco, Amazon, BusinessWeek, and even NASA.

Zeus implements its keylogging and screen scraping by way of an import hook to the application program interface (API): "user32!TranslateMessage." APIs are a set of routines, protocols, and tools for building software applications. The API specifies how software components should interact, and such APIs are particularly useful when programming graphical user interface (GUI) components. One of Zeus's interesting features is its ability to steal the certificate store (including private keys) by hooking the function "PFXImportCertStore." At the core of Zeus's usefulness is its ability to hijack banking sessions and inject custom data into returned hypertext markup language (HTML)-formatted web pages and HTML formatted hypertext files. Zeus then renders them into visible or audible web pages. The data to be injected is specified within the "webinjects. txt" file, which is later built into the Zeus configuration file.

One important feature of the Zeus bot is the ability to download and execute files from a remote location. This gives Zeus the ability to extend its framework or install additional malware. Zeus also performs cookie stealing through the function "InternetGetCookie" to retrieve cookies for the specified URL. The cookie data is then logged to the user.ds file.

The fact that Zeus hooks by way of "wininet.dll" limits the injection to browsers that utilize these functions, implying that Internet Explorer sessions will be vulnerable to injection but Firefox will not. A new version of Zeus that includes support for Firefox is reported to be undergoing beta testing.

SpyEye is similar to Zeus, which is its main rival in the hacking world. SpyEye incorporates many advanced tricks to hide its presence on the local system. The unpacked SpyEye bot image can begin execution either at the entry point specified in its portable executable header, at a private (non-exported) hook procedure executed when the bot has injected itself into a new process, or at one of two private thread routines that execute when the bot has injected itself into an existing process.

Zeus and SpyEye have impacted many companies during the period from 2005 to 2011 (Figure 10.7), but most impact fully against the financial giants—Society General, UBS, and Credit Suisse.

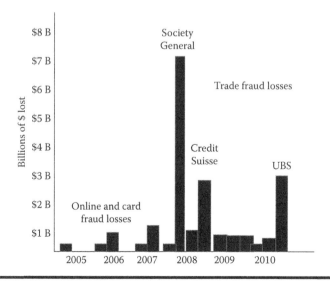

Figure 10.7   Zeus and SpyEye impacted three European banks from 2005 to 2010.

Zeus and SpyEye have attacked organizations spread across the globe on all continents, from North and South America to the counties of Europe and Russia, and the countries of Southeast Asia down to Australia. Their damage has been spread globally.

Since they begin by infecting a target's browser, Zeus and SpyEye can exercise some extensive damage and exhibit some sophisticated capabilities, allowing criminals to both impersonate the customer to the bank and the banks to the customer with capabilities nearing perfection.

The combined analysis of the Zeus and SpyEye Trojans offers an inside look into the methods that are common to most popular banking Trojans. Understanding the internal details of these Trojans provides a company with the opportunity to offset the underlying functionality of such common malware, rather than just relying on their detection and attempting to prevent individual agents using them.

Zeus and other similar malware lend themselves to many distinct detection methods, but the fact that a company implements a virtualized computer environment with associated isolation techniques offers the unique ability to implement protection that covers an entire range of malware and malware techniques. Physical and virtual memory monitoring can detect and prevent the placement of unwanted hooks and process injections. Having control of the virtual machine and virtual machine monitor offer a great opportunity for system-wide memory page monitoring and intrusion detection and the ability to apply static analysis to a possible malware image before it begins its execution process. Analysis focused on code sections and the detection of suspicious sections would consistently allow the detection of a persistent malware infection early in its infection process.

QUESTIONS

1. What type of attack is "man in the middle" and when does it occur?
2. This method helps hackers hide their trail through a person who receives and transfers money illegally on behalf of others. What is it?
3. What is the stealth strategy of the Zeus Trojan?
4. Give two ways in which SpyEye stays hidden.
5. What is Crypto Lock ransomware and how is it distributed?

Chapter 11

Web Application Security

Previously, web applications have been discussed with a technical analysis of the specific attack types that target them. Many of these high-profile attacks on companies use similar methods and tools to gain access, and some components of web services are especially vulnerable in comparison to others, especially at points where users are able to input text data. An open field, file, or form that will take input and allow server processing may not have properly cleansed that input, allowing the remote execution of hidden and embedded code in that data that was not intended to be run on that server. This type of attack uses structured query language (SQL), which is a language used to query databases and insert data within them. SQL is a special-purpose programming language designed for managing data held in a relational database management system (RDBMS), or for stream processing in a relational data stream management system (RDSMS).

Other attacks similar in nature to SQL include the cross-site request forgery (CSRF) approach, wherein an already-attacked website sends a request to a website it wishes to attack using previously obtained and valid credentials. CSRF is a type of attack that occurs when a malicious website, an e-mail, a blog, an instant message, or a program causes a user's web browser to perform an unwanted action on a previously trusted website for which the user is currently authenticated, and which is therefore trusted by that targeted but unsuspecting website. Cross-site scripting (XSS) also allows for an attack website to execute a script that extracts information from the web server being targeted for attack. XSS is a type of computer security vulnerability quite frequently found in web applications. XSS enables attackers to inject client-side script into web pages that are then viewed by other users.

Basics of SQL Injections

SQL injection is a code injection technique used to attack data-driven applications in which malicious SQL statements are inserted into an entry field for execution. For example, the goal may be to dump the database contents to the attacker's computer. SQL is an access and storage language used by most programmers against relationally stored databases. It is also frequently used by programmers who write in the PHP hypertext processor (PHP) programming language to access

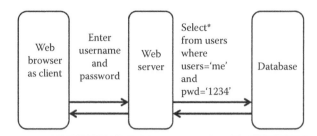

Figure 11.1   Querying a database by means of an infected (SQL injection) web server.

database information in order to provide front-end web services. In this case, the client accesses a desired web server and provides a username and password for authorization. Then, the client submits the normal SQL sequence of commands (select, from, where). The web server then submits those commands to the database server (or performs the database access function locally). The database determines the result of the query and then returns it to the client, as shown in Figure 11.1. This figure portrays a standard two-stage SQL (client to web server and then web server on to database server) access to a database wherein the SQL query has been infected with an SQL injection attack.

This two-stage design provides a separation or partitioning between the client, the web server, and the database server with the desired data to which the client seeks access. All processing, from initial log-on through authentication and then query request, are processed by the web server, which is separated from the back-end database server.

Once the entry web server has been infected by means of an SQL injection attack, the user input fields such as "user" and "pwd" are then overwritten by malicious PHP code with an input string that, once forwarded to the database server, would force that database server to perform an operation outside the security measures (which are meant to insure it as a safe data container) or the safe operating goals of the system. Figure 11.2 illustrates an example in which passwords would be overwritten by an SQL injection string.

This string will cause the login process to succeed, allowing a web-based attacker to move past the login screen and gain access to resources on an untraceable account. Beyond this method, the attacker may be able to add or remove users of the database and create the attacker's own user accounts for malicious purposes. Among the best methods to prevent these injection techniques from occurring is to only use tested and secured code supplied directly from a known and trusted vendor rather than to allow public apps (applications), which might be downloaded from invalidated sites. Furthermore, it is important to ensure that scanning and data cleansing are being carried out at any client-side input area and on the web server to reduce the risk of PHP parameter infection, resulting in an SQL injection risk.

ok = execute (SELECT …

WHERE user = " or 1=1 -- …)

Figure 11.2   Passwords overwritten by SQL injection attack.

More Examples of Injection-Based Attacks

Many entry points exist on a client machine. From e-mail messaging to SMS messaging and texting, there are many ways for an attacker to directly place malicious code on a user's machine and on web servers that are accessed by that user. So, the user may always be susceptible to infection by malicious code. It is difficult to secure many of these entry points without interfering with the functional process that the user's (and the web server's) applications perform. To secure against e-mail-based attacks, filters are placed to restrict the user from opening an e-mail from an illegitimate or unwanted source. However, fewer restrictions exist for text messages. Furthermore, the discovery and isolation of malicious spam e-mail is largely managed at high level by Internet service providers or corporate e-mail systems. However, a small spam e-mail, presented to an unwary user in such an attractive form that the user is compelled to click on it and follow its malicious link, is frequently all that is required for a chain of malicious processes to be triggered.

As an additional source of such malware infection, Adobe products have long been an easy and frequent target for infection because of their prevalence on user systems and their incorporation of automatic download processes for frequent upgrades. An infected Adobe PDF document has the potential to transmit malware code once an infected upgrade is downloaded and opened, since the PDF format has many rich options within the base of the file format itself. Additionally, the Java set of routines are universally present on user machines, and the launching of JavaScript code can then allow an attacker to launch malware on a user's system, if downloaded, in the following fashion:

http://path/to/pdf/file.pdf#whatever_name_you_want=javascript:code_here

This downloading and execution of code, scripts, and documents challenges the conventional notions of coding structure and the acquisition of program code from a limited set of trustworthy sources. Furthermore, scripts are normally intended to be executed in a narrow set of specific ways and areas of operation in order to promote efficiency and control security. With these new sources of threat, quite often the source of malicious coding is being executed in areas where the client did not expect code to be placed. This may be among images, frames, videos, and forms that may all load from remote sites onto a trusted site but can bring malicious code along with them as they are downloaded to the client's personal computer or mobile device.

A Review of the ScanBox Software

One of the attack tools that have been used in recent data breaches, such as the Anthem breach, is the downloaded ScanBox keystroke-logging software. It was triggered by the target client technician unwittingly clicking on an attractive spear-phishing or spam e-mail, which then triggered the ScanBox download. The ScanBox software was able to perform keylogging functions without the users ever noticing the installation of this malware on their machine. As long as the user was unwittingly heading to a compromised website, the resulting process of information collection from the now-compromised user's machine could continue. This phase of an attack quickly transitions into enabling a high-level corporate attack, infestation, reconnaissance, and information download phase, followed by the placement of software enabling a long-term anonymous persistent presence in the attacked corporate systems. The time elapsing from the compromise of a critical account to the occurrence of the actual attack, infection, and data theft has been reduced to within a day, and the anonymous persistent presence of the attacker and the attacker's installed malware are cloaked from detection.

QUESTIONS

1. How does a hacker perform keylogging functions without the user noticing?
2. What is SQL and what are some examples?
3. What are the commands for SQL injection?
4. CSRF relies on what four things?

Chapter 12

Session Management, User Authentication, and Web Application Security

Websites and web applications are frequently targeted environments for security attacks since they are the prime places that users are accustomed to accessing and utilizing. Given the constant user access to websites over the public Internet, the largest amount of security liabilities is the result of a by-product of these accesses. The following explores the components of web application management and the most common website vulnerabilities.

We have already discussed a number of these vulnerabilities that occur with website access. Among these are

- XSS: Cross-site scripting
- SQLi: Structured query language injection
- CSRF: Cross-site request forgery
- SSL: Secure socket layer corruption
- Session corruption
- Information leaking

Session Management and User Authentication

Security breaches commonly begin with the theft of valid user authentication credentials. It is important to understand how hackers use these vulnerabilities in session management and user authentication to gain access to data and network systems.

Session Management

A session is a sequence of requests and responses from one browser to one (or more) websites. Sessions can be long e-mail sessions (e.g., Gmail) or short texting sessions. Session management is the process of keeping track of a user's activity across sessions of interaction between the user's browser and the remote web server. Without session management, users would have to continually log back into websites to complete the sequence of work that the users wish to accomplish using a given website. Session management allows the user to be authorized once, after which all subsequent requests are tied back to that first authorized session and the recognition of that user.

Sessions at the browser level are called Hypertext Transfer Protocol (HTTP) sessions, which allow information to be associated with a particular session user. HTTP session management is made possible through the use of HTTP cookies and session IDs.

HTTP Cookies

A HTTP cookie is a small piece of data that is sent from a website and stored in a user's web browser while the user is browsing that website. Every time the user accesses the website, the browser sends the cookie back to the server to notify the website of the user's previous activity. Authentication cookies are the most common method used by web servers to determine whether the user is logged in or not and which account they are logged with. Without such a mechanism, the site would not know whether to send a page containing sensitive information or to require the user to reauthenticate themselves by logging in once again. The security of an authentication cookie generally depends on the security of the issuing website and the user's web browser and on whether the cookie data is encrypted. Security vulnerabilities may allow a cookie's data to be read by a hacker and used for inappropriate purposes.

Session ID

A session ID or session token is a small piece of data that is used in HTTP communications to identify a session. For example, a buyer who visits a seller's site wants to collect a number of items in a virtual shopping cart and then finalize the shopping by navigating to the site's checkout page. This typically involves an ongoing communication whereby several webpages are requested by the client and sent back to them by the server. In such a situation, it is vital to keep track of the current state of the shopper's cart, and a session ID is one way to achieve that goal.

A session ID is typically granted to a visitor on their first visit to a site. It is different from a user ID in that sessions are typically short-lived (they expire after a preset time of inactivity, which may be minutes or hours) and may become invalid after a certain processing goal has been met (e.g., once the buyer has finalized his order, he cannot use the same session ID to add more items). As session IDs are often used to identify a user that has logged into a website, they can be used by an attacker to hijack the session and obtain undue privileges.

A session ID is usually a long string of randomly generated numbers designed to decrease the probability of a potential attacker obtaining a valid ID by means of a brute-force search. Once generated, the session ID is sent from a server to a client to identify the current interaction session. The client usually stores and sends back the session ID as a HTTP cookie and also may send it as a parameter in GET or POST queries. Figure 12.1 illustrates the sequences of exchange that take place during the session login and ID validation process.

Your browser

Desired website

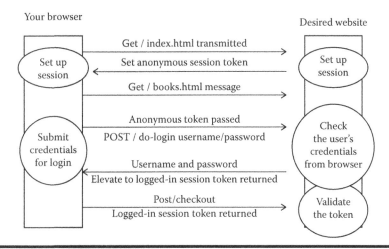

Figure 12.1   The session login and ID validation process.

Storing Session IDs

There are a number of ways to store session IDs over the course of a session exchange. The three most common are

1. Store the session ID as a browser cookie: (Set-Cookie: SessionToken=fduhye63sfdb)
2. Embed the session ID in URL links: (https://site.com/checkout?SessionToken =kh7y3b)
3. Store the session ID in hidden form: (<input type="hidden" name="sessionid" value="kh7y3b">)

In practice, none of these options is without its problems. Storing session IDs in browser cookies runs the risk that the browser will advertise the cookie with every information request during the session. This becomes an issue in CSRF attacks, which we will discuss later. Embedding session IDs in URL links leaks the ID through the HTTP reference header, allowing other users to obtain the ID from a public site. Hidden form-field storage is the most secure option, but this does not work for long-term sessions such as Gmail. Effective and secure storage of session IDs requires a combination of all of the foregoing options rather than reliance on a single one.

Web Application Security

Having discussed some of the components behind browser mechanisms, we will next examine in more detail the three most common forms of web application security vulnerability and the attacks that make use of these vulnerabilities:

1. SQLi
2. CSRF
3. XSS

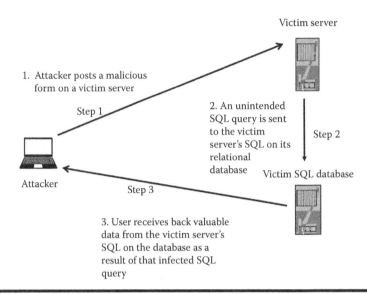

Figure 12.2 Basic SQL injection attack.

Structured Query Language Injection

We have previously discussed this common attack technique. SQLi uses the commonly employed SQL command sequence, which is submitted by a user or programmer to search for and retrieve information from a remote, relationally structured database system. The infection injects overwritten sequences that change the meaning of a database access and the SQL request for information command. The attacked browser will send a malicious request to the target server. Ineffective input checking on the target server can lead to malicious SQL queries containing the infected overwritten sequences, which have overwritten the user's normal query instruction sequence to the victim's SQL database, forwarding sensitive information back to either the infected user or to the attacker's browser (Figure 12.2).

An SQL Injection Example: The CardSystems Solutions Attack

In June 2005, it was discovered that CardSystems Solutions, a leading credit card processing company, had been the victim of an SQLi attack in which 43 million credit card numbers were stolen. The attack and marketing fallout eventually put that company out of business.

Cross-Site Request Forgery

CSRF is an attack that leverages a user's session on the victim's website server. A malicious website sends a browser request to a valid website using the credentials of a valid but innocent victim.

Some common CSRF characteristics are

■ They involve sites that rely on a user's identity.
■ They exploit the site's trust in that identity.

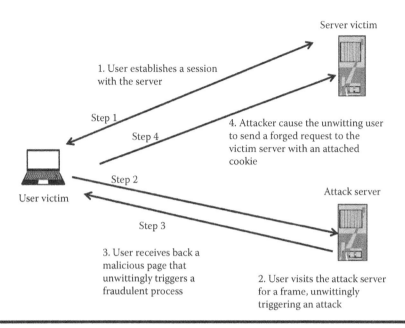

Figure 12.3 Basic cross-site request forgery attack.

- They trick the user's browser into sending HTTP requests to a malicious site.
- They involve HTTP requests that illicit side-effects such as financial transactions or data transmissions (Figure 12.3).

A CSRF attack secretly forces a user into submitting a malicious browser request to the user's server. First, the user establishes a session with a trusted site. While still on the trusted session, the user will unwittingly navigate to another site by means of a malicious link. Once selected, that link will assume the user's session authentication, in most cases by stealing the user's session cookie to disguise itself as a legitimate request sent by the victim. The attacker can then access the original session to steal data from the trusted site, sending the money to the attacker instead. The attack will comprise the following steps:

1. Building an exploit URL or script
2. Using social engineering to trick User A into executing the action

The social engineering aspect of the attack tricks User A into loading a malicious URL when he or she logged into the bank application. This is commonly done by means of one of the following techniques:

1. Sending an unsolicited e-mail with HTML content
2. Planting an exploit URL or script on pages that are likely to be visited by the victim while they are also doing online banking

The exploit URL can be disguised as an ordinary link, encouraging the victim User A to click on it. Once clicked, the browser will submit the request to bank.com without any visual indication that the transfer has taken place.

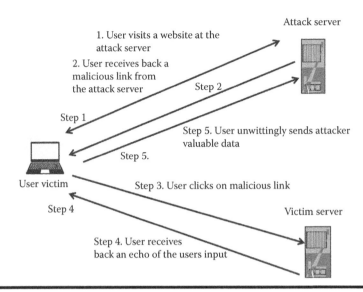

Figure 12.4 Basic cross-site scripting attack.

Cross-Site Scripting

XSS is an attack that injects malicious script into a trusted context in order to steal information from the valid site (Figure 12.4).

An XSS vulnerability is present when an attacker can inject scripting code into pages generated by a web application. There are several common methods for injecting malicious code:

1. Reflected XSS: The attack script is reflected back to the user as part of a page from the victim site.
2. Stored XSS: The attacker stores the malicious code in a resource managed by the web application, such as a database.
3. Others, such as DOM-based XSS attacks, arbitrary HTML, and scripts could be injected on the client causing forced errors.

Example of an XSS Attack on PayPal

In 2006, PayPal's user data was compromised on a large scale by an XSS social engineering attack. Attackers contacted PayPal users via e-mail and fooled them into accessing a particular URL hosted on the legitimate PayPal website. The attackers' previously injected code then redirected these PayPal visitors to a page that warned users that their accounts had been compromised. Victims were then redirected to a phishing site and prompted to enter sensitive financial data.

Session Management and User Authentication Conclusion

With increasing regularity, users traverse the Internet for personal tasks such as online banking, online shopping, and online bill paying. However, while companies tout the convenience of using the web for such purposes, the security threats associated with these activities and emanating from their usage continue to mount. Understanding the basic browser mechanisms and how they can be utilized by attackers is vital for preventing vulnerable data loss and network infiltration.

QUESTIONS

1. What are the four primary categories that network security falls under?
2. This acts as the heart of the Internet and is located in the backbone. What is it?
3. What is the role of a packet sniffer?
4. In what two ways can a packet sniffer usually be set up?
5. What are the general threats in Layer 1 and Layer 2 of the seven-layer model?
6. Why do hackers spoof the IP source address?
7. What does a DHCP server contain?
8. Why is it easy to attack DHCP?

Chapter 13

Web Security, DNS Security, and the Internet

To understand information security in regard to the Internet, we must start by discussing how the Internet works, examining the Internet Protocol (IP) and the Transmission Control Protocol (TCP), routing protocols, and Domain Name System (DNS) servers, including the technology employed as well as their various vulnerabilities.

The Internet is the global interconnection of computer networks (which we all use now on an everyday basis) that makes use of the TCP/IP to establish sessions between source and destination sites (TCP) and for addressing packets to be routed across the Internet to the desired destination.

Whereas the IP deals only with addressing packets that are to be routed across the network, TCP enables two hosts on both ends of the connecting network to establish a connection session and exchange a designated stream of data, which is transferred either individually or as a negotiated "window" of a specified number of IP packets. TCP guarantees delivery of the data and also guarantees that packets will be delivered in the same order in which they were sent by rearranging them in the transmitted order at the destination site. It also provides for retransmission of those packets if one of a "window" of packets is not delivered over a period of transmission time.

IP is the method or protocol by which data is addressed for transmission from one computer to another on the Internet. Each computer (known as a host) on the Internet has at least one IP address that uniquely identifies it among all the other computers on the Internet.

An IP address is a numerical label assigned to each device (whether it be a computer, printer, tablet, or smartphone) participating in a computer network that uses the IP for communication. An IP address serves two principal addressing functions: first, to identify a particular host or network interface with a unique identification; and second, to use that identity for the addressing of source and destination locations.

The Internet, then, is a network of various component subnetworks that have been interconnected. These can include public, private, academic, government, personal, and corporate networks that are spread across the globe. Making use of this interconnection are a variety of information services providing websites that connect to the Internet. The contents of such websites can be accessed via local routed networks or by means of an interconnected and interdomain-routed set

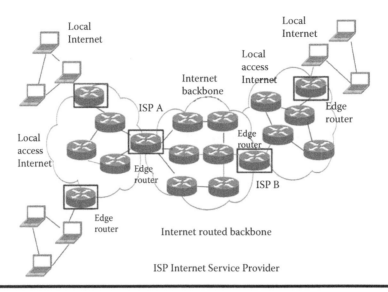

Figure 13.1   Local networks interconnected by backbone Internet network.

of networks. For this purpose, TCP/IPs and the DNS is required. Figure 13.1 shows an example of such interconnected local and backbone Internet networks.

TCP is a connection-oriented protocol that establishes the flow of packet transmission and reinstates the original order when they arrive at the destination in a different order than they were transmitted. When packets are transmitted across a network to another host (or network node), they have a transmission number inserted in a field that is then used to reorder them on the receiving end. Moreover, once the packets are received by the intended destination host, a receipt acknowledgment is sent back to the originating host. If any packets are missing, those are not included in the acknowledgments, resulting in the original sender resending the missing packets. While this is a nice control protocol, there are security flaws associated with it. For example, IP packets with TCP information can be intercepted and read by a packet sniffer such as Wireshark. Once the TCP state has been obtained, an attacker can send a "reset" packet to an open socket, which can create a denial of service for the original sender.

IP is the Internet addressing protocol that addresses packets, and those addresses are used to route and ultimately deliver packets to the destination host. For destinations outside a given network, the IP address will be the location of the default gateway. Although there is no error reporting if a packet is dropped (requiring non-acknowledgment as an indicator), a time-to-live field helps prevent endless loops of packets continually being transported and clogging up the network bandwidth. However, a security downside of the IP is that there is no authentication of the source IP address. This means that attackers can send packets from a fake source IP address to launch anonymous denial-of-service attacks or attempt to send an overwhelming amount of "ping" messages and essentially ping a server to death.

Beyond our discussion of the TCP and IP, there are a number of routing and associated protocols, which include Address Resolution Protocol (ARP), Border Gateway Protocol (BGP), Open Shortest Path First Protocol (OSPF), and Cisco's Enhanced Interior Gateway Routing Protocol (EIGRP), as well as the original Routing Information Protocol (RIP). A security flaw of ARP is that proxy traffic can inject large amounts of broadcast packets into a network seeking a particular hardware address and blocking legitimate traffic. Also, with BGP, hackers can hijack a route to a

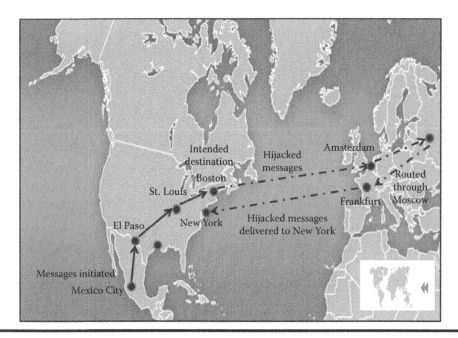

Figure 13.2   How Russian attackers could sniff packets.

victim of an attack, most likely as part of a denial-of-service attack, and can eavesdrop on packets that are being routed on a specific network. An example of this process is the situation wherein Russian attackers are reputed to have rerouted and sniffed packets that were not meant to have been routed through the Russian network (Figure 13.2).

Another important component to know is the DNS. Domain names provide a means of translating an alias destination name, such as jjstone@bsu.edu, that stands in place of a real IP address such as 176.52.27.12, which is the real IP address (although in binary form). When a user's browser requests the IP address of another user or website by entering the alias name (jjstone) and the destination domain name (bsu.edu), the website's DNS server will respond with the IP address to be inserted in packets to be routed to that specific user's computer or to a specified website. These entries are cached at the local DNS server, allowing for a quick response time for repeated transmissions. There are security flaws in this system that can be exploited by hackers. For instance, interceptions of DNS requests or compromised DNS servers can send malicious responses to the requesting host. This can result in DNS poisoning attacks, which can send user packets to websites for which they were not intended.

The Internet is a large and complex interconnection of networks that is in no way free from the numerous hackers and the vast array of threats that are lurking and searching for appropriate and vulnerable victims.

QUESTIONS

1. Describe what IPSec is and what layer it is in.
2. What two encryption modes does IPSec support?
3. Which one encrypts both header information and data?
4. What is the function of secure socket layer?
5. Snort is used for a distributed intrusion detection. What is its advantage over a firewall?

Chapter 14

Network Security and Defenses

Network security is a large part of information security for many different types of networks, whether they are public, private, government, or academic. Whether attacks are malware, denial of service (DoS), sniffing, or man in the middle (MitM), networks need to be properly secured against them to avoid a complete shutdown of services. To do this, it is important to get an understanding of network security threats in order to better understand how to protect networks against these threats with proper defenses.

Network security threats fall into four primary categories: confidentiality attacks, integrity attacks, availability attacks, and common attacks. Confidentiality attacks can include packet sniffing, or the fact that data being transmitted over Internet Protocol (IP) may be subject to decryption by a malicious attacker. For example, if a user is connecting to a server via the File Transfer Protocol (FTP), a malicious attacker could use a packet-sniffing software such as Wireshark to sniff critical information that can include the destination server IP, your user name, and your password.

Integrity attacks can include cross-site scripting (XSS). In these attacks, which prey on vulnerable web pages, an attacker will inject malicious code to essentially hijack a user's session. Once the session is hijacked, the attacker can have the malicious code executed and send the victim's data to a malicious database to be retrieved later by the hacker. However, this isn't the only form of integrity attack. Recently, MitM attacks have preyed on weak computer cryptography protocols to intercept "encrypted" packets that may contain personal information (often banking information).

Availability attacks are most often DoS attacks. Attackers will use these methods when they would like certain networks to be rendered unreachable or temporarily disabled. There are two subclasses of integrity attacks: local DoS and remote DoS attacks. Local DoS attacks can include the injection of IP packets into a network, saturating the bandwidth to unusable levels and thus bringing the network to a halt. An example of remote DoS attacks can include the pinging to death of a web server, which can bring websites down for hours, even days, at a time. Availability attacks are performed on a daily basis throughout the Internet, and as their sophistication grows it becomes harder to defend against these attacks.

Common attacks can be attributed to address translation poisoning attacks and other routing attacks. A common tactic can include domain name system (DNS) spoofing. In this attack, the attacker will inject data into the DNS resolver's cache. Once this has been performed, the name server will provide an IP address that was not originally requested but can navigate the victim's traffic to another computer or server.

While these network attacks can be very menacing, there are plenty of defenses against them. For IP defense, a firewall can be put in place within your local network to help prevent malicious traffic from entering or exiting your network. Another defense that can be used is packet filtering. Packet filtering can help in common attacks by blocking incoming packets based on certain specific ports. Another key element of network security is the use of an intrusion detection system. These detection systems look for anomalies to see if there has been unauthorized access into a system. While these systems are not perfect, there is at least some mechanism in place if a drastic intrusion has occurred that a user might not be able to see.

Overall, network attacks are inevitable. However, there are proper defense mechanisms that can be put in place to at least combat attacks if they happen on a system.

Network Security: Recap

We started out looking at a case study (the Anthem break-in) and tried to understand how the break-in happened and what tracking efforts were deployed by the company in an attempt to understand the events that took place. A combination of social engineering, watering-hole techniques, and spear phishing was used to infiltrate the company and inject potent combinations of spyware and malware to penetrate the systems more deeply. Through under-the-radar testing, hackers gained relevant knowledge concerning the capability of their software to infiltrate trial systems.

We evaluated the details and strategies that hackers used. Their attacks were composed of various types of malware and spyware, which included viruses, rootkits, worms, and so on. We also evaluated algorithms and Rivest–Shamir–Adleman (RSA). We briefly discussed browser security and web applications security, and then we looked at the domain name structure. Finally, having looked at the domain applications, we will now examine network security itself.

Protocols

When we evaluate the network, we will primarily focus on evaluating Layer 2, Layer 3, and Layer 4 protocols. This is not to say that we should disregard the other layers in the seven-layer

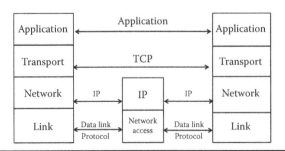

Figure 14.1 Layers of the TCP/IP process.

model (illustrated in Figure 14.1), but for now, we will focus on specific vulnerabilities affecting the access, link, and transport layers.

Starting with Layer 2, and given our familiarity with the MAC layer, we know that the Media Access Control (MAC) addresses in the network access layer are associated with the network interface card (NIC) and use 48 bits out of the available 64 bits. Frequently, Layer 2 is a point-to-point protocol over private lines. It tends to be a simple protocol, but it is nevertheless useful. At Layer 3, we've examined the IP, whose job is to address source and final destination segments that are passed to the network. We will also talk a little bit about Transmission Control Protocol (TCP) and will touch briefly on port numbers, which are used to create a connection between an application and TCP. This will establish a contextual reference that will set the stage for an exploration of the vulnerabilities found at all of the different network layers.

Note that there is an issue between MAC addresses and IP addresses. This is because, typically, users will use IP to go across the Internet. But when the packet gets close to the destination, the packet is delivered over Ethernet. Generally, it doesn't need to look at the IP address to complete that transition. But given the nature of the situation, it essentially requires a translation process. The edge router will basically broadcast the request on that network, which may elicit responses from any device on that network. This serves to highlight the fact that previously, many of the communications taking place within the network were directed under inherent trust. Individuals' operating devices trusted that other devices on the network were authorized devices. Therefore, it becomes obvious that vulnerabilities are built into this early model.

Also, part of the discussion will include border gateways, which act as the heart of the Internet. These are generally located in the backbone. Essentially, an area network and another area network are bridged through the use of border area gateways. These are subject to vulnerability.

Specifically, the following threats will be discussed in detail:

Packet sniffing (confidentiality issues): When packets go across the network, there are several ways in which a packet can be sniffed by several devices on the network.

Session hijacking (integrity issues): This involves diverting traffic to a different service.

Address translation poisoning attacks (common issues): This involves Address Resolution Protocol (ARP) and route table corruption, which is a common occurrence, as any device can respond to an ARP request.

Further, there are more concrete security problems. The following include ARP, which is not an authenticated protocol. Source IP addresses do not typically get checked. This poses a threat because seldom do devices check the veracity of the IP addresses. This provides hackers with the ability to give themselves a different IP address. However, MAC addresses provide some buffering for these issues. Additionally, network packets that are sniffed by untrusted hosts are also a concrete security problem. TCP state also poses a security risk as it can easily be guessed by hackers.

Address Resolution Protocol

ARP is a broadcasting protocol that is primarily used to translate IP addresses to Ethernet MAC addresses. Each host (PC or server) on the network has a table of the IP and MAC address, and every switch also stores a table of the MAC and IP addresses. Together, they serve to provide address resolution between these two layers. Figure 14.2 illustrates the way ARP works. ARP represents a vulnerability because it is easy to spoof ARP requests and replies.

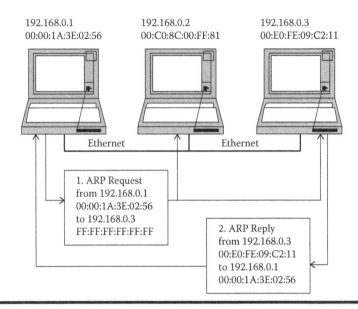

192.168.0.1
00:00:1A:3E:02:56

192.168.0.2
00:C0:8C:00:FF:81

192.168.0.3
00:E0:FE:09:C2:11

Ethernet   Ethernet

1. ARP Request
from 192.168.0.1
00:00:1A:3E:02:56
to 192.168.0.3
FF:FF:FF:FF:FF:FF

2. ARP Reply
from 192.168.0.3
00:E0:FE:09:C2:11
to 192.168.0.1
00:00:1A:3E:02:56

Figure 14.2   Basic Address Resolution Protocol (ARP) process.

ARP spoofing or poisoning occurs when hackers send fake or spoofed ARP messages to an Ethernet local area network (LAN). This allows hackers to trick machines into associating their IP addresses with the attackers' MAC address. In other words, hackers are basically falsely putting in their MAC address and beating the authentic reply, and then essentially getting all the traffic from the associated IP addresses. What are the defenses for this type of spoofing? Prebuilding a static ARP table is one of the solutions; however, this is messy and hard to sustain as it does not easily allow for dynamic changes and requires a significant amount of maintenance. Other defense methods include Dynamic Host Configuration Protocol (DHCP) snooping, which allows users to leverage access control lists to ensure that hosts only use the IP addresses that are assigned to them and only enable access to authorized DHCP servers. Arpwatch can also be used to send out information, in the form of e-mail, to cycle through a verification process and improve transparency.

Internet Protocol

Note that IP is unreliable by design. In other words, it is a best-effort protocol that only serves an addressing purpose. The routers along the network path essentially only look at the destination IP address, and the routing tables are set up so that they provide the router with information concerning the output port and the respective MAC address associated with the device sending the packet, as opposed to the destination IP address. Routing does not make any attempt to get the packet to the destination but instead functions more as a distributed process. This type of protocol is different from the way specific types of networks work. Multiprotocol label switching (MPLS) is a good example of a network that attempts to identify the best path to the destination. However, IP is an addressing and routing protocol and not much else. This best-effort concept, realistically, creates some vulnerability. One of the key issues associated with IP vulnerabilities is packet sniffing.

Packet Sniffing

Networks can be composed of host devices, switches, routers, and various network end-point devices, including servers. The vulnerability of some designs is observable when promiscuous listeners are attached to that network. Since generally the traffic going over both private and public networks is unencrypted, access to the network may compromise the integrity of the data traveling through the network. Having servers on multiple sides has made some networks particularly vulnerable to this kind of intrusion. As an example, consider corporate networks, such as that of Anthem. It is not uncommon for parts of their network transmissions to be completely encrypted, such as information coming from the outside. The problem then becomes more relevant when one notices that the information traveling within the corporate network is often not encrypted. If hackers acquire access to the inside of the network, data may be compromised, as was the case for Anthem. However, as a method of prevention, many corporations are putting in an effort to encrypt most of the data traveling through their networks based on the RSA encryption standards and IP security (IPSec).

User Datagram Protocol (UDP)

UDP is a protocol that acts at Layer 4. It operates similarly to IP, which means that it doesn't have a verification mechanism that ensures data receipt. There are minimal guarantees, as with UDP there are no acknowledgments, no flow control, and no message continuation. It differentiates itself from TCP, as its main responsibility is to separate traffic by port, whereas TCP segments each message and negotiates with the destination TCP device in order to transmit relevant data via IP. Given that it is dependent on the integrity of the data transmission, TCP is a connection-oriented protocol as it provides an acknowledgment of receipt at most stages of data retrieval, and lost packets are generally resent and reassembled in the correct order. Concerning TCP, one of the ways that hackers slow down networks is through the use of edge routers. These will be controlled so as to send small packets to reduce the window size, and then each one gets acknowledged. However, while UDP's focus is smaller and provides no guarantees, it's important to note that UDP still has value as most network management uses UDP.

TCP sequence numbering is yet another technique to which networks are particularly vulnerable. This takes place because hackers are able to guess and spoof the sequence number of the following packet in TCP communications. For example, take the basic three-way-handshake approach: In the first step, the sender chooses an initial sequence number that is ideally chosen at random. The destination then sends back an acknowledgment that it received that packet coming across, and it takes that sequence number and adds a unit to it. Every time a new set of communications is issued between the two nodes, there is a degree of predictability to each sequence number issued, so hackers tend to take advantage of this by predicting the number and then issuing counterfeit packets. While hackers don't have full control of the network, they can easily introduce packets with fake source IP addresses and compromise the integrity of the data traveling the network. One defense measure commonly used for this type of hacker spoofing is to turn off the three-way-handshake mechanism.

Blind TCP Session Hijacking

There are many ways to hijack TCP sessions, and one of these is to use a malicious server in the sequence. These types of servers can be outside the corporate network and outside the firewall but

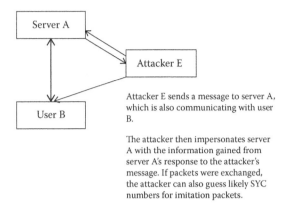

Attacker E sends a message to server A, which is also communicating with user B.

The attacker then impersonates server A with the information gained from server A's response to the attacker's message. If packets were exchanged, the attacker can also guess likely SYC numbers for imitation packets.

Figure 14.3 Attacker impersonation of server.

still doing the same basic process. As illustrated in Figure 14.3, Attacker E is attempting to set up a connection. Attacker E is essentially trying to impersonate that server and other PCs that might be behind that server.

Attacker E sends a message to Server A, which is also communicating with User B. The attacker then impersonates Server A with the information gained from Server A's response to the attacker's message. If packets were exchanged, the attacker can also guess likely SYN numbers for imitation packets. SYN is the series or sequence numbers used with TCP segment in IP packets, especially during the TCP three-way handshake.

There are foreseeable risks that corporations take relative to session hijacking. The first element is data encryption. For example, inside corporate networks, data is often not encrypted. A potential solution to this is to create encryption tunnels within corporate environments to prevent malicious attacks from bogus clients and devices in the environment.

DoS is a type of attack that results from these types of vulnerabilities. Hackers can easily guess sequence numbers and then send and resend constant requests throughout the network to shut down connections. For efficiency, many systems are set up where a large window is negotiated, which enables a range of sequence numbers to be arranged. If the range of these sequence numbers is guessed, hackers have an opportunity to cause a lot of damage in the form of network package flooding.

DoS attacks have two main goals. One is to stop services in the network from operating, and the other is to exhaust the resources available in that network (Figure 14.4).

	Stopping services	Exhausting resources
Locally	• Process killing • Process crashing • System reconfiguration	• Spawning processes to fill the process table • Filling UP the whole file system • Saturate comm bandwidth
Remotely	• Malformed packets to crash buggy services	• Packet floods (Smurf, SYN flood, DDoS, etc.)

Figure 14.4 Two main goals of issuing denial-of-service attacks.

Stopping Services

Locally, these attacks are focused on process crashing and forcing system reconfiguration. Remotely, the attacks are predominantly focused on sending malformed packets that crash buggy services.

Exhausting Resources

Hackers try to send spawning process commands to fill the process table. Additionally, hackers tend to fill up the whole file system and saturate the communications bandwidth. Remotely, packet floods are used to block the network from utilizing its resources properly.

SYN Flooding

Synchronize (SYN) flooding is one of the standard approaches in which hackers send a string of messages after they have successfully guessed the sequence number. This string of SYN messages looks valid, and victim devices tend to not look at the source for further authentication. The victim allocates resources for each request as the data is stored and forwarded, which engenders a vicious cycle of continuous forwarding until timeout, which is capped by the new incoming packets. In essence, resources are exhausted, and incoming real requests are rejected as the network devices are operating at full capacity and bandwidth. It is no more effective than other channel capacity–based attacks today.

Smurf DoS Attacks

In this attack scenario, hackers tend to send ping requests to broadcast addresses via Internet Control Message Protocol (ICMP) echo requests. The result is a lot of responses as every host on the target network receives that ping and, therefore, generates another ping reply to the victim. This, in turn, overloads the victim with the resulting ping reply stream. To prevent this type of attack, users must not allow any remote ICMP echo request to come through, especially those with broadcast address destinations.

Internet Control Message Protocol

This is a core part of network management. Frequently, workgroups will have a responsible individual that will leverage ICMP to determine if there is a valid connection. Its primary uses include providing feedback about the network operation via error reporting, reachability testing, and congestion control.

Distributed Denial-of-Service Attacks

An attacker will create a botnet out of zombie devices. The attacker basically triggers the zombie devices to attack another victim network. The trigger will contain valuable information or details concerning the attack, and the devices will leverage this data to complete the attack.

There are a number of methods that hackers will leverage in order to hide the fact that they are trying to achieve a DDoS attack. First of all, they pursue companies that have a big distributed network. This makes it hard to distinguish whether the traffic coming in from zombie devices is false or whether it is authentic. Another technique they use is called *pulsing zombie floods*. This creates stop-and-start flooding, which also makes it difficult to identify the source of the attacks.

Cryptographic Network Protection

Internet Protocol Security

We assume that Layer 7 is where the applications programs are located. Layer 6 contains all kinds of routines related to remote procedural call software; this is also where encryption is housed. The next layer up containing TCP then passes it on with further information attached and moves the data through all layers. Generally, IPSec is what is used at Layer 6 for solving encryption issues. The commonly used technique known as clocking has been too easy to guess, so random number generators have become the desired approach for assigning sequence numbers.

Network Attacks

While examining Layers 2, 3, and 4, consider Layer 1 as well. There is a common semantic misunderstanding as to what Layer 1 actually is. Layer 1 is not the media by which data is transmitted. Instead, Layer 1 is in the computer, and it is the connection to the transport media. An example is the Ethernet card, which enables communication between the Ethernet cable and the port on the computer. The physical layer encodes the bits that are sent out over the network. Layer 2 is in charge of the framing and transmission of a collection of bits into individual messages sent across a subnetwork.

Physical/Link-Layer Threats: Eavesdropping

Eavesdropping (also termed *sniffing*) is one of the threats found in Layers 1 and 2. This is becoming a particular phenomenon affecting cell phones. There are many ways to sniff at the physical layer. Multiple tools including Wireshark and tcpdump/windump are enabling the scanning or capturing of relevant transmission components such as MAC addresses. There's a multitude of techniques that enable hackers and attackers to steal photons as well. The physical/link-layer threats do not just pick up the signal but also disrupt the signals.

Physical/Link-Layer Threats: Spoofing

Spoofing must have root administrative access to do damage, but the basic concept behind this kind of attack revolves around gaining physical access to a subnetwork. Once the attacker has gained access, they can easily create false messages. Spoofing poses a greater threat when it is combined with eavesdropping, as the attacker is able to determine the state of the victim's communication. This further allows the attacker to create his or her own spoofed communication traffic, which matches that of the authentic network. The combined technique is known as *bling spoofing*.

Layer 3 Threats

Typically, the most vulnerable areas for Layer 3 components are the source and destination addresses, plus the routers and their routing tables. Keep in mind that the routers have a designated algorithm that they use to build their routing tables. They sustainably build and maintain the routing tables for themselves. Therefore, it becomes interesting to see how malicious devices create false links and routing processes to disrupt this process. Source IP addresses are never checked because the router does not care where things came from. It leverages the IP addresses solely to determine the next forwarding output port. Each output port has an associated MAC address attached to that port, giving hackers the flexibility to set packets with bogus or arbitrary source and destination addresses to disrupt the operation of these devices.

Fragmentation of the packets is another method commonly used by hackers to evade network monitoring. They also utilize timed fragmentation to avoid rotating monitor systems. By manipulating areas such as the time-to-live and the identification fields, hackers gain more flexibility, which helps them evade security checkpoints.

Layer 4 TCP and UDP Threats

A variety of issues affect both TCP and UPD protocols at Layer 4. Among them it is not uncommon to find:

▪ Disruption threats
▪ Injection threats
▪ Spoofing threats

TCP is not involved directly in the network. TCP is the sender and the receiver that sets up a flow control mechanism. The only place that TCP is involved in the network is when it acts as a slowdown mechanism that essentially reduces the window size to slow down the network for a temporary period of time. In most cases, we observe that there are only two TCPs talking to each other. Also note the specifications surrounding port numbers. The source and destination ports are built for a set of standard or known programs. Specific sets of ports are used for specific applications, and the remaining ephemeral ports are used mostly ad hoc. Also note that the upper limit for these ports has expanded in the last years.

The sequence number is then used as an authentication by that mechanism. TCP sends a FIN control message if it wishes to terminate (finish) a session with a destination site. The destination site must then reply with its own FIN control message to acknowledge receipt and acceptance of the finish of the transmission. If only one site wishes to terminate (finish) the transmission session, it sends an RST control message, which does not require acknowledgment. Given that it requires this acknowledgment, hackers have tapped into this and have issued false FIN messages to disrupt the process. This, again, is dependent on authentication that relies on sequence numbers, which, in turn, are easily guessed by hackers. By injecting data into the packet data field, hackers can also cause damage to the packet. But perhaps one of the most important areas of concern is servers that are attached to networks in which routers have been compromised. From here, traffic is diverted easily via that corrupted router.

Hackers use a technique termed *blind spoofing* to guess specific sequence numbers. Keep in mind that each host tells its initial sequence number to the other host. From here, hackers can easily guess the spec used to determine the sequence numbers and can prepare the remaining pieces of information to stage the attack (Figure 14.5).

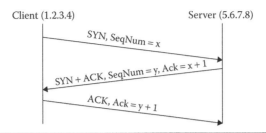

Figure 14.5 Using blind spoofing to guess specific sequence numbers.

Once they've compiled all relevant data and have launched an attack that has given them access to a trusted network, hackers can then create a fake connection to leverage a server's trust or to frame a given client. As a precaution, network engineers can leverage the use of a random number generator. However, this can become difficult to implement every day as routers don't have a built-in random number generator.

Other varieties of network attacks include, but are not limited to, attacks that target

- DHCP for bootstrapping Internet access
- DNS for mapping hostnames to IP addresses
- TCP cheating on fairness

DHCP Threats

DHCP is a bootstrapping technique. If a new PC does not yet have an IP address, the device sends out a discovery message to a central DHCP server (frequently supplied by a corporation with a large number of employees requiring IP addresses), and the DHCP server will respond with loaned temporary IP number to be used by that device—frequently for that particular day but possibly for longer. In some situations, the DHCP server will provide static addresses, but the working assumption is that the company will leverage the DHCP servers to distribute, by lending, a more limited set of corporate IP addresses for temporary usage by its employees. Figure 14.6 illustrates the IP leasing process as it occurs via a DHCP server.

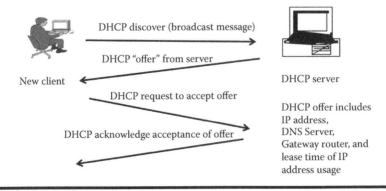

Figure 14.6 Dynamic host configuration process.

Historically, network engineers set up proxy servers on the edge of a corporation's network. These proxy servers would loan external IP addresses to internal company workers to communicate with networks, particularly the public Internet, outside of the working corporate "intranet." Using the inside private corporate intranet, users employ a private 10.0.0.0 set of IP addresses, which can be duplicated around the world since they only address within private IP networks. At the edge proxy server, the user is lent an outside public IP address to replace the local private 10.0.0.0 address. Given this mechanism, there are many types of threats that can impact this process. Attackers can position themselves at locations where they can listen in on new host DHCP requests. From there, hackers can spoof the entire process, even attempting to beat the DHCP server in its offer of a loaned external public IP address. If the "fake" IP address is accepted by the client requesting the address, then the next IP address issued by the DHCP server will be misaligned, causing disruption in the proxy server process.

If a threat is attached to the local internal Ethernet network, hackers listen to that internal network and send false replies, which will enable them to substitute a fake DNS server or substitute a fake gateway and to launch attacks including invisible MitM attacks.

Domain Name System Threats

When users send a message and a connection must be established, the alias name must be translated to a valid IP address expressed in binary (such as 176.142.76.12) via the use of an organization's or an Internet Service Provider's (ISP) DNS server. An example is if a message is to a distant DNS server that acts as the root DNS server. If that local DNS server is unfamiliar with that destination alias name, the local DNS sends the request on to the public Internet's servers, which are provided in duplicate fashion at specific sites across the Internet. The public Internet's DNS servers know all the local DNS servers that can provide the required alias to IP address translation. They forward the request to that destination local DNS, which provides the translation; this is returned to the original sender's browser, which then substitutes that real binary IP address in the message to be transmitted. Meanwhile, the sender's local DNS will remember that translation for a limited time, in case it is required again. If it is a repeated request, it is stored on a more permanent basis.

The DNS server process, then, is constructed in a hierarchical fashion, according to which only the local DNS servers know how to provide the local address translations for their local community. The public Internet's DNS servers know where all the local DNS servers are located and which address translations they specialize in serving. Local DNS servers will contain all the local information, while the higher-level public Internet DNS servers have knowledge of the DNS servers' availability, capability, and location; however, they don't perform specialized address translations themselves, nor do they maintain the knowledge to do so. This equates to all translations being performed at the distributed lower levels of the DNS hierarchy. As a precaution, note that since all translations are performed at the local DNS level, if these become damaged or infected, communication becomes blocked or corrupted.

There is a formal protocol with a particular identification feature for the header. This is part of a UDP message that is included with the source and destination port number. Given that UDP is a best-effort protocol, much of the DNS functioning and network management is unacknowledged. If it doesn't work, it doesn't work. All communication over public and private networks depends on the DNS because individuals don't know specific IPs but rather textual English aliases. Additionally, these IP addresses change on a constant basis; therefore, a system is used to reconcile the differences. The question is now what happens when attackers eavesdrop on DNS queries. The short answer is that they are, once again, empowered to cause a lot of damage to the network.

More specifically, they gain the ability to redirect us with misinformation through corrupting of DNS tables. Again, since the DNS is subject to very little validation, this represents a big vulnerability in this system.

Blind spoofing is one of the primary ways to leverage information from the DNS to mislead users. Again, given the nature of UDP, there is no acknowledgment that can be provided to safeguard users. As a defense, it's important to know a valid set of source and destination ports. However, keep in mind that valid ports can easily be spoofed. A random source port then can be used as a fix.

Concluding Highlights

DHCP is a major source of vulnerability, given that broadcast protocols are inherently at risk of spoofing. When systems are first initializing, they are particularly vulnerable because they lack a trusted foundation. Finally, MitM attacks are insidious, given that there are no indicators that they are occurring.

DNS attacks tend to be opportunistic kinds of attacks. They tend to be fairly straightforward and are designed to poison the cache or the DNS. Specifically, attackers are trying to manipulate victims into engaging in vulnerable activity. Finally, attacks of this nature appear technically remote but can become real practical issues as they are often unforeseen.

QUESTIONS

1. Describe four primary categories that network security falls under.
2. Give an example of each network security attack.
3. What is considered the heart of the Internet and why?
4. What is used to translate an IP address to an Ethernet MAC address?
5. Why is ARP vulnerability important?
6. Explain what a pulsing zombie flood is.
7. What threat is found in Layer 1 and Layer 2?
8. What are the most vulnerable areas for Layer 3?
9. What is the primary way to leverage information from the DNS to mislead users?

Chapter 15

Network Security Protocols and Defensive Mechanisms

Network Security Protocols

We are increasingly concerned that we are not using wired Ethernet for PC access to the networks but are wirelessly connecting to access points, and our access link tends to be a variation of the 802.11 standard, with Wi-Fi Protected Access (WPA)2 for wireless security and Internet Protocol Security (IPSec) for encryption and routed network security. However, security issues continue to plague our networks. Border gateways between certain autonomous networks are used at the borders to facilitate communication across networks. Since these are located at the border of networks, they tend to be more vulnerable; therefore, we use Secure Border Gateway Protocols (S-BGP) to provide a level of security. Domain Name System (DNS) rebinding also has a secure version, which we've also started using. This is known as a *Domain Name System Security Extension* (DNSSEC). Further, network engineers have developed perimeter defenses, which look like firewalls. Their functions are varied and include packet filtering of stateless and stateful packets. Specifically, these filters look for things that should be allowed through. In this chapter, there will also be an evaluation of anomalies that could represent a threat to the network. More specifically, time-of-day markets will be examined in further detail.

Basic protocols that will be assessed in this section include Internet Protocol (IP), Transmission Control Protocol (TCP), User Datagram Protocol (UDP), Border Gateway Protocol (BGP), and a combination of DNS and Dynamic Host Configuration Protocol (DHCP). There are a multitude of security issues with these protocols. Regarding IP, there is no source validation, and it is also fairly easy to sniff these packets and spoof connections by guessing TCP sequence numbers. Concerning BGP, it's fairly easy for hackers to advertise bad routes and close good ones. And in the case of DNS, cache poisoning and rebinding are quite common and affect overall web security mechanisms that rely on the DNS for address resolution.

IP Security (IPSec) Protocol

This is one of the key IP security and encryption protocols. One of IPSec's sub-protocols is the Internet key exchange (IKE), a standard protocol used to ensure security negotiation for virtual private networks (VPNs) and, in particular, the negotiation of remote access by hosts or edge devices to an IP network. IKE's primary task is concerned with negotiating the IPSec security association (SA), which is a relationship between two or more entities that describes how the entities will use security services to communicate securely. IKE (or IKEv2) is the protocol in the IPSec protocol suite that is used to set up an SA. IKE builds on the Oakley protocol and the Internet Security Association and Key Management Protocol (ISAKMP), which is a protocol defined for establishing SAs and cryptographic keys in an Internet environment. IKE uses X.509 certificates for authentication—either preshared or distributed using DNS (preferably with DNSSEC) and a Diffie–Hellman key exchange—to set up a shared session secret from which cryptographic keys are derived. This process requires that the IPSec systems authenticate themselves to each other and then proceed to establish ISAKMP (IKE) shared keys.

Phase 1

The source IKE sends an IKE message, which creates a secure channel between two IKE peers, the source and destination IKE peers. An encryption key is used as the Diffie–Hellman key agreement. This type of agreement is considered a superior encryption to the popular Rivest–Shamir–Adleman (RSA) encryption discussed in Chapter 8.

Phase 2

The source IKE negotiates an IPSec SA and generates the required key materials for encrypting and decrypting. The sender offers a set of transformations. The receiver then accepts one of the transformations.

The sequence of exchanges is portrayed in Figure 15.1.

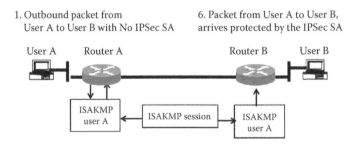

1. Outbound packet from User A to User B with No IPSec SA

6. Packet from User A to User B, arrives protected by the IPSec SA

User A   Router A   Router B   User B

ISAKMP user A ← ISAKMP session → ISAKMP user A

2. Then, User A's IKE/ISAKMP negotiates with User B's IKE/ISAKMP.
3. The two IKEs set up a secure channel to negotiate the IPSec Security Associations (SAs).
4. Router A and Router B then negotiate an IKE Phase 2 session.
5. Information is transmitted via the arranged IPSec tunnel.

Figure 15.1   IKE/ISAKMP process of negotiating an IPSec security association.

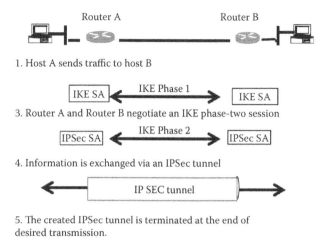

Figure 15.2   Process of creating an IPSec tunnel for transmitting encrypted packets.

Frequently, a certificate of authority is added to the process. A message is sent out to a radius server, the purpose of which is to have the radius server authenticate the message that is being sent across the IP network.

The sequence for this process is illustrated in Figure 15.2.

This process includes a set of access lists that, in combination with the encryption, increase the level of security components.

Layer 2: Link-Layer Connectivity of Wireless

Our society's growing need for mobility has led to the increased use and adoption of the 802.11i wireless connectivity standard, which specifies security mechanisms for wireless network connection. In this protocol, the network attempts to set up the secure transfer of information from the source to destination. This includes a supplicant, an authenticator, and an authenticating server (usually a radius server). On one side of the communication is the supplicant; in the middle is the authenticator and the authenticating radius server. The authenticator uses the radius server to supply encryption keys that will provide secure communication with the supplicant over an unsecure IP network. For this protocol, there are five layers of communication that require agreement between the source and destination.

TCP/IP Basic Layer 2–3 Security Problems

The following all comprise big issues for IP/TCP:

- Eavesdropping
- Packet sniffing, which enables controlling of machines
- TCP state can be guessed, which enables spoofing
- Session hijacking

Defense Mechanisms That Can Be Employed

Virtual Private Network

For protection over unsecured IP networks, companies increasingly employ VPNs using IPSec as the encryption algorithm and IKE as the requesting mechanism for passwords.

There are three different modes used for VPN:

1. Remote access client connections
2. LAN-to-LAN internetworking
3. Controlled access within an intranet

Several Different Protocols Then Apply to These Modes

PPTP: Point-to-Point Tunneling Protocol
L2TP: Layer 2: Tunneling Protocol
IPSec: Layer 3: network layer (includes the Diffie–Hellman encryption process)

IPSec

There are two varieties of IPSec, one of which is an extension for IPV4 and the other for IPV6. Furthermore, IPSec includes an IP authentication header. This safeguards the authentication and integrity of the payload and the header itself. An encapsulation protocol is used to enhance the confidentiality of the payload and the headers. Encapsulating security payload (ESP) is another member of the IPSec protocol suite. In IPSec, it is used to provide integrity check values that can be combined with other prior tools to provide confidentiality and data origin authentication.

Basic Packet Formats

The basic packet formats in the TCP/IP variation of the Open Systems Interconnection (OSI) seven-layer data communication model include a message originating in Layer 7 (application layer), which is usually broken up into 1500 byte parts, and then each part of the message is separately included in a data field of a Layer 4 (transport layer) segment with a TCP header. That Layer 4 segment is then included as the data field in a Layer 3 IP packet with an IP destination address. Next, the IP segment is included as a data field in a link-layer frame at Layer 2, with its own header containing a Layer 2 address, frequently an Ethernet address. Thus, the resulting unit to be transmitted contains a portion of the original message plus a series of Layers 6, 5, and 4 headers, if there are any, plus TCP, IP, and Ethernet headers. There are as many of these units transmitted as can contain all of the 1500 byte portions of the original message to be transmitted. The headers and data fields created at each layer of the transmission model are illustrated next to their respective layers in Figure 15.3, which shows the sequence of the inclusion of those successive headers included with the transmitted unit sent out over the network.

A source will encrypt its packet data in the header, and it is sent over an encrypted tunnel. The receiving device will then decrypt the packet. However, prior to this, it will receive authentication keys to ensure the integrity of the packets when IPSec is used.

Figure 15.4 provides a more detailed view of the process, which now includes IPSec protocol.

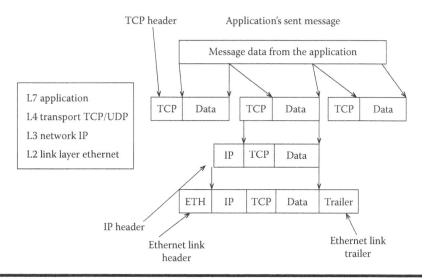

Figure 15.3   Packet formats and layers.

IPSec tunnel mode: IPSec header + IP header

Internet Protocol Security (IPSec) is a protocol suite for secure Internet Protocol (IP) communications by authenticating and encrypting each IP packet of a communication session. With IPSec tunnel mode, in addition, IPSec encrypts the IP header and the payload.

Layer 4 TCP/UDP					TCP header	Upper layer header	Data part

Layer 3 IP				IP header	TCP header	Upper layer header	Data part

	Encapsulating IP and IPSec datagram						
IPSec between L2-L3	New IP header	AM header	ESP header	IP header	TCP header	Upper layer header	Data part

Layer 2 ethernet	L2 ETH-NT header	New IP header	AM header	ESP header	IP header	TCP header	Upper layer header	Data part

Figure 15.4   IPSec tunneling mode and TCP/IP layers.

Filtering Network Traffic at the IP Level

Network traffic at the IP level is often filtered through a firewall at the perimeter of the receiver's network. A firewall is typically placed at the connection point of the local company network and the public Internet to filter traffic that comes from the public Internet and goes to the local company network. Firewalls of this nature implement a set of access rules defining what packets are to be allowed, blocking all others that do not meet those access parameters. All packets between the local area network (LAN) and the Internet are routed through the firewall. The firewall screens the packets coming in and evaluates them based on a stored set of valid parameters. If they match the valid criteria, packets are allowed through, and if not, they are blocked. Outbound packets may also be screened but generally under less stringent criteria.

Basic Packet Filtering

Several steps are involved in basic packet filtering. First, the firewall will evaluate incoming packets that are arriving. They will be evaluated based on a set of specified criteria. Often, the set of valid criteria against which incoming packets are matched up will include a list of valid IP source addresses and destination addresses. The next step is to use Layer 3 transport layer header information, TCP, or UPD data. An evaluation of valid protocol information, specific TCP and UPD ports, specific flags that are allowed or not, and ICMP message type should be included. The Internet Control Message Protocol (ICMP) is one of the main protocols of the IP suite used by network devices such as routers to send error messages indicating that a requested service is not available or that a host or router could not be reached.

An example of a proper port relationship to protocol or device would include a DNS that uses port 53. A filter can be provisioned with the specification to block incoming port 53 packets, except those associated with a known trusted server.

Concerning capability, filters may be programmed to look for source or destination address forgery. However, as with all security systems, some main issues arise concerning firewalls. Stateful filtering is hard to achieve, encapsulation via address translation may lead to complications, and fragmentation may throw off comparisons to valid rule information. The filtering examples in Figure 15.5 portray the evaluation of inbound Simple Mail Transfer Protocol (SMTP) packets.

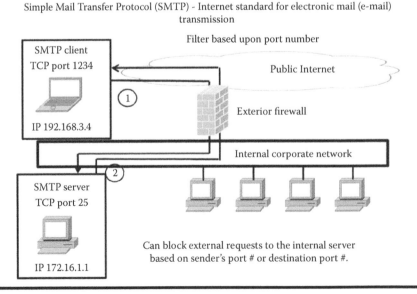

Figure 15.5 Filtering example of INBOUND SMTP message.

SMTP is an Internet standard for electronic mail (e-mail) transmission. SMTP by default uses TCP port 25.

Firewall Stateful Packet Filtering

Keep in mind that third-generation firewalls maintain records of all connections passing through the firewall. This process is commonly recognized as stateful packet inspection. Firewalls can determine whether a packet is part of an existing connection or if it contains parts of a new connection. If a user inside a company network requests information from outside the network, the firewall will likely let this type of traffic through; however, if the traffic is coming in from the outside without an initiated request from the inside, the traffic will not be allowed, unless a specific firewall specification enables this type of traffic to be allowed through.

Other Protocols of Concern

Telnet is a protocol used by an external client to open up a channel for a client to connect with a server. Telnet is a user command and an underlying TCP/IP protocol for accessing remote computers. Through Telnet, an administrator or another user can access someone else's computer remotely. The client sends a message requesting to set up a connection to the respective port on the server. The server will then acknowledge the submitted request. However, if the acknowledgment bit is not set while the connection is established, then the server will not provide this acknowledgment.

The *TCP three-way handshake* is similar. The client establishes a communication channel, and the server then proceeds to acknowledge the channel. However, as an additional step, the client sends another acknowledgment affirming the connection (acknowledging the returned acknowledgment).

File Transport Protocol (FTP) also operates with a similar process of establishing communication channels and acknowledgments. However, it differs in that the issue of the data and the command ports set on the FTP server are separate. However, acknowledgments between the FTP client and the FTP server continue to be transmitted. The FTP is a standard network protocol used to transfer computer files from one host to another host over a TCP-based network, such as the Internet. FTP is built on a client–server architecture and uses separate control and data connections between the client and the server.

IP Fragmentation

Normally, the data to be transmitted is separated into 1500-byte sections, with each section placed into the data field of an IP packet. However, in specific cases, data that is to be transmitted into smaller 596-byte sections for special transmission situations may be fragmented down to a 596-byte section plus header packet. Smaller packets tend to pass through some networks more quickly due to their smaller size. Note that despite this fragmentation of the initial message, it is the sum of all packets containing the message parts that comprise the transmission of the complete message. Figure 15.6 showcases an example of the fragmentation of a 1500-byte packet into three 596-byte packets.

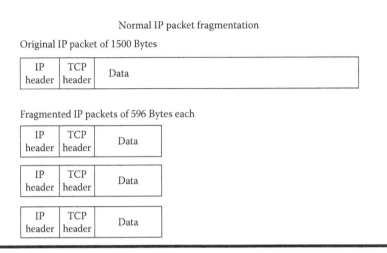

Figure 15.6   Normal IP packet fragmentation process.

Abnormal IP fragmentation is also commonly performed by hackers. Although this can be done by users performing normal, valid activities, it is also frequently employed by hackers. The discrepancies in the way these packets are fragmented are found in abnormal or inconsistent uses of IP headers and TCP headers. Other problems such as data overlapping can be part of the hacker routine. Figure 15.7 illustrates this non-standardized IP packet fragmentation technique.

As a result of this fragmentation practice, hackers have learned to leverage this process as an attack. This in turn has resulted in what we call *packet fragmentation attacks*, a common practice. Hackers leverage this by sending in fragmented packets. This causes the firewall to ignore the second packet of a complete packet message that is fragmented in the appropriate way. The result: damage due to the subsequent included information.

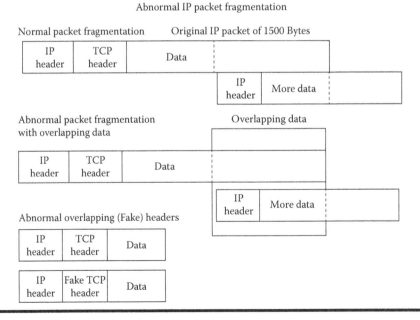

Figure 15.7   Abnormal IP packet fragmentation processes.

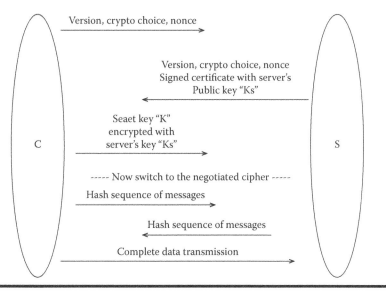

Figure 15.8   SSL security process.

Transport Layer Security

Secure Socket Layer (SSL) was the predecessor to transport layer security. SSL is a computer networking protocol that manages server authentication, client authentication, and encrypted communication between servers and clients. These protocols allow a client to authenticate a server and establish an encrypted SSL connection, which is designed to enable secure communication from one area of the network to another through the use of authentication and encryption. A choice notice is sent to the server by the client. The server responds with a certificate. The client then sends back a secret key. This communication is followed by a negotiate cipher, which then culminates in the exchange of hash sequence messages from both sides.

The process is illustrated in Figure 15.8.

Proxy Firewall

Corporations use local IP addressing inside their local network using the IP addresses in the form of 10.0.0.0. When leaving the local network, the normal IP address scheme is employed in the form of 176.221.54.10 on the outside worldwide networks. This local address scheme is used because there are only a limited number of addresses available, particularly with version four of IP (IPV4). Corporations will place a proxy server at the edge of the network. This will allow the outgoing traffic to apply for a loaned outside IP address. Traffic will then be sent with an appropriate outside source and destination address to the outside destination. Everything that is going outside is passed from the edge router to the proxy server, which validates the mapping of the external network. For returning traffic, the proxy server will then translate the external IP addresses and map them to internal local network destinations to ensure proper communication.

IP proxy servers are not only located at the edge of the network. Corporations often employ specialized proxy servers, which range in types from Telnet to FTP to SMTP proxy servers. Application-level proxies are also available for use. These are specific to predetermined applications.

Web Traffic Scanning

It is possibly useful to scan and examine outgoing and incoming web traffic, especially when corporations and network administrators have a specific set of well-known dangerous sites. The traffic for these known bad sites can be scanned and intercepted if necessary. Additionally, these scanning tools can block attachments of certain specified types. JPEGs, GIFs, bitmaps (BMPs), attached pdfs, and other file types can be blocked through the use of this feature. Blockings can take place based on the types of protocols, types of content, and the numbered port to which the message intends to connect.

Intrusion Detection Systems

Intrusion detection systems tend to be placed on networks with increasing frequency as a direct result of the increasing amount of network attacks attempting to penetrate organizational security systems. In combination with modern personal techniques that range from social engineering to spear phishing, these types of attacks can pose a significant threat to the network. Intrusion detection systems monitor activity on the local company network. They can be network or host based, or a combination of both. There are two basic models:

1. Misuse detection model
2. Anomaly detection model

Note, however, that the primary task of these systems is to search for abnormal network traffic and behavior. There is a whole set of systems. One example of these systems is called *Snort*. Snort works with UNIX-based systems. It operates with Windows. It is able to see and decode packets. It is looking for specific criteria, and if it identifies those criteria in the packet, it sends an alert message to the network administrators.

Some of the challenges affecting Snort and other intrusion detection systems concern the amount of rules observed in the databases. These databases tend to grow very large, and they may allow known intrusions to avoid detection. Snort also spends up to 80% of its time running string matches, which is simply one task. Finally, given the fact that Snort works on an anomaly detection pattern basis, the probability of identifying new attacks is diminished, as most of these anomalies are older.

There are many problems with anomaly detection patterns themselves. For these systems, it becomes hard to distinguish between abnormal traffic behavior and normal behavior. Another hindrance that adversely affects these systems is the need for training data. Further, note that much of the data that is actually captured during these training data phases is normal data and contains little evidence of realistic attacks. Assuming this, it is not uncommon for misidentifications concerning the nature of network traffic and data to be made.

Two Critical Infrastructure Protocols: BGP and DNS

The BGP and DNS systems represent areas of major vulnerability for networks since they both serve a between-network function, with BGP routers physically located at the edge of two networks. If affected, damaged, or compromised, they can disrupt the networks they are attached

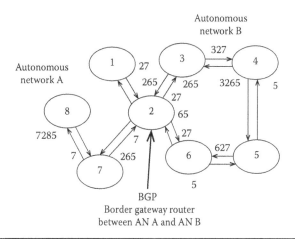

Figure 15.9   A Border Gateway Protocol (BGP) example.

to. They are typically built in sets. The border gateway area is a place where traffic can be blocked, and it is typically also a target area for hackers to attempt router poisoning. Similarly, poisoning of the DNS is also quite common. Observe the set for BGPs shown in Figure 15.9. Routers 1–8 are border routers, containing the structure of the networks on each side and providing the routing information for interarea bridging of transmission. BGP provides each area network with the physical and logical interarea bridge function for interarea routing of communications.

Note that BGP is used for all routing between Internet service providers (ISPs). Benign configuration errors impact 1% of all routing table entries at any time. BGP routers are extremely vulnerable to malicious attacks as well as human errors. When those attacks are successful, one area network is unable to communicate with neighboring area networks. To enable a secure BGP design, it's important to leverage IPSec and also to leverage public-key infrastructures, distributed valid certificates, and digitally signed authorizations.

Infrastructure Protocols for DNS and DNSSEC

Figure 15.10 shows a user PC with a stub resolver, a local recursive resolver DNS server in the center; a set of root zones, each with their own local DNS servers, then create a multilevel local DNS. Every Internet low-level DNS can do all these translations. When one DNS server is down, others can pick up the slack.

DNS by design is insecure. Packets to and- from the DNS server are all UDP with no acknowledgment. This means they are best-effort transmissions. There is a great deal of reliance on the source port, with no real evidential reliance on whether it is valid, and the caches are easily poisoned. A more secure approach will be presented with DNSSECs. The DNSSEC is a future system that would require a very elaborate DNS system, which would change the apparatus of the DNS. Resource records would all be secured and encrypted, and all of the source and destination addresses would have to be validated.

If a human error occurs when typing in an alias, then it is assumed that when the DNS lookup takes place, the DNS system should return a denial-of-existence message. A large portion of the

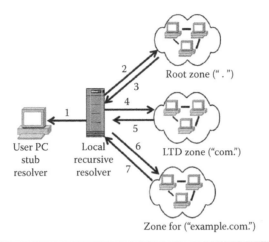

Figure 15.10 DNS and DNSSEC infrastructure protocols.

communications or messages going into the local and Internet DNS servers will result in no translation, and a lot of excess traffic ends up with no translation result.

A DNS rebinding attack is a form of computer attack wherein a malicious web page will cause visitors to run a client-side script that attacks machines somewhere else in the network. In many cases, the DNS will allow these attacks through. In the example, the message looks valid. The DNS lookup also looks valid. Given these two assumptions, if the DNS system is corrupted, then it will forward the message under the assumption that the information is valid. Some defense mechanisms for DNS rebinding attacks include the following:

■ Browser mitigation
■ Server-side defenses
■ Firewall defenses

Network Control Firewalls

The intent of network control firewalls is to determine a hardened set of parameters that would block externally sourced attacks. If the incoming messages don't meet the criteria outlined in the firewall, they should be blocked. One approach is to have each system turn off unnecessary network services. Certain kinds of things will always be blocked. Management packets are typically blocked if they are issued from outside.

Another example of what might be blocked is associated with SMTP, which is an Internet standard for electronic mail (e-mail) transmission. SMTP by default uses TCP port 25. The protocol for mail submission is the same but uses port 587. SMTP connections secured by SSL, known as SMTPS, default to port 465 (non-standard, but sometimes used for legacy reasons). Although electronic mail servers and other mail transfer agents use SMTP to send and receive mail messages, user-level client mail applications typically use SMTP only for sending messages to a mail server for relaying. We might decide to only allow connection to port 25 and block connection to ports 587 and 465.

```
allow tcp *:* -> 1.2.3.4:25
Allow tcp 1.2.3.4/24 :* -> *:*
drop * *:* -> *:*
```

Figure 15.11   Firewall packet filter allowances and drops.

Firewalling is a very complex process. A potentially more scalable defense would be to reduce risk by blocking or restricting network access to any outsiders. There are chokepoints associated with firewalls, and such chokepoints can cover thousands of hosts.

Selecting a security policy is complex. One rule could be that any user can connect to any service and any user outside. Another option is to limit certain services and websites by incorporating a list of invalid sites. External users can be limited to certain applications and services. The default for these policies is to allow external access to services and deny non-well-known or insecure services. Basic packet filters with a set of access control rules also need to be set up via the router. These access control rules are combinations of source and destination information and addresses at multiple layers.

A basic kind of firewall is considered a packet filter. The access control rules are used to examine and filter IP packets. The rules specify simply whether these packets are allowed to pass through to the local network or are denied entry. For example, any TCP/IP packet that looks a certain way will be allowed or denied. There's a specific rule that sets IP and another for TCP or for allowed combinations of TCP ports and IP addresses. The most stringent ones include explicit drop and allow parameters. We certainly want to be careful when it comes to allowing all IP addresses. Rule sets look like that shown in Figure 15.11.

Incoming packet types need to be distinguished as well. For example, when the website responds to our query, then general rules apply, such as the allowing in of any incoming packet that was associated with an outgoing connection.

Security Principle Reference Monitors

As a best practice, network administrators should introduce reference monitors to oversee the flow of traffic across their network. Reference monitors should always be invoked to examine all packets going across the network. All operations have to be mediated, which means that if these monitors don't like the communication, they can block the packet. A good portion of the scanning of these devices' performance is based on observing behavior. Factors such as time of day, type of communication, content, and source and destination are all closely monitored to detect abnormal behavior. This is behavior over and above what a firewall would normally be able to oversee and block.

Potential problems associated with these reference monitors include wireless network access points. Users can easily access or leverage these unsecured access points, and this may pose a security threat to the internal network. A program called NetStumbler allows hackers and prospective attackers to drive by a wireless-enabled laptop and gain access to an internal network. Ideally, reference monitors are tamper resistant. This is to protect the monitor itself and to protect the integrity of the data it is monitoring. As a maintenance approach, network administrators should connect locally to these devices in order to reduce the risks of a breach. Unfortunately, there are a variety of other risks that can affect or subvert firewalls. Poor administrative practices and IP tunneling can weaken reference monitors.

Overall, there are many advantages associated with implementing firewalls. They have a central point of control, they are easy to implement, and there's also a lot of experience regarding their implementation and access control rules. The disadvantages of these defense systems include the fact that some applications are immune to or incompatible with firewalls. Firewalls may lead to some functionality loss as there might be less connectivity. Finally, older firewalls are becoming less and less effective.

In summary, we have performed an evaluation of network security protocols and defense mechanisms, specifically examining firewalls.

QUESTIONS

1. What is DNSSEC and why is it important?
2. What are two ways IPSec provides security service?
3. IKE provides three different methods for peer authentication. What are they?
4. What is the difference between an intrusion detection system and an intrusion prevention system?
5. Is an intrusion detection system the same as a firewall?
6. An intrusion detection system has two basic models. Explain the role each performs for the intrusion detection system.

Chapter 16

Denial-of-Service Attacks

A denial-of-service (DoS) attack is a malicious attempt to make a machine or other computing resources unavailable. There is also a distributed DoS attack that comes from many unique Internet Protocol (IP) addresses that renders a machine or other computing/network resource unavailable. In fact, each of these types of attacks exists in two different forms, which are known as *bugs* and *floods*. While both types can come in many different forms, they are all devastating to the victims whom they affect. However, as with most malicious attacks, there are steps that can be taken to help prevent these attacks from causing damage to host computers or other network nodes.

A modern version of the DoS attack is a Domain Name System (DNS) amplification attack. This type of attack is a distributed DoS attack that relies on the use of vulnerable DNS servers. To perform this attack, an attacker will issue a DNS look-up request using a spoofed IP address. The request then gets relayed through a series of botnet computers so that each in turn also requests the same DNS look-up to separate DNS servers, which thus amplifies the original numbers of the same DNS request to a number of DNS servers. The resulting traffic appears to be coming to the target server from a number of different directions, hiding the source that originated the attack (Figure 16.1).

Another example of a DoS attack is a SYN flood. This is when an attacker will exploit Transmission Control Protocol (TCP) connections. Normally, when a user wants to connect with a server, a series of messages are exchanged between the host and the server. During a SYN flood, an attacker will send multiple connection requests to a server. The server will initiate a SYN-ACK (acknowledgment) back to that host to make sure the originating host is ready to use and thus acknowledge the impending connection. However, the attacker will not have his machines respond to the server's acknowledgment and therefore there will be multiple half-open connections that will take up all of the server's resources. This will not allow any further hosts, legitimate or not, to connect to the server, thereby creating the DoS. A solution to this DoS attack, if it comes from an IP address outside the server's network, is to block all outside connections from being established. While this may prevent outside connections, if the server is primarily serving a corporation, at least the corporate employees on the corporation's own internal network will still be able to access the server through the corporate intranet. An example of a SYN flood is demonstrated in Figure 16.2.

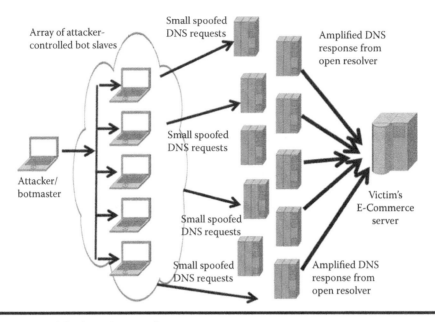

Figure 16.1 Denial-of-service attacks.

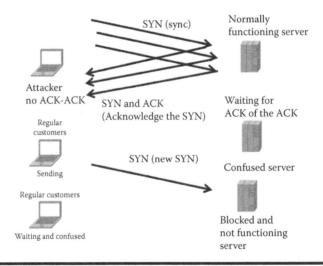

Figure 16.2 A SYN attack to deny service.

Hackers are motivated by a wide variety of reasons to initiate these malicious DoS attacks. They can be based on a personal vendetta toward a particular company, extortion, as a political statement, and even as an act of general cyber warfare. For these attacks to cease, system administrators must carefully lay out guidelines for user authentication. Reliable authentication allows for these administrators to know who is trying to utilize a server's connections and services. In addition to reliable authentication and identification of users, careful testing of servers, codes, and report reviews is of the utmost importance when dealing with information security regarding DoS.

QUESTIONS

1. How many forms of DoS attacks exist?
2. What are the two primary forms of DoS attacks?
3. Explain how a DoS works.
4. How do you block a DoS attack?
5. Explain the process of a SYN attack.

Chapter 17

Mobile Platform Security

People are increasingly relying on mobile devices to perform the majority of their daily tasks, leading many attackers to focus their efforts on mobile operating systems within the top-tier markets. Android has about 50% of that market, whereas Microsoft has 23% and Apple iOS has 21%. While these are different operating systems, the attack vectors to which they are vulnerable are quite similar. Nearly all smartphones allow the installation of externally supplied applications (apps). These apps, once downloaded to the phone, are the linked to messaging services capable of launching many forms of remote media. Many of the vulnerabilities associated with mobile devices were previously associated with non-mobile desktops, laptops, and tablets. The following summarizes three of these mobile platforms.

Comparison of Mobile Platforms

Many companies will carefully evaluate the security risks across mobile platforms to determine what may be the best fit for their company-sponsored mobile device deployment (if a bring-your-own-device [BYOD] policy is not implemented). In this case, an evaluation of the company's "security model" should be performed. Security needs to be implemented and viewed as a whole, which is why it is best represented as a model or architecture.

The Apple iPhone iOS operating system is based on the Objective-C programming language and separates its platform into four key areas. Apple has a highly regulated app-development environment as compared with the Android and Windows platforms. All Apple devices have built-in hardware encryption, remote wiping, and a protocol stack that is current with the latest secure transmission standards. The area most at risk is the ability to download from an external source and install user apps. When apps are installed, they are "sandboxed" into their own separate environment and are unable to access other areas of the system. When an app is created and then distributed to and made available from, or "published," by the app store and compiled using the Xcode platform, it must be signed using a certificate that can only be granted by Apple. Figure 17.1 illustrates how the sandbox isolation works.

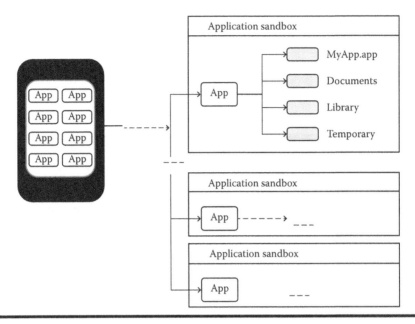

Figure 17.1   How sandbox isolation works.

Apple iOS Operating System

At the highest level, iOS acts as an intermediary between the hardware and apps you have on your phone. Apps talk through a set of defined system interfaces. This allows apps to work consistently on devices that have different hardware capabilities. The iOS technology can be viewed as a set of layers, which are shown in Figure 17.2. The OS is implemented in C and Objective-C.

Core OS Layer

The core OS layer (the bottom layer) contains low-level features on which most technologies are built. Some examples include explicitly dealing with security or communicating with an external hardware accessory.

Core Services Layer

The core services layer (one of the middle layers) contains fundamental services for apps. The key services are the core foundation frameworks, which define the basic types that all apps use. This layer also contains individual technologies to support features including iCloud, social media, and

Cocoa touch
Media
Core services
Core OS

Figure 17.2   The Apple iOS layers.

networking. It also includes SQLite, which allows you to embed a lightweight Structured Query Language (SQL) database into your app without running a separate remote database server process. This layer also includes POSIX threats and UNIX sockets.

Media Layer

This layer (the upper middle layer) contains graphics, audio, and video that you would use to implement multimedia experiences in your apps. This layer makes it easy to build apps that look and sound ideal.

Cocoa Touch Layer

The Cocoa Touch layer (the top layer) contains key frameworks for building iOS apps. These frameworks define the appearance of your app. They also provide the basic app infrastructure and support for key components such as multitasking, touch-based input, push notifications, and other services.

Development of iOS Applications

The development of iOS apps is done in Objective-C using Apple SDK or Xcode (Figure 17.3).

Apple iOS Security

Apple has four primary security focuses: system, data, app, and network security.

Apple uses touch ID and passcodes to protect a phone's information. Users are encouraged to use strong passcodes, and to have both an expiration and maximum number of fail attempts. For

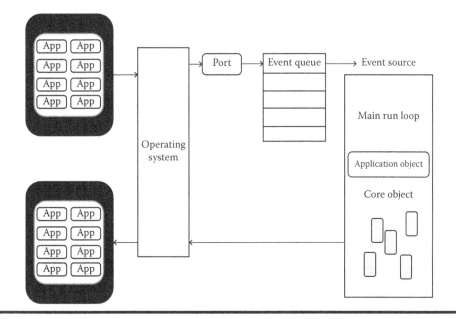

Figure 17.3 Apple iOS app development.

data security, it provides hardware encryption, remote and local wiping of your data, encrypted configuration profiles, and encrypted iTunes backups. For security, it keeps current accepted network security protocols, such as Internet Protocol Security (IPSec), Layer 2 Tunneling Protocol (L2TP), pocket transport network (PTN), and virtual private network (VPN). PTNs are frequently associated with MPLS networks. Secure Socket Layer (SSL) VPN is available via app store apps, SSL/Transport Layer Security (TLS) with X.509 certificates, and Wi-Fi Protected Access (WPA)/WPA 2 Enterprise with 802.1x.

Android Mobile Smartphone

As with Apple's iOS operating system, the Android phone is based on a Linux operating system kernel (which was derived from the standard historical UNIX kernel). The Android programming is in the C language (similar to Apple's Objective-C language utilization). When apps are downloaded, installed, and run, they are executed by the Java platform.

In comparison to Apple iOS, Android apps can be "self-signed," whereby the individual user is in complete control of what apps are installed. This is a point of vulnerability due to the widespread use of Android and limited education concerning the potential security risks associated with downloaded apps. Even app stores for the Android marketplace may unknowingly distribute malicious software.

Android has a similar approach to the app containment methods used by Apple iOS. Android runs each app on the device as its own user with its own permission and restrictions. Each of these apps runs in a mini virtual machine provided by Dalvik, much like Apple's sandbox. If one app wants to access resources from another, they must communicate through the "inents" app framework.

Android Security Model

The Android Platform Outline-Android is built on the Linux kernel and is currently developed by Google. The other layers include libraries, app frameworks, and apps. Android is open-source software and is written with C with a Java platform for running apps (Figure 17.4).

Because Android is open source, this allows for a vast amount of apps to be developed by third parties, which enhance your mobile capabilities but also can expose your phone to self-signed apps (uncertified) or permit actions on installation. When malware is downloaded in the form of an unsecure app, the malware app escalates from being a remote exploit outside the device to being installed inside the device and now having privilege escalation status on the device. Under privileged escalation, a bug—or merely a design flaw or configuration oversight in an operating system or software app—can be exploited to gain elevated access to resources that are normally protected from an app or user. The malware app, once downloaded and installed on the mobile device, then gains a privileged status for exploitation of the user's device's facilities.

The shift has then moved from being a remote external potential exploit to having privilege escalation status on the mobile device. This privilege escalation is essentially the exploitation of an installed bug, or of a design flaw or configuration oversight in an operating system or software app, which is used to gain elevated access to resources that are normally protected from other apps or users.

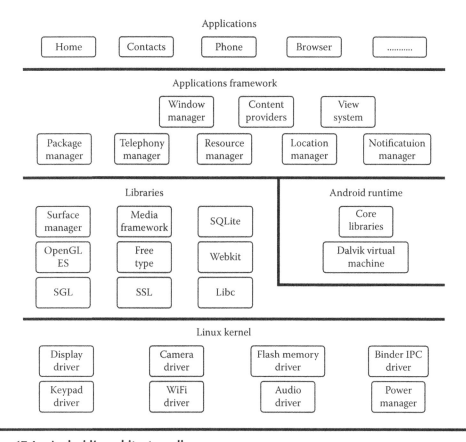

Figure 17.4   Android's architecture diagram.

Security Features

One of the key features in an Android phone is that it uses a multiuser Linux operating system. In other words, each app normally runs as a different user, preventing them from having access to one another. Communications between apps may share the same Linux user ID. If they do, they can access files from each other. Another key feature of an Android phone, although not specifically a security feature, is its battery life. Both Android designers and application developers have attempted to extend battery life by employing power conservation methods. Apps store state so they can be stopped (to save power) and restarted for power conservation purposes.

Figure 17.5 shows a chart of the app development process.

App Development Concepts

The five key components to consider when developing an app are activity, service, intents, content provider, and broadcast receiver. Activity refers to a one-user task. An example would be scrolling through your inbox. An e-mail client comprises many activities. Service refers to a Java daemon that runs in the background. An example would be an app that streams an MP3 in the

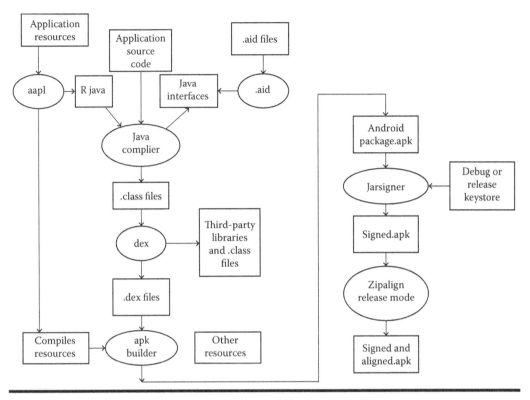

Figure 17.5   The app development process for mobile apps.

background. Intents are an asynchronous messaging system. When you fire intent, you switch from one activity to another. An example would be an e-mail app that has an inbox, compose activity, viewer activity, and so on. When the user clicks on the inbox entry, an intent is fired to the viewer activity, which then allows the user to view the e-mail. A content provider looks at where and how to store and share data using a relational database interface, and a broadcast receiver looks at "mailboxes" for messages from other apps.

Exploit Prevention

There are hundreds of libraries and over 500 million lines of new code with those libraries. The goal of mobile security is to prevent remote attacks and privilege escalation. One large defense is the app sandbox. A sandbox is a security mechanism for separating running programs. This provides central processing unit (CPU) and memory protection (Figure 17.6).

Layers of Security

Each app executes as its own user identity. Android middleware has a reference monitor that mediates the establishment of intercomponent communication (ICC). Applications (apps) announce permission requirements that create a whitelist model giving users grant access.

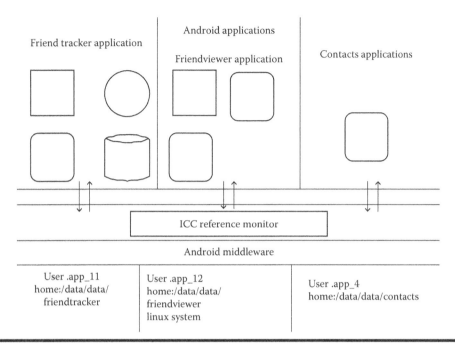

Figure 17.6   The Android app model.

Java Sandbox

The Java sandbox is a security measure in the Java development environment. When a browser requests a web page with applets (a program designed to be executed from within another app), the applets are sent automatically and can be executed as soon as the page arrives in the browser. If the applet is allowed unlimited access to the memory and operating system resources, it can be harmful in the hands of an attacker. The sandbox creates an environment in which there are strict limitations on what system resources the applet can request or access. Sandboxes are used when executable code comes from unknown or untrusted sources, and they allow the user to run untrusted code safely.

The Java sandbox relies on a three-tiered defense. If any one of these three elements fails, the security model is completely compromised and vulnerable to attack. These three elements are

- Byte code verifier
  - This is one way that Java automatically checks untrusted outside code before it is allowed to run. When a Java source program is compiled, it only compiles down to the platform-independent Java byte code, which is verified before it can run. This helps to establish a base set of security guarantees.
- Applet class loader
  - All Java objects belong to classes, and the applet class loader determines when and how an applet can add classes to running Java environment. The applet class loader ensures that important elements of the Java run-time environment are not replaced by code that an applet tries to install.

- Security manager
  - The security manager is consulted by code in the Java library whenever a dangerous operation is about to be carried out. The security manager has the option to veto the operation by generating a security exception.

Apple iOS versus Android Operating System Comparisons

Below is a list of comparisons between the Android and Apple iOS operating systems.

App approval process: Android apps are downloaded from an open app store, while Apple iOS apps are downloaded from a vendor-controlled store of vetted apps.

App permissions: Android permissions are based on an install-time manifest, while all Apple iOS apps have the same prespecified set of sandbox privileges.

App programming language: Android apps are typically written in Java with no buffer flow, while Apple iOS apps are typically written in Objective-C.

Windows Mobile Models 7 and 8 Devices

Windows Mobile devices have been on the market far longer than either Android- or Apple iOS-based devices. Furthermore, the Windows security model is far simpler and more streamlined than its competitors, especially for the Windows Mobile 8 operating system. Figures 17.7 and 17.8 show the Model 7 and Model 8 security models.

Microsoft describes its "isolation" boundaries as "chambers," but its isolation techniques are similar to that of its competitors. Each chamber has a preset amount of permissions and process capabilities. Memory data is completely isolated, and there is no direct communication between apps; such communication must go through cloud-based services. When an app is switched, the app is entirely shut down, which differs from the way Apple's iOS operates.

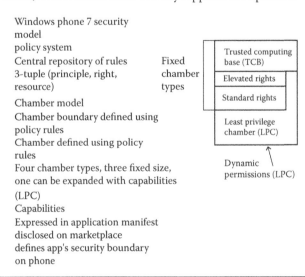

Figure 17.7 Windows 7 phone security.

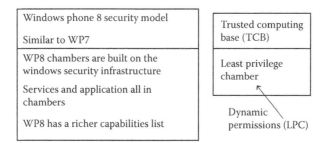

Figure 17.8   Windows 8 phone security.

Windows Phone OS 7.0 Security Model

The Windows security model has the principles of isolation and least privilege. Each app runs its own isolated chamber. Each chamber provides a security and isolation boundary and is defined and implemented using a policy system. The security policy of a chamber is that it specifies the operating system capabilities that processes in that chamber can access. The isolated chamber cannot access the memory or data of other apps, including keyboard cache. No communication channels are permitted between apps, except through the cloud. Non-Microsoft apps that are distributed via the marketplace are stopped in the background. In other words, when a user switches apps, the previous app is shut down. The reason for this is that apps cannot use critical resources or communicate with Internet-based services while the user is not using the app.

There are four chamber types. Three types have fixed permission sets, while the fourth is capabilities driven. Apps that are designed to run in the fourth chamber type have capability requirements that are honored at installation and at run time. Apps that are designated to run in the fourth chamber type have capability requirements that are honored at installation and at run time.

The four chamber types are as follows:

Chamber 1, the *trusted computing base (TCB)*, has unrestricted access to most resources and can modify policy and enforce the security model. The kernel and kernel-mode drivers run in the TCB. Minimizing the amount of software that runs in the TCB is essential for minimizing attack surfaces in the Windows Phone 7 and 8.

Chamber 2, the *elevated rights chamber (ERC)*, can access all resources except the security policy. It is intended for services and user-mode drivers.

Chamber 3, the *standard rights chamber (SRC)*, is the default for preinstalled apps that do not provide device-wide services.

Chamber 4, the *least privileged chamber (LPC)*, is the default for all non-Microsoft apps and is configured using capabilities.

The overall goal of isolation and chambers is to give apps the least amount of privilege as possible. The app should get the amount it needs but no more. Developers use the capability detection tool to create the capability list. The capability list is included in the app manifest. Capabilities are resources associated with user privacy, security, cost, or business concerns. Each app discloses its capabilities to the user. It is listed on the Windows Phone Marketplace, and there is an explicit prompt on app purchase. Lastly, there is a disclosure within the app for the first time the user is about to use the location capability.

```
Class native methods

{
        // This is a call to unmanaged code. The execution of this
        // method requires employing "UnmanagedCode" security
        // permission. Without this permission, an attempt to call this method
        // cause a security exception.
        [DllImport" ("msvcrt.dll")]
        Public static extern puts(string.str);
        [DllImport" ("msvcrt.dll")]
        Internal static extern int_flushall();

}
```

Figure 17.9   Code requiring permission.

.NET Code Access Security That Can Be Exploited on Windows Phones

The .NET framework is a proprietary, partially open-source freeware software framework developed by Microsoft that runs primarily on Microsoft Windows. The default security policy is part of the .NET Framework. Default permission for code access is permitted to protect resources. Permissions can limit access to a system's resources. "Deny and revert" denies access to a resource, and "revert" can cancel a previous deny command. Figure 17.9 shows an example of code requiring permission.

Figure 17.10 is an example of code denying permission because it is not needed.

The following is a summary list of Windows characteristics.

■ The approval process for apps:
  – The market is both vendor controlled and open
  – App signatures are also both vendor and self-signed
  – User approves permissions

```
[Security Permission(Security.Deny, Flags =
      SecurityPermissionFlag.UnmanagedCode)]
   private static void MethodToDoSomething()
   {try

     {
         Console.WriteLine(" … ");
         SomeOtherClass.method();
     }
     catch (SecurityException)
     }
       …
     }
   }
```

Figure 17.10   Code denying permission because it is not needed.

	Apple iOS	Android	Windows
UNIX	X	X	
Windows			X
Open market		X	
Closed market	X		X
Vender signed	X		
Self-signed			
User permission approvals			
Managed code		X	X
Native code	X		

Figure 17.11   Summary chart: Differences between, Apple iOS, Android, and Windows phones.

■ The programming languages employed:
- – The managed execution is in Java, .NET
- – The native execution is in Objective-C

Figure 17.11 provides a summary of overall comparisons between the different platforms.

Mobile Platform Security

Mobile platform security is a leading topic regarding the future of information security. More often than ever, people are using their smartphones to deal with critical tasks such as banking, investing, and even health care. Knowing this, hackers and malicious coders are looking for ways to exploit present security vulnerabilities in Apple iOS, Android, and Windows Mobile platforms. Luckily, security measures have already been implemented within these operating systems to combat potential issues. However, they are certainly far from perfect. Understanding the potential risks of mobile information security is important for understanding each operating system's current security platform.

Apple's iOS is one of the leading mobile operating systems in the world. In fact, it is estimated that Apple has sold almost half a billion iPhones within the past seven years! Apple's iOS is a kernel-based operating system, much like Apple's computing operating system OS X. It is coded in the C and Objective-C programming language, which is a fairly efficient computing language. While at rest, Apple's iOS is fairly secure. There are lock-screen passwords that enable a user to lock their phone at the simple click of a button. However, if the phone is stolen, the data integrity may be compromised by third-party apps that could rip data off the iPhone. Luckily, Apple has a remote erase feature that can wipe the iPhone of all its data if it has been stolen. However, there have been iPhone worms that have affected users. Ikee is the most famous

```
*/
    People are stupid, and this is to prove it so
    RTFM. its not thats hard guys
    But hey who cares its only your bank details at stake.
*/
// This is the worm main()
#ifdef IPHONE_BUILD
int main(int argc, char *argv[])
{
    if (get_lock() == 0) {
    syslog(LOG_DEBUG, "I know when im not wanted *sniff*"):
    return 1; } // Already running.
    sleep (60); // Lets wait for the network to come up 2 MINS
    syslog(LOG_DEBUG, "IIIIIII Just want to tell you how im feeling");
    char *locRanges = getAddrRange ( );
    // Why did i do it like this i hear you ask.
    // because i wrote a simple python script to parse ranges
    // and output them like this
    // THATS WHY.
```

Figure 17.12   Source code for Ikee with developer comments.

of these iPhone worms. While it isn't considered malicious code, Ikee changes the background to a picture of Rick Astley with text on the top screen that reads, "Ikee is never going to give you up."

While the developer had no malicious intent, it was supposed to be a commentary on the fact that users do not adequately change their passwords. In fact, this code could have been written maliciously and taken bank information from the users. Figure 17.12 shows the source code for Ikee with developer comments.

The Android phone has another vulnerable operating system. One billion Android phones were shipped in 2014 alone. Needless to say, this is a fairly popular operating system. As with iOS, Android is written in the C programming language and utilizes a Linux kernel. The apps for Android users are written in Java, which can be a security risk itself. Another glaring security flaw is the Android applications. In the Android model, users could potentially create malicious apps to be downloaded by other Android users. DroidDream is a perfect example of one of these apps. DroidDream conducted data theft on Android user's phones by utilizing 58 bad apps. It got its name because the malicious apps would run between 11 p.m. and 8 a.m., when most users would not be utilizing their telephones. While Google has removed DroidDream, variations of it have hit the market since. Some of these variations include DroidDream Light, which hit the market in 2011.

Mobile security is the next big topic of the future regarding information security. The statistics for vulnerabilities and exploits presented in Figures 17.3 and 17.4 will corroborate this belief. Mobile operating system vulnerabilities have grown from 18 to close to 200 from 2006 to 2012, while mobile exploits have risen from near zero to 14 in the same time period.

More users need to proceed with the same caution in using their mobile devices that they use on their computers, if not more so. With this being the next frontier for hackers and malicious coders, there is no telling what the possibilities are for security threats within iOS and Android devices.

Worldwide mobile operating system share change Dec 2008 to Dec 2012	
Apple iOS	from 33 % to 26%
Nokia	from 43% to 22%
Android	from 0% to 38%
Blackberry	from 0% to 4%

Figure 17.13   Worldwide mobile operating systems (phones) market share.

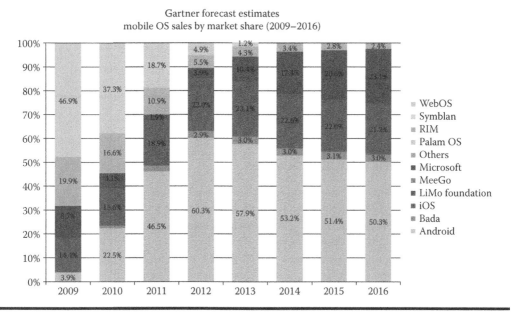

Figure 17.14   Gartner group estimate of mobile operating systems sales market share 2008–2016. (From Gartner, Forecast: Mobile devices by open operating system, worldwide, 2009–2016, 2012.)

Mobile Platform Security

In this section, we will further discuss mobile platforms and the potential threats they each face. Specifically, we will again focus on the Apple iOS, Android, and Windows 7 and 8 security models. Figures 17.13 and 17.14 show a graph representing the mobile phone operating system market share from 2008 to 2012.

As you can see, Android has been rapidly growing in popularity. Apple has remained steady in its market share, but Microsoft has begun growing significantly in the past 4 years. For each operating system, there are dozens of apps providing similar services. Figure 17.15 is a list of displayed icons that represents some of the Android advertised apps.

However, apps for all mobile phones can be broken down into eight broad categories (Figure 17.16).

With the rise in mobile devices and apps, more and more threats and attacks will continue to occur following the pattern of operating system vulnerabilities and exploits previously discussed.

Android advertised apps for phones and tablets			
CCC app for Android	Samurai II Vengeance	Cordy	Pulse News Reader
Gun Bros	Fruit Ninja THD	Accu Weather.com	Androidify
Grocery iQ-Tablet	Movies	Monster Madness	Breaker THD
Google Sky Map	Angry Birds Seasons	Rocket Bunnies	Talking Tom Cat Free

Figure 17.15 Some Android advertised apps.

Broad categories for available apps			
Business	Education	Entertainment	Family and kids
Finance	Food and drink	Games	Health and fitness

Figure 17.16 Eight broad categories of mobile apps on the market.

Attack Vectors for Mobile Devices

There are two attack vectors for mobile platforms, the web browser and installed apps, both of which are increasing in prevalence and sophistication. Phones are unique in that they have short message service (SMS) messages, identity location, and records of phone calls, and they log a certain number of your SMS messages. They are similar to desktops in that they can connect to botmasters, can steal data, and are vulnerable to phishing and malvertising. Some broad examples include DroidDream (Android), Ikee (iOS), and Zitmo (SYmbian, BlackBerry, Windows, Android). DroidDream was malware that was placed in over 58 apps and then uploaded to the Google app market. It conducts data theft, sending credentials to attackers. Ikee has worm capabilities (targeted default ssh pwd), but it only worked on jailbroken phones with ssh installed. Zitmo is malware that propagates via SMS, claiming to install a "security certificate," but it actually captures information from the SMS. It's aimed at defeating two-factor authentication. Zitmo works with Zeus botnet and is timed with user PC infection.

QUESTIONS

1. List the Apple iOS layers and describe each.
2. What are the five key components when developing an app?
3. What is a Java sandbox?
4. A Java sandbox relies on a three-tiered defense. What is it?

Chapter 18

Cellular Access Security: 4G LTE, Mobile WiMAX, 5G, and MIMOs

Mobile computing device (mobile devices) are information systems that are capable of storing and processing large amounts of data without having a fixed-in-place or set physical location, all while being portable. Examples of mobile computing devices include smartphones, mobile devices, personal digital assistants (PDAs), and notebook/tablet computers. Since the introduction of these devices into society, the impact of the change on our everyday lives has increased significantly. Mobile devices have provided the user with the ability to multitask like never before. They allow people to send and receive e-mails and text messages, all while surfing the web and streaming high-definition video.

The cellular wireless generation (G) denotes a change in the overall nature of the service being provided, non-backward-compatible broadcast technology, and new bands of frequency for data and voice transmission. A new generation has appeared approximately every 10 years since the first generation (1G), the analog generation, to the second generation (2G), the digital generation (Patil and Wankhade, 2014). After 2G came the third generation (3G), allowing the use of graphics, video, and audio applications, followed by the fourth generation (4G), which uses an Internet Protocol (IP) switched network with a focus on supporting broadband-level performance, as well as enabling both video and voice multimedia applications. Over the past two decades alone, the cellular industry has witnessed major growth in terms of its subscribers and its overall mobile technologies. By the end of 2010 alone, the number of cellular subscriptions was four times higher than that of fixed telephone lines.

First-Generation Cellular Network

1G cellular networks are the only ones to use analog transmissions. These were introduced in 1980 and continued to be used until they were replaced by 2G cellular networks. They were first commercially launched by Nippon Telegraph and Telephone (NTT) in Japan. This was followed by the launch in 1981 of operations in Denmark, Finland, Norway, and Sweden controlled by Nordic Mobile Telephone (NMT. NMT was the first to launch international roaming. Advanced mobile phone system (AMPS) was the first mobile phone system widely deployed in North America.

Security Issues and Drawbacks

1G was unencrypted and vulnerable. Anyone with an all-band radio receiver could listen in to the conversation. The frequency division multiple access (FDMA) mechanism was used, which required large bandwidths. Different countries followed their own standards, which were incompatible, and 1G also had poor sound quality.

Second-Generation Cellular Network

2G mobile services were commercially launched on the GSM standard in Finland by Radiolinja in 1991. Radio signals on 2G networks are digital, and fast out-of-band phone-to-network signaling is used. The primary benefits of a 2G network over its predecessor were more efficient service, signals that were digitally encrypted during the transmission, and the provision of data services. 2G was followed by newer technologies such as 2.5G, 2.75G, 3G, 4G, and 5G.

Depending on the type of multiplexing used, 2G technologies can be categorized into two types of systems: time division multiple access (TDMA) and code division multiple access (CDMA). The main 2G standards are GSM, IS-95 (CDMA One), PDC, and iDEN.

The capacity of a 2G network is much greater than that of its predecessor, due to the use of digital signals instead of analog signals for the transmission of data between the network and the end user. More calls can be transmitted within the same bandwidth by employing compression and multiplexing techniques. The only problem is that the weaker digital signal that is transmitted by a mobile phone may not be sufficient to reach the cell tower. However, this will only be a problem when the signal is transmitted on higher frequencies. Since telecom regulations vary between different countries, this problem may not persist everywhere. Digital signals tend to perform better when the signal strength is strong, but they become worse when the signal strength is poor. Digital calls are free from static (white noise) and background noise (noise from the environment).

The 2.5G and 2.75G technologies were implemented to help bridge the gap between 2G and 3G cellular networks. 2.5G implemented packet-switched networks in addition to circuit-switched networks. This is where the introduction of the general packet radio service (GPRS) takes place. 2.75G was brought into existence along with enhanced data rates for GSM Evolution (EDGE) networks, which employed 8PSK (phase-shift keying) encoding schemes. This is a backward-compatible digital mobile phone technology that brought forward enhanced rates for data transmission. GPRS provides a data transmission rate of 50 kbps (40 kbps practically), whereas EDGE offered speeds of up to 1 Mbps (500 kbps practically). Internet service was first launched by NTT DoCoMo in Japan in 1999. 2G made services such as text messaging, call forwarding, and caller ID possible. Most network operators are planning to phase out 2G services by 2017.

Security Issues and Drawbacks

2G does not perform proper authentication. The lowest level of encryption is easily crackable with a laptop. No data integrity algorithms are used either. Cryptographic algorithms used for security (A5/1 and A5/2) are exploited only for authenticating the user to the network and not vice versa.

Third-Generation Cellular Network

3G cellular networks are the networks that comply with IMT-2000 specifications. The first precommercial and commercial launches were done by NTT DoCoMo in Japan. 3G offers greater security as mutual authentication between networks and terminals is used. Universal Mobile Telecommunications System (UMTS) and CDMA2000 phase 2 are two of the most important 3G technologies. Since it is an IP network, 3G and its users are exposed to all kinds of threats that are currently being faced by Internet service providers. As it is an IP network, 3G and its users are exposed to all kinds of threats that are currently being faced by Internet service providers.

Security in UMTS was boosted with enhancements such as mutual authentication and strong encryption with 128-bit key lengths. Network access security in UMTS is achieved by Authentication and Key Arrangement (AKA) Protocol. This is an enhanced version of the authentication mechanism used in GSM 2G networks. Unlike GSM, wherein only networks authenticate users, AKA provides a mechanism for mutual authentication.

The three main entities involved in this process are the user (MS or USIM),* the serving network (visitor locations register [VLR] or serving GPRS support node [SGSN]) and the home environment (home location register/authentication center [HLR/AuC]). The serving network is the actual network that the user connects to, and the home environment is the network to which the user originally subscribed. Circuit-switched and packet-switched services are handled by VLR and SGSN respectively. HLR plays a vital role in the process as it is the place where the user database resides, next to the AuC (Figure 18.1).

The three stages in AKA are (1) initiation, (2) transfer of credentials, and (3) challenge-response exchange. During the first initiation stage, the mobile station sends its

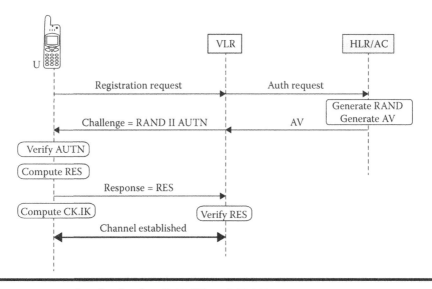

Figure 18.1   AKA authentication in 3G UMTS and CDMA2000.

---

* MS is a mobile station in a GSM mobile system that contains a USIM application module. USIM is Universal Subscriber Identity Module, a software application for UMTS mobile telephony, which runs on a UICC and is inserted in a 3G mobile phone.

IMSI/TMSI* number to the network. Based on the type of identity received by the mobile station, the network initiates the authentication procedure. In the second transfer-of-credentials stage, the security credentials of the user are transferred by the HLR to the VLR. These credentials are also referred to as authentication vector (AV). The HLR may send multiple AVs to the VLR for a specified user. Mobile Application Part (MAPsec) Protocol might be used for the establishment of secure channels between the HLR and VLR. In the third stage, the challenge and response transmissions occur.

CDMA2000 made significant improvements to previous CDMA security schemes for the following reasons:

- Weakness of CAVE, CMEA, and ORYX algorithms
- Weakness of 64 bit keys
- Lack of mutual authentication

CDMA2000 adopted AKA Protocol with some changes. These changes can be seen in the implementation of new cryptographic functions such as f11 and UMAC.† The UIM‡ authentication key (UAK) is generated by f11 to be included in AV and UMAC, which is the message authentication function of UAK. Rogue shell attacks can be prevented by using UAK. Rogue shell refers to a mobile unit that does not remove its CK and IK even after its UIM is removed.§ In this attack, a mobile unit can still make fraudulent calls by using the still active CK/IK until the registration is removed or a new AKA challenge is initiated. UMAC also provides an efficient reauthentication method.

Security Issues and Drawbacks

3G falls back on 2G when the 3G network is not available, compromising the security of the user. International mobile subscriber identity (IMSI) is sent in clear text when allocating temporary mobile subscriber identity (TMSI) to the user. The transmission of IMEI¶ is not secured. The user can be lured to camp on a fake base station (BS). Once this connection is established, the user will be out of reach of the paging signals of the signaling network.

In AKA, the authentication of the user by the network is done by a one-pass challenge-response mechanism, but the user verifies the network only by the message authentication code (MAC) address, so AKA in its present form does not provide full mutual authentication. Full mutual authentication can only be done by using a challenge-response mechanism. However, it is not implemented for performance reasons.

---

* An international mobile subscriber identity (IMSI) is a unique number, usually 15 digits, associated with Global System for Mobile Communications (GSM) and Universal Mobile Telecommunications System (UMTS) network mobile phone users. The IMSI is a unique number identifying a GSM subscriber. MSI is a local country mobile subscriber number.
† A UMAC is a fast and secure message and authentication system using message authentication code that employs universal hashing.
‡ User identity modules (UIM), particularly R-UIM, i.e., removable user identity modules, are cards in phones that allow them to connect to both CDMA wireless networks and GSM wireless networks.
§ CK and IK are session keys for confidentiality (CK) and for integrity (IK).
¶ IMEI is an international mobile station equipment identity, which is a number to identify 3GPP, GSM, UMTS, LTE, and iDEN mobile phones, as well as some satellite phones.

Information Security

In order for security to be efficient in all the main sectors, it must be implemented in all portion of the network and processing components. Regrettably, this is not something that comes easy for cellular and wireless networks. In attempting to avoid security problems like the ones that overwhelmed the 1G cellular systems, network designers must implement security into any new technology, as it can't be added as an afterthought. In order for all security aspects in 4G technology and cellular networks to be implemented and maintained properly, these major players (government regulators, network infrastructure providers, equipment providers, service providers, and the end-device user) must work together and apart to create a secure wireless system.

Before pursuing the design and implementation of wireless security, you must first understand what the vague concept of security really means. In this specific case, wireless security is a blend of wireless channel security, or the security of the radio transmissions; and network security, or the security of the wired network through which data is transmitted.

Security Analysis

The infrastructure for cellular networks is immense and intricate with numerous entities working together, such as the IP Internet working in part with the core network. Thus, a challenge is presented for the network to provide security at every possible communication path.

Goals and Objectives in Security

Some of the goals and objectives of security are as follows:

1. Making sure that information generated by or relating to a user is suitably protected against misapplication or misappropriation
2. Ensuring that the resources and services provided to end users are sufficiently protected against misapplication and misappropriation
3. Guaranteeing that security features are compatible with worldwide availability
4. Making sure that security features are sufficiently homogeneous to ensure worldwide interoperability and roaming between the different service providers
5. Guaranteeing that the level of security afforded to users and service providers is better than the security in a modern-day fixed and mobile network
6. Ensuring that the application of security features and mechanisms can be drawn out and enhanced as demanded by the rise of new threats and services
7. Making sure that security features permit new "e-commerce" services and other advanced applications

The above-stated goals are a representation of what the policies and technologies used in wireless cellular networks should achieve when analyzing and implementing security. These objectives can be used as guidelines for better directing the efforts of security when defending against certain security dangers.

Boundaries and Limitations in Security

1. Open wireless access medium: Since the actual transmission of information and data is being completed through wireless connections, the physical barrier keeping an attacker from accessing the network is non existent.

2. Limited bandwidth: Due to channel conflict, users are forced to share the same medium, resulting in limited bandwidth.
3. System complexity: With the evolution of mobile cellular networks, the complexity behind the networks has evolved as well, thus constantly bringing new security weaknesses to light.
4. Relatively unreliable network connection: When comparing the reliability of wireless cellular networks to wired cellular networks, the wireless medium is much more volatile. Wireless networks have a much higher error rate.

Types of Security Issues

With the design of new cellular mobile systems over the past 30 years, the mobile devices that have followed have also become more and more complex. The physical layer of these devices has not changed much during the transition from 1G to 4G devices, but now that we are in the fourth generation, new layers of software have been implemented, adding a whole new weakness to mobile cellular devices. 4G wireless devices are known for their software applications, which provide advanced new features for users. Although these software applications can be beneficial and afford easier use, they introduce new types of security risks that can provide easier access and more avenues for hackers to attack.

The following are different security issues that need to be noted when examining cellular systems and their security risks:

1. Authentication: Cellular networks have large quantities of subscribers, who have to be authenticated to guarantee that the correct subscribers are using the network. Its location is a very important factor in guaranteeing that the correct subscribers are using the network. As the number of subscribers using the network is getting bigger and bigger, issues relating to cross-region and cross-provider authentication arise.
2. Integrity: With a growing number of ways to share information and communicate with one another, it's important to guarantee that the data being transmitted does not get altered or corrupted. With services such as short message service (SMS), chat, and file transfer, it is important that the data arrives without any modification.
3. Confidentiality: It is very important to ensure that the information being transmitted gets to the end user securely and successfully. Since there has been a major increase in the use of cellular phones for sensitive communication, there is a major need for secure channeling in order for information to transmit.
4. Access control: Cellular devices may have files that need restricted access to be added to them. The device might also access a database where some form of role-based access control is required.
5. Operating systems (OSs) in mobile devices: Cellular devices have progressed from having low processing power and ad hoc supervisors to having high power processors and fully functional OSs. Issues may become apparent in the OS, which could expose security holes that can be exploited by attackers.
6. Web services: A Web service is a component that offers functionality, available through the web, using the Hypertext Transfer Protocol (HTTP) standard. This leaves the cellular device open to a number of different security issues such as viruses or malware, denial-of-service attacks, and eavesdropping or hijacking.
7. Location detection: The physical location of a cellular device needs to be kept disclosed for the privacy of the user. With the move to IP-based networks, the issue has arisen where a user may be linked with an access point, causing their location to be compromised.

8. Device security: The mobile devices should have a fail-safe or application set in place that can be opened from another device, allowing the user to delete all the important information stored on the device, just in case of theft.

9. Viruses and malware: With an increase in functionality being provided in cellular systems, problems arise in systems such as viruses and malware. A device that has been infected can also be a tool for attackers to attack the infrastructure of the cellular network by being part of a large-scale denial-of-service attack.

10. Downloaded contents: Spyware or adware can be downloaded by the user, by accident or unwittingly, creating the potential for security issues to arise. Digital rights management is another major problem. Users can accidentally download unauthorized copies of videos, music, and games.

This analysis of the issues relating to wireless cellular networks and with wireless mobile devices is just a basic overview and does not define an overall solution for security. Instead, the concepts that have been listed are intended to help in the understanding of security problems that have become apparent through previous wireless generations or ones that may arise in future generations, such as 5G.

Types of Security Attacks

1. Theft: One of the most common forms of attack, especially with the portability of mobile devices, is through physical theft of the device. The mobile device user runs the risk of losing all information and data stored on the device, including financial documents or personal pictures, when their device is stolen. Even more importantly, the people who use their device for business or work-related functions run the risk of devastating business implications, such as divulging sensitive customer and employee information as well as a host of other highly guarded corporate assets.

2. DoS: One of the most dangerous types of attacks is a DoS attack. It has the ability to bring down an entire network infrastructure due to the excessive transmission of data to a network, resulting in users being denied access to network resources.

3. Distributed denial of service (DDoS): It could be hard to launch a large-scale DoS attack from one single or original host. Instead, a large amount of hosts can be used to launch an attack. An attacker tries to make a network resource or machine inaccessible to its anticipated users, with the intention of momentarily or indefinitely disturbing or suspending service. The big differentiation between a DoS and a DDoS attack is that during a DDoS attack, there is more than one, and often thousands, of unique IP addresses involved.

4. Channel jamming: Jamming the wireless channel is a method used by attackers to deny access to any authorized users in the network.

5. Unauthorized access: If the proper authentication method is not deployed, then attackers may gain unrestricted access to a network, using it for services that attackers might not be normally allowed to access.

6. Eavesdropping: This involves listening to the private conversations of others without the conversationalists' consent. Eavesdropping may also be done over telephone lines, e-mail, and various other methods of private communication. A publicly broadcast message is not considered eavesdropping.

7. Message forgery: When the network channel isn't secure, attackers can intercept message going and coming from both directions and can modify the message without the users ever being informed.

8. Message replay: Even if the network channel is secure, attackers can intercept an encrypted message and then replay it back at a later time. The victim of the attack may never know that the encrypted message received is not the original one.

9. Phishing: These attacks make use of network communications to mislead users into installing malevolent software that leads the user to provide information that is sensitive or personal. A very common type of phishing on e-mail-enabled mobile devices is e-mail phishing. Other common forms of phishing are referred to as "vishing," the phishing of voice calls; and "smishing," the phishing of SMS/MMS messages.

10. Malware: There are always software applications that seem authentic and non volatile. Almost anyone who has the capability and knowledge can create and develop apps for some of the most widely used service providers and mobile OSs. Some service providers provide access to third-party applications that have had no analysis of their safety for the end user. Users can even completely bypass their operating system lockout mechanism by jailbreaking a mobile device. Some quality examples of malware are applications running in the background of the user's device that can build up long-distance bills, and code that self-propagates and infects devices and then spreads from one device to another through the address book.

Architecture of Security

When examining the security of cellular networks from a broad perspective, the overall architecture of security should have five important characteristics. The security architecture should be complete, efficient, effective, extensible, and user friendly.

The architecture should be efficient and effective, with security features and functionalities that are independent of their counterparts but still complete their overall purpose. The architecture should be extensible, constructed in such a way that new ideas and technologies can be implemented and built on to the existing architecture in a methodical way. Lastly, the architecture should be friendly to the user. The end users should have to learn about security and how it works. If the user must interact with security, it should be easy for the user to understand.

4G Security (LTE and WiMAX)

Worldwide Interoperability for Microwave Access (WiMAX) and LTE are the two leading wireless technologies of the 4G mobile networks. Here, their history, architecture, and security overview are explained.

WiMAX Introduction

The demand for broadband wireless access technologies has been growing over recent years due to the increasing request for mobile Internet and wireless multimedia applications. WiMAX is a part of 4G wireless communication technology. Developed under a trademark of the WiMAX forum (a not-for-profit association that certifies and promotes the compatibility and interoperability of broadband wireless products based on the Institute of Electrical and Electronics Engineers IEEE Standard 802.16), WiMAX is based on the IEEE 802.16 standard and was developed to deliver non-line-of-sight (NLoS) connectivity between a subscriber station and a base station. Mobile

WiMAX was the first mobile broadband wireless access solution based on the IEEE 802.16e-2005 standard and adopted into the International Telecommunication Union (ITU), and it has become a leading global cellular wireless standard. However, if WiMAX wishes to continue being a leading wireless standard, focusing on security will be extremely important.

History of WiMAX

WiMAX technology expansion and fruition was due to the cooperation of the WiMAX Forum, the ITU, and the IEEE 802.16 Working Group (Working Group of Broadband Wireless Access Standards). The IEEE 802.16 Working Group develops standards and recommended practices to support the development and deployment of broadband wireless metropolitan area networks and is one of the numerous working groups (WGs) within the LAN/MAN Standards Committee (LMSC). The purpose of the LMSC is to develop and maintain networking standards and recommended practices for local, metropolitan, and other area networks, using an open and accredited process, and it advocates them on a global basis. The IEEE Working Group 802.16, along with the WiMAX Forum, became sector members of ITU-R (radio communications) in 2003. Recognition within the ITU gave WiMAX technology international credibility.

Evolution of Mobile WiMAX

IMT-2000, commonly known as 3G, became the foundation of the personal mobile communications industry due to its availability almost everywhere in the world. In 2011, ITU-R completed the next generation of global broadband technology, International Mobile Telecommunications—Advanced (IMT-Advanced), commonly known as 4G. IEEE 802.16 WG announced the amendment of the previous Mobile WiMAX standard, IEEE 802.16e, to the transition of IEEE 802.16m, which was to meet or surpass the current specifications of IMT-Advanced. Some of the upgrades with IEEE 802.16m included higher bandwidth, from 30 mbps to 100 mbps; extensive wide coverage area, which increased from 1–3 miles to 30–100 km; and interoperability with other technologies. Scalability in both network architecture and radio access technology also allow Mobile WiMAX, IEEE 82.16m, to have a great deal of flexibility with network offerings. Some of the most prominent features with Mobile WiMAX include

- High data rates and speed: Wireless connectivity can be offered in a very short amount of time for operators while enabling the Mobile WiMAX technology to support 1000 mbps for mobile stations (MS) and 1 Gbps for fixed locations.
- Mobility: Short latencies allow users to run multiple real-time applications without any interruption in service or quality and allow operators to provide a wide variety of different applications.
- Quality of service (QoS): IEEE 802.16m supports revisions of service flow QoS parameters. Mobile stations (MS) and base stations (BS) negotiate the possible QoS parameter sets during set up of the service flow (Ahmadi, 2009). UGS, Rtps, Nrtps, Ertps, and BE are all types of QoS that WiMAX supports.
- Cost: When compared with 3G, 4G is cheaper for cellular carriers to deliver.
- Deployment opportunities: WiMAX allows operators to design their own networks. This allows them to capitalize on a strong market to receive a high return on investment (ROI).

Mobile WiMAX Architecture

The mobile WiMAX architecture has four main components. Figure 18.2 displays the basic components of an IP-based WiMAX network architecture.

The MS was added in the 2005 IEEE amendment, IEEE 802.16e standard, instead of a subscriber station. The MS provides wireless connectivity when there is movement between BS through handoff procedures.

Physical and medium access control (MAC) are the main layers of a BS. The BS acts as a connection or gateway point to other networks. Functions such as mobility and tunnel establishment, radio management, and handoffs are all performed through the BS.

Access service network gateway (ASN-GW) acts as the entrance point to the WiMAX network and controls location management, caching, network discovery and selection, and handover. The ASN gateway also acts as a Layer 2 traffic connectivity point with the MS (Figure 18.2).

Connectivity service network (CSN) involves routers, servers, and devices that provide all core network functions to the IP and connectivity to the Internet and various other networks. To add an additional authentication processes for devices and users, an additional authentication and accounting server is added.

The protocol level is divided into two layers, the Media Access Control (MAC) layer and the physical layer (PHY). The MAC layer consists of three sublayers:

1. Service specific convergence sublayer (CS): Classifies and maps MAC service data units (MSDUs).
2. Common part sublayer (CPS): Responsible for bandwidth allocation, connection establishment, and connection maintenance.
3. Security sublayer: Handles authentication, encryption, and exchange issues.

The PHY layer handles physical transportation, transmission, and reception of data as well as power control.

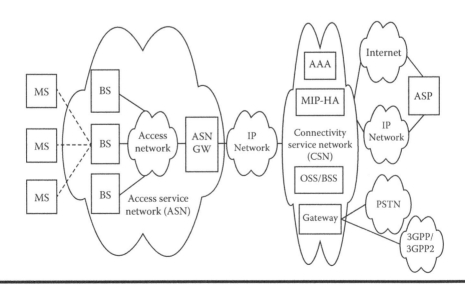

Figure 18.2 IP-based WiMAX network architecture.

WiMAX Security, Threats, and Solutions

Although WiMAX is known for its mobility, attackers do not need to be at a stationary location to make an attack, leaving the network more susceptible to an attack. In WiMAX's protocol architecture, the security is implemented in the security sublayer, leaving the physical layer exposed and unprotected. Jamming, scrambling, and water-torture attacks cannot be prevented easily. Although many of the amendments focused on securing the MAC layer, threats on the PHY layer remain unresolved. Almost all security issues in a mobile WiMAX network reside in the sublayer. Man-in-the-middle attacks, DoS due to the continuous sending of packets, and threats to the physical layer are the largest threats to WiMAX security.

- Threats to the physical layer: The two largest threats to the physical layer are blocking and rushing. Blocking triggers a strong frequency to the channel, which creates a DoS to all stations. Although detectable with a radio analyzer device, it is not preventable and can only notify the user of an attack so that the proper recovery steps can be taken.
- Authentication: WiMAX networks use a privacy key management (PKM) protocol for management (Ahuja and Collier, 2010). PKM provides better privacy for traffic data through authentication and key management. It only allows three types of authentication:
  - RSA
  - Extensible Authentication Protocol (EAP)
  - RSA followed by EAP authentication
- The authentication mechanism in the PKM protocol can cause a breach leading to man-in-the-middle attacks, which can cause subscribers to have confidentiality attacks. Man-in-the-middle attacks are when an attacker intercepts information being exchanged between two parties and tampers with the data. This makes it seem like the two parties are still communicating with one another. EAPs were amended to IEEE 802.16e to help reduce the chances of attacks.
- Encryption: Advanced Encryption Standard (AES) is the main encryption tool used by WiMAX, although it does use triple data encryption standard (3DES) as well. Encrypted data can only be exchanged through the WiMAX network after the successful exchange of keys. The AES was brought in by an amendment in IEEE 802.16e allowing the confidentiality of data traffic. Attackers can collect information in the area because standard management frames are not encrypted, allowing the possibility of an attack.
- Availability: WiMAX uses RF Spectrum, which is a downfall as the higher the frequency, the more the BS range decreases. Legacy management frames effectively used by an attacker can cause legitimate stations to be disconnected. It wouldn't be too difficult for an attacker to cause a jamming attack on all planned deployments as well.
- DoS: Using the IP address to overflow the user's network, DoS attacks are used to block communication and computer resources, making the user's network unavailable. They are carried out by flooding the user with a large number of messages to authenticate. Although unpreventable, firewalls and other shared authentication information (SAI) protocols can be used to alert the user and resolve the issue as quickly as possible.

Although WiMAX is known to have reliable security, it is not a flawless system. We can expect WiMAX to take extensive measures in the future to clear up its security issues as it has done with its previous standards. When the aforementioned security threats are resolved, the security capabilities of WiMAX will be significantly increased.

4G LTE Introduction

4G Long-Term Evolution (4G LTE) is 4G wireless communication technology. The 3rd Generation Partner Project (3GPP) had developed a strong security framework for the 4G LTE network based on five security feature groups. Although the strong outline of the architecture appears to have been put in place, many security vulnerabilities have been identified, particularly with mobile network operators (MNOs). Because of LTE's open, all IP-based architecture, attackers can target mobile devices and networks with relative ease and attack their networks with a wide variety of options. Although a strong framework has been put in place, MNOs play a critical role in the maintenance and security of their 4G LTE networks.

History of 4G LTE

LTE is the brand name based on the 4G technology development efforts from the 3GPP. In order for LTE to succeed the 3G technology, the 4G technology had to meet a specific high-level requirements, including

- Higher spectral efficiency
- Reduced cost per bit
- Increased service provisioning by lowering the cost and increasing efficiency and experience
- Open interfaces as opposed to the closed technologies of the past
- Power consumption efficiency
- Scalable and flexible usage of frequency bands

The 3GPP was in charge of bringing together technical specifications and developing telecommunications standards for the LTE network. Orthogonal frequency division multiplexing (OFDM) and multiple-input multiple-output (MIMO) were the technical specifications determined by the 3GPP. OFDM was chosen because it makes it possible to extend wireless access across wide systems, and MIMO was chosen because it allows enhanced throughput for given bandwidths. This higher throughput is one of the many advantages for network operators as well as low latency and operating costs. For the user, LTE allows faster data downloads and a vast improvement of the user experience.

4G LTE Architecture

The 4G LTE architecture has a few key differences compared with 3G architecture. Figure 18.3 shows the basic LTE system architecture. First, it only contains two types of network components: the eNode B, which incorporates all radio interface tasks in Evolved UMTS Terrestrial Radio Access Network (E-UTRAN); and the Access Gateway, which incorporates all Evolved Packet Core (EPC) functions. The EPC's task is to connect the user to the IP network. The user

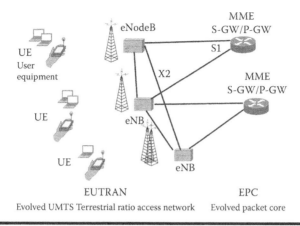

Figure 18.3   The 4G LTE system architecture.

equipment (UE) connects through the eNode B, which is located within the E-UTRAN. From there it is connected to the EPC, which connects to the network. This allows LTE to have greater efficiency due to its meshed architecture. All signaling protocols are IP based within the LTE network.

4G LTE Security, Threats, and Solutions

The 3GPP, taking security into deliberation, developed the 4G LTE architecture based on five security features:

1. Network access security, to provide the user with secure access to the service
2. Network domain security, to protect the network elements and secure the signaling and user data exchange
3. User domain security, to control secure access to mobile stations
4. Application domain security, to establish secure communications over the application layer
5. Visibility and configuration of security, bringing the opportunity for the user to check if the security features are in operation

However, as stated earlier in the introduction, security vulnerabilities have been identified because these features are discretionary. These features can only help as much as the MNOs understand about their LTE network security and choose to take action against threats, which causes a large number of inconsistencies in security implementation. These enhancements, although meant to help better protect the system, created the following potential security issues that need to be addressed:

■ Open architecture threats: LTE's IP-based end-to-end deployment and open architecture configuration causes the MNO to share their security risks to other end users as everyone is interconnected. In order to prevent this from occurring, interoperability standards were set with the agreement that each MNO would secure their network using preventative measures to make sure that any subscriber or user on their network is never compromised.

■ Location tracking and privacy: Although it is not considered a direct security threat, location tracking compromises privacy and security, which could become a direct security threat. Location tracking is caused when there is a UE presence in the network and it is being fed false authentication requests from an attacker. Attackers can further replay the intercepted authentication request and determine the presence of a specific phone in a certain location. When the UE receives a replay of an intercepted authentication request, it will send a synchronization failure request. This attack has the potential to enable location tracking, thus compromising privacy and security.

■ Infrastructure sharing: Due to varying security standards from multiple MNOs interconnecting with one another on a shared network, these types of arrangements pose high security threats. Lack of consistent security measures can increase the chance of an attack.

■ Risk of data loss: 4G LTE UE stores more data on the actual UE than any other generation due to the capabilities of the broadband network, but this can cause severe security issues, as UE lacks management tools. If an MNO allows an unsecure device on their network, access to user data can lead an attacker to have access to the user's identity. This can lead to financial loss, personal information loss, breach of privacy, and even identity theft.

■ DoS: Perhaps the most serious threat because the entire network could be shut down, the risk of DoS attacks is possible in LTE networks. Each new UE that gets added to the network will increase the complexity of the network. An attacker can enter the system undetected due to interconnectivity and pose a threat to the network if the situation isn't resolved.

The 3GPP developed a strong architecture for 4G LTE, but it is the responsibility of the MNOs to understand their networks and take proper precautions to maintain their network. Through proper design and deployment, proper protection can minimize the impact of various security threats inside a 4G LTE system network.

A 5G Future

The next evolutionary step in the mobile telecommunication standard is known as fifth generation or 5G. Currently, there is much discussion about what is expected of this new network, but much like the previous generations, it is anticipated to roll out 10 years after the previous generation, sometime around 2020.

5G is still in its infancy, and research regarding the architecture is still quite limited. Much of the discussion of 5G in this section will focus on the demands that 5G is anticipated to handle by its introduction, the possibilities of security, network architecture, and spectrum use.

To understand what is expected of 5G, it is important to understand what the network is expected to handle in the coming years. In May 2015, Cisco released its Cisco Visual Networking Index (VNI): forecast and methodology, 2014–2019. The VNI is a forecasted global traffic analysis for a 5-year span, relatively close to the rollout of 5G. All of the data relates to some form of global traffic, but some is directly related to mobile technology. The following are some of the forecasts.

1. Over half of all IP traffic will originate with non-PC devices by 2019. In 2014, only 40% of total IP traffic originated with non-PC devices, but by 2019 the non-PC share of total

IP traffic will grow to 67%. PC-originated traffic will grow at a CAGR* of 9%, while TVs, tablets, smartphones, and machine-to-machine (M2M) modules will have traffic growth rates of 17%, 65%, 62%, and 71%, respectively.

2. Traffic from wireless and mobile devices will exceed traffic from wired devices by 2019. By 2019, wired devices will account for 33% of IP traffic, while Wi-Fi and mobile devices will account for 66% of IP traffic. In 2014, wired devices accounted for the majority of IP traffic at 54%.

3. The number of devices connected to IP networks will be three times as high as the global population in 2019. There will be three networked devices per capita by 2019, up from nearly two networked devices per capita in 2014. Accelerated in part by the increase in devices and the capabilities of those devices, IP traffic per capita will reach 22 GB per capita by 2019, up from 8 GB per capita in 2014.

4. Globally, mobile data traffic will increase tenfold between 2014 and 2019. Mobile data traffic will grow at a CAGR of 57% between 2014 and 2019, reaching 24.2 exabytes per month by 2019.

5. Global mobile data traffic will grow three times faster than fixed IP traffic from 2014 to 2019. Global mobile data traffic represented 4% of total IP traffic in 2014 and will make up 14% of total IP traffic by 2019.

Not listed in the VNI is the projected use of wearable technology or the Internet of Things (IoT). The ITU in 2012 defined IoT as a global infrastructure for the information society, enabling advanced services by interconnecting (physical and virtual) things based on existing and evolving interoperable information and communication technologies. The ITU has two notes regarding IoT: (1) "through the exploitation of identification, data capture, processing and communication capabilities, the IoT makes full use of things to offer services to all kinds of application, while ensuring that security and privacy requirements are fulfilled" and (2) from one perspective, the IoT can be perceived as a vision with technological and societal implications.

Much of the research focuses on not only the mobile demands of 5G but also the demands that IoT will have as well. Communications companies such as BEEcube and Ericsson have all acknowledged that IoT is an important factor of 5G with billions of miscellaneous devices as a contributing factor.

Cisco places the number of IoT devices at around 50 billion by 2020. 5G will also provide wireless connectivity for a wide range of new applications and use cases, including wearables, smart homes, traffic safety/control, and critical infrastructure and industry applications, as well as for very high-speed media delivery. It is quite clear that 5G will have plenty of demanding applications in the near future.

With the anticipated growth in mobile use between now and 2020, much of the research has concluded that 5G will have to achieve higher data throughput and capacity than 4G. Because 5G is still in its infancy, the expected rates of 5G are anticipated to be over 1 Gbps to well over tens of gigabits per second.

5G Security

Even though security will be one of the top issues for 5G, very little has been published on what is necessary to secure all that data. Unlike the previous generations (2G–4G), 5G will in all likelihood have to establish a new trust model. A trust model is nothing more than the experience we

---

* CAGR is the compound annual growth rate for global mobile units and global mobile data traffic.

have had with the previous generations. As the usage of mobile devices, wearable technology, and IoT expands, and the need to secure all the data collected with ever-growing privacy concerns, security measures that are put in place for 5G will have to build a new form of trust far beyond that of current generations.

One noted departure from the traditional cryptographic techniques is that physical layer security is identified as a promising strategy, providing secure wireless transmissions by smartly exploiting the imperfections of the communications medium. Two advantages of using physical layer security instead of cryptology are reducing the need for computational complexity and high scalability.

It is suggested that physical layer security regarding computational complexity be utilized based on the assumption that current devices lack the ability to compromise the computational complexity; next-generation devices may have that ability.

Device-to-device (D2D) communication is also an important aspect of security but will be addressed in another portion of this book. With billions of devices expected to rely on 5G, scaling computation security becomes more complex.

We must understand that different services/devices will rely on different network requirements. Monitoring sensor networks (assumed to be connected to 5G) use less bandwidth throughput and require different delay times compared with that of virtual reality. Because of the increased demand and individual requirements for all the expected devices, the computational requirement to address the billions of devices on 5G will become increasingly complex. Physical layer security can be used either to provide direct secure data communication or to facilitate the distribution of cryptographic keys. To illustrate the difficulty in securing data from all of these devices, Cisco VNI forecasts that global IP traffic will surpass 2 ZB (2 billion TB) per year in 2019. This means that IP traffic will only continue to increase and will increase almost three times the original amount during the next five years.

HetNets

Many companies have begun to aim at the use of heterogeneous networks, or HetNets, for 5G use. HetNets are the provisioning of a cellular network through a combination of different cell types (e.g., macro, pico, femto cells) and different access to technologies using 1G, 2G, 3G, 4G, or Wi-Fi.

Supplementary features of a HetNet are nodes that have different coverage areas, transmitting powers, and radio access technologies that are created for the purpose of forming a multitier hierarchical architecture (Figure 18.4).

Much current research is suggesting that the current network architecture will not be able to handle 5G, and that a multilayered network (HetNet) is a possible solution. The overall aim of HetNet is to deliver an energy-efficient and spectrum-efficient solution that satisfies the dramatic progression in demands for data in future wireless applications. Ericsson has had some success in testing small HetNets to achieve data rates exceeding 5 Gpbs over the air. This was achieved by using new antenna technology for wider bandwidths, higher frequencies, and short transmission time intervals and by building BSs for 5G with baseband and radio units.

D2D will be an important factor in 5G as well as HetNets. Not only will D2D have to address security issues, but it will be an integral part of HetNets as potential providers of data. It has been suggested that D2D communications should not only be considered when developing the architecture of 5G but that direct D2D communication should extend the capabilities and enhance the overall efficiency of the wireless-access network. With the opportunity to transmit data from one device to another, there have been a number of suggestions as to its potential. One note is to use

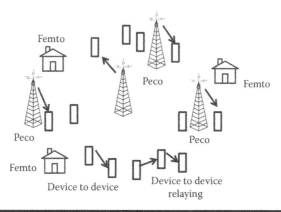

Figure 18.4 A heterogeneous cellular network.

the D2D communication to have one device with better geometry, so that the transmitter device may act as a relay for the receiver device. This would essentially allow network access anywhere, as long as you are within the proximity of another device. The caveat to this is, of course, the significant security protocols that must be addressed to ensure the relaying device isn't compromised.

Massive MIMO

Massive multiple-input multiple-output (massive MIMO) is another suggested component of 5G, including the possibility of its use as physical layer security. By deploying a very large number of antennas (e.g., a few hundred) at BSs to serve multiple users at the same time, massive MIMO gains all the benefits provided by conventional MIMO but on a much larger scale.

Massive MIMO relies on the ability to have multiple data paths to multiple devices (Anritsu, 2015), while "the number of antenna arrays at the BSs is much larger, for example, 10 times, than the number of data streams served to all users in a cell." Comparatively, a current MIMO uses 2 or 4 antennas to transmit (Tx) and receive (Rx), massive MIMO may be using 128 antennas (Figure 18.5).

Low power consumption and artificial noise (AN) are two more benefits of a massive MIMO. Low power consumption allows a reduction in eavesdropping in two ways:

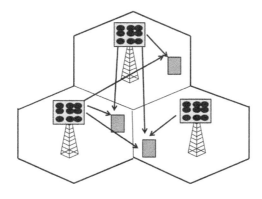

Figure 18.5 Cellular network with the deployment of massive MIMO.

1. Since the transmit power level is cut, the received signal-to-noise ratios (SNRs) at the eavesdroppers are highly reduced. This leads to a significant decrease in the eavesdroppers' channel capacities.
2. Given the transmit power and expected secrecy rate at the transmitter, the secrecy outage probability can be arbitrarily small when the number of antennas grows unbounded.

AN is currently used in MIMO systems, but the possibility for its use in massive MIMO hasn't been fully examined. AN proves an effective way to cause interference to the eavesdroppers and degrade their reeved signals. However, researchers have stated that AN signals in a spatial null space may not be practical since the computation complexity of the null space is extremely high for the large-dimensional channel matrix.

Massive MIMO is still being researched, and while many suggest its possibilities, it is not without its technical hurdles. The following is a list of potential concerns:

1. High-order MIMO can have issues with radio interference, so technology is required to help mitigate this problem. This tends to focus on the need for the radio network to adjust its beam to take into account the specific orientation of the antenna at any given time.
2. The digital signal processor (DSP)* processing power required to implement high-order modulation schemes across many antennas and many sectors, as with massive MIMO, is immense. Tens of thousands to hundreds of thousands of multiply-accumulate (MAC)[†] units will be required, with each running at hundreds of megahertz.
3. Considering wireless signal propagation characteristics, the massive MIMO antenna and millimeter wave communication technologies will obviously reduce cell coverage.
4. To date, the processing power required means that the deployment of massive MIMO is not suitable for portable devices due to its size and power consumption, and so first deployments are focused more on fixed wireless access schemes and the provision of wireless backhaul to a dense deployment of small cells.
5. A significantly more advanced baseband computation is required to meet the complex requirements of new solutions such as mass-scale MIMO.

Currently, OFDM is the multiplexing scheme suggested for 5G, mainly because it is the trusted model currently used with 4G. As previously mentioned, the amount of devices that will rely on 5G may have a significant impact on whether OFDM will be used. Duplexing will also likely have to change for 5G. While frequency division duplexing (FDD) will likely stay for low frequency bands and is currently used for MIMO systems, many have indicated that in a massive MIMO, time division duplexing (TDD) will be a likely solution because the frequencies will be above 10 GHz.

TDD is when the transmitter and receiver transmit at different times but use the same frequency. TDD has many qualities that will give it an important role in 5G, specifically because

---

* A DSP is a specialized microprocessor with its architecture optimized for digital signal processing. The goal of DSPs is to measure, filter, and/or compress continuous real-world analog signals.
† In networking, media access control (MAC) and MAC addresses are commonly described since all wire or fiber networks connect directly to a MAC unit, which is the unit that directly attaches the device to the media whether it be wire or fiber transport media. However, in wireless networks, the MAC acronym is reused to indicate multiply-accumulate units, once again MAC. A multiply-accumulate unit (MAC) is the main computational kernel in DSP architectures. The MAC unit determines the power and the speed of the overall system; it always lies in the critical path. Developing high-speed and low-power MAC is crucial to using DSP.

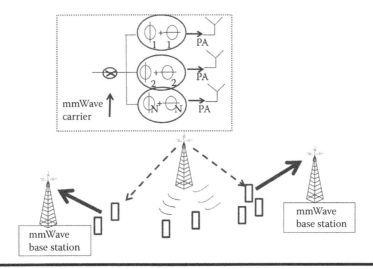

Figure 18.6   Deployment of mmWave BSs.

FDD limits the number of antennas, unlike TDD. TDD is significantly more secure than FDD. TDD not only allows for more dynamic use, but is expected to be employed in dense deployments accessing low-power base-stations deployed both indoors and outdoors at street level.

The BS with massive antenna arrays obtains the uplink channel state information (CSI) via uplink pilot signals from the users. It then obtains the downlink CSI, relying on the reciprocity between the uplink and downlink. As such, it becomes difficult for eavesdroppers to determine the CSI between themselves and the BS, as well as the CSI from other users to the BS. From TDD, the next consideration has been full-duplex; this means simultaneous transmission and reception on the same carrier frequency, which essentially doubles the capacity of FDD or TDD. Much research still needs to be conducted to determine if full-duplex will be useful for 5G, but the key issue with full-duplex will be to resolve the transmit–receive isolation problem.

Millimeter Wave

Current cellular providers have a limited carrier frequency spectrum of between 700 MHz and 2.6 GHz, and these limits are nearly occupied. Many have suggested that to overcome the frequency allocations, research needs to be done into the mmWave spectrums, which occupy range frequencies from 30–300 GHz. One of the most noted benefits of mmWave currently is not only the expansion of bandwidth channels but also higher data transfer. Much like massive MIMOs, mmWave isn't without its problems. Besides the need for further research into the development and distribution of mmWave, its technological and regulatory challenges are yet to be addressed, including its limited transmission range (Figure 18.6).

Conclusion

Understanding the evolution of wireless security is important as we look at the fourth and fifth generations. It becomes clear that security in the generations has been reactive to threats. 4G saw significant strides in design, capacity, security, and efficiency. Although these improvements were made, new security threats and risks are created and developed with each new wireless network. Also, with new designs come new expectations and innovations.

The IoT will come with security procedures and solutions that can only currently be speculated about as we look toward the unknown 5G. Just as the previous generations have shaped the ones that follow, 4G is providing insight into the dynamic requirements needed to launch the 5G network. For the next few years, securing 4G communication should remain a top priority while the research and development of 5G continues.

While capacity, security, and connectivity are sure to increase, there are still a lot of questions that are yet to be answered about 5G. Security for 5G should be proactive and should be established prior to its official launch in efforts to secure data and reduce attacks. Regulatory issues regarding spectrum use and security should also be addressed in efforts to ensure that 5G is more successful and dynamic than the previous generations. This is especially important if this generation is to be the final evolution.

QUESTIONS

1. WiMAX is based on which IEEE standard?
    a. IEEE 802.17
    b. IEEE 802.16
    c. IEEE 802.18
    d. IEEE 802.15
2. Which cellular generation brought with it the use of graphics, video, and audio applications?
    a. 1G
    b. 2G
    c. 3G
    d. 4G
3. What type of security threat has the ability to bring down the entire network infrastructure?
    a. DoS
    b. Channel jamming
    c. Theft
    d. Message forgery
4. What is not an AKA protocol stage?
    a. Initiation
    b. Transfer of credentials
    c. Strong encryption
    d. Challenge response exchange
5. Which cellular generation is known as the analog generation?
    a. 1G
    b. 2G
    c. 3G
    d. 4G
6. By the year 2019, the non-PC share of IP traffic is estimated to grow by how much?
    a. 45%
    b. 90%
    c. 67%
    d. 52%

7. Which architecture component acts as a connection or gateway point in mobile WiMAX networks?
    a. Mobile station (MS)
    b. Base station (BS)
    c. Access service network gateway (ASN-GW)
    d. Connectivity service network (CSN)
8. Which was not a specification that 4G LTE needed to meet in order to succeed 3G?
    a. Higher spectral efficiency
    b. Power consumption efficiency
    c. Scalable and flexible usage of frequency bands
    d. Packet-switched network implementation
9. Which 5G communication method could allow network access anywhere within the proximity of another device?
    a. Device to device (D2D)
    b. Massive multiple-input multiple-output (MIMO)
    c. Artificial noise (AN)
    d. Frequency division duplexing (FDD)
10. Which multiplexing scheme is currently being suggested for 5G?
    a. Code division multiplexing (CDM)
    b. Orthogonal frequency division multiplexing (OFDM)
    c. Polarization-division multiplexing (PDM)
    d. Time division multiplexing (TDM).

Chapter 19

Wireless LAN Security

A wireless local area network, referred to as *WLAN*, is a network that is able to connect two or more devices within a defined area without physical connectivity, such as cable. An example of a WLAN may exist right in your home and consist of a network access device (router) that connects to your high-speed Internet service and doubles as a routing device and a switch. This creates the WLAN to connect your home computer, iPad (tablet), or other wireless device. WLAN has exploded in popularity based on the ease of access to the Internet that it can offer. An overly simplistic WLAN can be vulnerable to many different threats as was proved with early forms of wireless security, which didn't really provide any security at all. Figure 19.1 shows a basic diagram of a wireless LAN.

The simplest way to give a more detailed description of WLAN is to break it down into its major components. The first and most important component of a WLAN is the radio card, which is more commonly referred to as a station (STA). The STA can be either an access point (AP) or a client. The client is the receiver's radio card, which operates on the standard 802.11 protocols, and consists of devices such as a smartphone or computer. The AP refers to the device that communicates with all of the devices on the current WLAN. The AP works as a gateway through which the client devices can achieve an Ethernet connection. This may not be the case in every WLAN setup, however. Sometimes, the AP is a stepping-stone to another AP, which is then the connection to the Ethernet.

The last two components of a WLAN device are an antenna and the ability to operate under the 802.11 protocol standards. Since all clients exist on the same set of protocols, they all compete equally for the right to gain connection to an AP. When attempting to connect to an AP, a client must either find or receive that point's service set identifier (SSID). The client accomplishes this by scanning, which can be either active or passive. Active scanning is when the client sends out a probe pulse request to all of the available APs in the area. Passive scanning, on the other hand, is when the client waits to notice the beacon that all APs constantly em it.

Regulatory WLAN Security Standards

The Institute of Electrical and Electronics Engineers (IEEE) originally set the 802.11 standards in 1997. These standards represent all of the operating procedures that a device

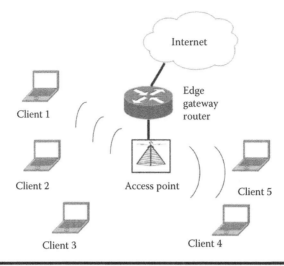

Figure 19.1 Basic wireless local area network.

communicating over a WLAN must follow. Since their inception, these standards have been modified many times, and each time, they are given a new letter at the end (such as 802.11a). The Federal Communications Commission (FCC) is most impactful on WLAN in regulating the spectrum of bandwidth that is allotted for Wi-Fi technology. The FCC does not issue WLAN encryption minimum requirements for businesses and individuals using a WLAN. However, the FCC does strongly recommend using Wi-Fi Protected Access II (WPA2) encryption for any wireless network. It also recommends a number of other measures for individual and business networks including using a firewall, changing the password regularly, changing the default name of the network, turning off network name broadcasting, and using the media and access control (MAC) address filter.

The FCC defers to the IEEE in their recommendation for WPA2. The IEEE sets the industry standards for wireless security in the 802.11 protocols. These protocols are a set of specifications for the MAC physical layer in a WLAN. The first 802.11 standard was released in 1997, and currently the IEEE is working on 802.11ad, which would set the standards for WLANs with throughput capabilities of 7 gigabits per second by utilizing a frequency of 60 GHz.

WPA2 became the industry standard in June 2004, when the IEEE ratified 802.11i-2004 (802.11i-2004, 2004). 802.11i-2004 implemented the standard for WLAN security standards that still exist today—WPA2. WPA2 replaced Wi-Fi Protected Access (WPA), which was implemented in 2003. WPA was implemented as a stopgap to replace Wired Equivalent Privacy (WEP) because of its glaring deficiencies, which are detailed later in this chapter. The IEEE plays a vital role in security and data, as their standards are frequently the standards adopted by regional, national, and international standards bodies. The following section describes some of the technical definitions of the different 802.11 standard.

802.11a

This standard operates at 5 GHz and provides data rates between 1.5 Mbps and 54 Mbps. 802.11a was originally common for APs in both the corporate and residential settings, but this is no longer the case; this is because of its limited range and high level of attenuation when traveling through objects. 802.11a is also more expensive than many of the other standards that the IEEE has released, because its limited range made it necessary for more equipment to be bought.

802.11b

This standard uses an unregulated 2.4 GHz band with a throughput of 11 Mbps. Since this standard uses unregulated frequencies, there is the likelihood of interference in the normal consumer's home from appliances such as microwaves. 802.11b also offers a lower throughput than 802.11a but has a greater range, which gives it the ability to service a whole home with only one AP. This factor made 802.11b more popular than 802.11a in the residential setting.

802.11g

Created in 2003, this standard attempted to offer the best of both the 802.11a and 802.11b standards. 802.11g supports a bandwidth of 54 Mbps and utilizes the 2.4 GHz unregulated band. This made AP utilizing either the 802.11a or 802.11b obsolete in both the residential and industrial setting.

802.11n

Created in 2009, 802.11n has a speed of up to 600 Mbps. This standard operates in both the 2.4 GHz and 5 GHz bandwidths by using multiple input/output antennas. These two features made it so that 802.11n could provide greater range with less interference.

802.11ac

Created in 2013, 802.11ac offers a speed of 1.3 Gbps and operates on the 5 GHz bandwidth. This technology has just recently been implemented, but it is expected to be deployed in upward of 1 billion devices by 2015. It is also important to note that the 802.11ac standard also offers more channels than previous standards.

802.11af

This type of standard has not yet been implemented, but it is very interesting because it uses the TV white space spectrum. Its throughput is low, however, and it has a maximum throughput at 35 Mpbs. The added frequency bands that are available in the TV white space are a way to begin to increase the spectrum's capacity as it becomes more popular. In addition, the frequencies are below 1 GHz, thus it can offer a large amount of range compared with other standards.

802.11i

802.11i is an amendment that defines wireless security concerning WPA2. This is especially important to understand since this is what superseded WEP. The largest difference that separates WPA2 from WPA and WEP is its use of the advanced encryption standard (AES) block cipher. This amendment is also interesting because it is one of the few that does not deal specifically with a new form of signaling for a WLAN (Doherty, 2016).

Wire Lined to Wireless Transition

Since their commercialization, both telephones and computers have been hugely successful. This success came for computers in two ways. The first was the invention of the personal computer (PC), and the second was the implementation of wireless networks. In this section, we will focus on how wireless networks came to be part of computer technology.

When wireless technologies were created, networks were actually of very little use. This is because of the lack of existent and/or legal frequencies that could be used to carry a signal for a wireless network. This all changed after the FCC opened up several bands of radio spectrum for unlicensed use. The bands included 900 MHz, 2.4 GHz, and 5.8 GHz, which were originally reserved for appliances such as microwaves.

After these bands opened and wireless networks were made commercially available, users began to prefer a slower wireless connection to the regular wired connection. This convenience did not just affect consumers; businesses also bought into the trend of wireless network access. This brought about many different trends in the business world, such as bring your own device (BYOD), which is the idea that employees can bring their own devices into the workplace. This soon became a popular method for consumer products too. The demand for a more convenient connection to information made the industry of wireless technology explode, which had a large societal and economic impact.

WNIC

The wireless network interface card (WNIC) is a card used to connect a device to a WLAN. This WNIC device can also be employed for hacking wireless networks that use the WEP wireless security protocol. Every mobile device that has Wi-Fi capability comes equipped with a WNIC, but WNICs come in a huge range of different types because both their signal strength and protocol communication language have been continually changing.

WINCs do not necessarily have to be inside your device; they can be purchased and attached to the device through a simple USB port. It is the external WNICs that have proved to be problematic for wireless security networks. An external WNIC is not only a threat to information that moves over a wireless network, but it can also attack and access grounded sources that companies may think are protected and only accessible on site.

Corporate Background of Wireless Networks

As stated before, the simplicity of always being on the network is something that is lucrative in both a residential and industrial setting. A wireless environment in the workplace has the capacity to eliminate much of the aggravation that comes with being tied to a desk to be on a company's network. There are also many risks to a company becoming wireless. This was especially prevalent during the early days of wireless networks when WEP was the primary form of security. When wireless was first introduced into the corporate setting, there was also no way to control how far the signal of an AP would reach. Based on this information, many computer users were able to access company networks when they were in the parking lot or even down the street from the AP. In 2004, Red M. Ltd. did a survey of companies to see what the state of their wireless security was. Within this report, they stated that the wireless industry is doing everything imaginable to protect wireless networks. The weakness comes when end users fail to secure not just their wireless networks, but also their fixed networks. Every wireless notebook represents a clear and present danger to the security of your computer network.

According to a new survey from Red M, for which the company gathered statistics for six months on 100 companies, including large multinational corporations, 80% of corporate networks are accessible from outside their buildings. Within that 80%, 66% of banks, 69% of financial services institutions, 100% of educational institutions and 79% of information technology companies were broadcasting confidential and sensitive information. And 100% of the e-mail messages on insecure corporate networks could be intercepted, read, and manipulated.

Wireless corporate networks have become more insecure in recent years due to several factors:

1. Wireless technology itself has changed and has become much more secure due to developments such as the move from WEP to WPA.
2. Industries recognize the benefits of better protecting themselves when using wireless networks. Although there is a cost imposed by setting up wireless security, the benefits of wireless access outweigh the potential harm.

Wireless Network Security Methods

Networks can require different types and amounts of security, depending on the purpose of the specific network. There are hundreds of ways to secure a network, but networks typically follow one of three intrusion prevention concepts. The first scenario is ideal for smaller networks, such as homes or small businesses. This simple method is to configure restrictions in the APs. These restrictions may include the settings of media access control (MAC) address filtering and SSID broadcasting, potentially paired with a wireless intrusion prevention system (WIPS). Another security tactic is to have a completely open and unsecure network but total isolation. This is usually done by larger businesses or commercial hot spots. Security is achieved through an intranet portal, which then authorizes the user. This method is not as secure, as someone could easily bypass all the security if he or she was to gain an authorized user's credentials. It is also more prone to denial-of-service attacks. Finally, some parties use full end-to-end encryption, with additional authentication on private resources. This configuration can be more difficult but can give the best results.

CIA Triangle of Confidentiality, Integrity, and Availability

Before securing a network, one must first determine what good security will look like. Confidentiality, integrity, and availability are at the core of every secure network, according to the Central Intelligence Agency (CIA). When a user connects to a wireless network, these three components are the basic expectations that the user has regarding his or her privacy. Confidentiality refers to the information being transferred, stored, and processed. In a secure network, only the designated owner will ever be able to see the information (unless other permissions are explicitly given). Integrity is the expectation that data will not be modified. Lastly, availability is the expectation that users will be able to access the data at the time they want and the speed they want. Bandwidth or downtime should not be a major issue in a secure network.

There are a few other concepts that are important to be familiar with when discussing security. One term is *authorization*, which is checking to make sure that the users are allowed to do what they are trying to do. For example, when someone wants to edit a file, the system will make sure that the specific user has been given edit rights to that file (or is inheriting rights from someone else who does). Authorization can apply to users, processes, or programs.

Accountability is also an important factor in security. In order for a system to be accountable, it must be able to keep track of who is doing what on the system at any given time. Similarly, non-repudiation is the idea that users should not be able to deny performing an action that they performed (because of the accountability of the system).

When users want to gain access to a restricted system, the first step in the process is identification. This is when users ask to be authenticated, and the system verifies that they are who they say they are. For better security, multifactor authentication should be used.

There are three main authentication factors: something you know (such as a password or personal identification number [PIN]), something you have (such as a security key or smart card), and something you are (biometrics). For best results, at least two different factors should be used for multifactor authentication implementation. Since authentication is so important, the next two sections will outline a few new ways to securely authenticate.

Smart Cards

We are all familiar with the magnetic strip that occupies the back of our credit and debit cards. Although magnetic-strip technology is effective and pervasive in the United States, it does lack the stringent security reliability that is desired when it comes to access to payment card information. The security inadequacy of magnetic-strip technology is the reason it will become obsolete in the years to come, when it will almost certainly be replaced by smart cards. Outside the United States, there have been examples of switching to Europay, MasterCard, and Visa (EMV): smart-card technology that decreases fraud and card counterfeiting. In 1992, France introduced these cards and saw a 78% drop in card counterfeiting, accompanied by a 50% drop in total fraud losses.

Smart cards look like any other credit or debit card but are equipped with either a microcontroller or a memory chip that can connect to a smart-card reader to transmit payment information. The microcontroller chip has its own processing power, which allows it to carry out its own encryption protocols and mutual authentication features that allow it to prove its identity to the smart-card reader. The microcontroller is essentially its own computer with the ability to store much more data. A memory chip merely has the ability to store the payment information with a small level of security. They are less expensive than microcontroller chips, but they depend on the smart-card reader's processing power and encryption to protect the data.

The cards can also be broken down into contact and contactless cards. Contactless cards communicate with the card reader via radio frequencies at a very short distance, between one to three inches. Contact cards must have direct connection to the smart-card reader via a conductive plate on the card. In addition to its obvious implications in the payment card industry, smart cards are also used in employee ID badges, driver's licenses, passports, and portable medical records cards.

Security Tokens and Software Tokens

Security or authentication tokens are a hardware solution that can help to mitigate the risk of data breaches. A security token could be in the form of a smart card, key fob, or USB drive. Security tokens allow for two-factor authentication, in which the network recognizes the object as an authorized hardware, and then the network will also require the user to have a PIN.

A software token is software that can be installed on an authorized device such as a laptop, PC, or smartphone. While software tokens are cheaper and do not require the user to carry a physical item, they are somewhat more susceptible to attacks and data breaches. Because a security token is a physical item, the user is more likely to notice that it has been stolen or has gone missing. This is not always the case with a software token. If the software is duplicated and installed on another device, it is possible that it could happen without the authorized user being made aware of it.

Wireless Security History, Standards, and Developments

Ever since the mid-1990s, wireless technologies have been rapidly deployed. As a result, the issue of wireless security needed to be addressed. The first encryption standard, wired rquivalent privacy (WEP), was developed in the late 1990s, and was a basic and flawed protocol. Its limitations required serious improvements for the wireless networks to be considered secure. Since then, two main protocols have surfaced: Wi-Fi Protected Access (WPA) and WPA2. WPA2 is synonymous with 802.11i, which is the standard recommended for use today (Figure 19.2).

Wired Equivalent Privacy

WEP was developed in 1997 as part of the original 802.11 standard. The goal of WEP was to provide security on the same level as wired networks through the use of CRC-32 checksum and RC4. CRC-32 is an integrity tool used to detect changes in data. RC4 is a cryptography method that was exploited in 2001 by attackers listening on the network to intercept the keys used. The keys used in wireless security are referred to as preshared keys, or PSKs. PSKs are shared by both the client and the AP and are used for authentication.

Protocol	Encryption	Authentication	Key management
WEP	RC4 with 40 bit key/28 bit hash	Pre-shared keys	Manual key rotation; no key management
	Static keys also	Open system (SSID)	
WPA	TKIP with 128 bit key (over RCA) Constant key rotation	802.1X with EAP and radius	Per packet key rotation
802.11i	TKIP with 128 bit key (over RCA)	802.1X with EAP and radius	Per packet key rotation (TKIP)
	AES-CCMP Constant key rotation	Preshared keys	Per session key rotation

Figure 19.2   Wireless security protocol comparisons.

In 2004, enough vulnerabilities were discovered that WEP was officially condemned. In 2005, the U.S. Federal Bureau of Investigation (FBI) was able to easily penetrate a WEP-secured network in fewer than 3 minutes. In 2007, after a massive hack against T.J.Maxx, it was discovered that major business were still using the notoriously weak and outdated WEP standard.

Wi-Fi Protected Access

WPA was created as a quick link-layer security fix after the vulnerabilities were discovered in WEP. It was not an infallible solution but rather an interim solution to be used while the more complete WPA2 was being developed.

Temporal Key Integrity Protocol (TKIP)

Encryption was implemented through the use of a preshared key technology, TKIP. TKIP is based on RC4, and each packet generates a different 128-bit key (unlike WEP technology, which had a shorter key and was static for each AP). This combats integrity attacks, since every packet has its own unique key. In addition, packets must be in the correct order to be accepted by the AP. Finally, TKIP uses an additional 64-bit message integrity check (MIC), named Michael, which is an improvement on WEP's CRC-32 checksum method. Michael's goal was to prevent attackers from changing packet data (Greenfield, 2003). Unfortunately, hackers were still able to find ways to alter packets. Since TKIP is based on older WEP technologies, it has since been identified as insecure and thereafter disapproved.

Extensible Authentication Protocol (EAP)

EAP is a user authentication framework first introduced in WPA security. Unlike WEP, which only authenticates using MAC addresses, EAP uses various authentication methods to verify a user's identity. Some examples of EAP technologies include token cards, public-key encryption, and one-time passwords. When a user tries to connect to a network, the AP will confirm the user's identity with an authentication server, such as RADIUS. RADIUS stands for remote authentication dial-in user service, and it is used by Internet service providers (ISPs) to verify usernames and passwords.

Lightweight Extensible Authentication Protocol (LEAP)

There are a few different methods of implementing EAP. LEAP is a proprietary method developed by Cisco Systems. It is based on MS-CHAP, which is a Microsoft authentication protocol that has since been deemed unsecure. The LEAP method is popular but rather weak. Cisco recommends that any user who must use LEAP should be sure to have a complex password. Since LEAP works only on a Cisco-based networking gear, it lacks compatibility with non-Cisco products.

Protected Extensible Authentication Protocol (PEAP)

PEAP is a form of encapsulation that exists within EAP. Encapsulation is the way in which communication is constructed to be sent between two units. In this case specifically, PEAP both encapsulates and encrypts a security access transmission so that it cannot be easily intercepted and decoded. PEAP was created by Microsoft, Cisco Systems, and RSA Security.

Wireless Transport Layer Security (WTLS)

WTLS was the security level for the Wireless Application Protocol (WAP) version 1.1. WTLS provided privacy, data integrity, and authentication of WAP devices. WTLS ensured that the connection between the device and the server remains secure and encrypts the transmission of data. WTLS was largely based on TLS but is adapted for mobile devices. TLS and WTLS are both initialized in the application layer (Layer 5) in the OSI Model and operate in the presentation layer (Layer 6).

WTLS mainly relied on the compression of packet size and on web-content developers creating separate WAP web pages that have less content and will work in WAP format. Today, WAP 2.0 browsers are able to support HTML formats. The improvement in the processing power of devices and in wireless/cellular network throughput capabilities has enabled more powerful mobile devices to display web pages in their original format without needing to use WAP.

With the release of WAP 2.0 in 2002, WTLS was replaced by TLS. Instead of decrypting the data from WTLS and then reencrypting it using secure sockets layer (SSL), servers are able to accept the TLS transmission directly and no longer need to go through the extra step of changing between encryption types.

Wi-Fi Protected Setup (WPS)

One major flaw in WPA was the creation of WPS. WPS enabled less experienced computer users to secure their network using WPA. To add new devices to the network, users could use an eight-digit PIN method. Unfortunately, these PINs could easily be cracked using brute-force attacks, thus making WPS extremely unsecure. To avoid this vulnerability, WPS should be disabled.

WPA2

WPA2 was implemented in 2004 and was based on the newly developed 802.11i standard. The terms *802.11i* and *WPA2* are commonly interchangeable. WPA2 comes in two main types: personal or enterprise. Personal use involves PSKs and does not require an authentication server. Enterprise scenarios use EAP and involve the client (supplicant), AP (authenticator), and authentication server.

802.11i also defines a robust secure network (RSN), which introduces and implements security primarily through a four-way handshake and group-key handshake. The RSN ensures that the network communication and data transfer are secure through authentication and keys. If a device has been authenticated before, then it joins a robust security network association (RSNA). One downside to WPA2 is that some older hardware may not be compatible with the new protocol or might require a firmware upgrade. Testing and certification from the Wi-Fi Alliance ensure that a network is WPA2 secure and must be done in order for a device to have a Wi-Fi trademark on it. With WPA2, various keys are used to encrypt the traffic as shown in Figure 19.3.

It begins with the pairwise master key (PMK), which is derived from the master session key (MSK). Both the client and AP know the PMK, and the goal is to change this into encrypted temporal keys. The PMK initiates the four-way handshake and then produces the unicast pairwise transient key (PTK) or multicast group temporal key (GTK). The four-way handshake is a method used to establish secure connections in four steps. It enables the AP and client to prove that they know the keys without ever actually stating them.

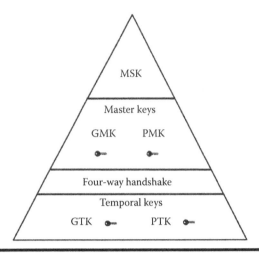

Figure 19.3   WPA2 encryption keys used to encrypt traffic.

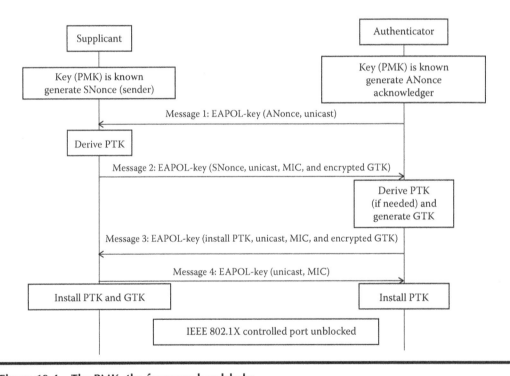

Figure 19.4   The PMK, the four-way handshake.

The WPA2 process begins with the AP and client choosing security methods that they both support. This includes the type of authentication method (e.g., 802.1X—also known as EAPOL [Extensible Authentication Protocol over LAN] or PSK) and the security protocols (e.g., CCMP and TKIP). The variation here depends on the usage (personal or enterprise). Next, the AP requests the client's identity and, after successful authentication, a PMK is created. After both devices know the PMK, the four-way handshake begins (Figure 19.4).

The AP sends the first message to the client, called ANonce. This is a randomly generated authenticated number that is used only once. The client then generates a PTK (set of encryption keys) from this. Next, the client sends a SNonce (a supplicant/client number that is used only once) protected by a MIC, and then the AP sends back the MIC-protected PTK and GTK (for unicast and multicast traffic) that it has calculated. Finally, the client sends a confirmation message to the AP to confirm that it's ready for encrypted communication. The pairwise and group transient (temporary) keys are used by the CCMP protocol to confirm integrity and confidentiality. If the GTK needs renewing, a similar group key handshake occurs.

The most notable part of WPA2 security is the mandatory requirement for using the AES-CCMP algorithm. This stands for advanced encryption standard, counter mode cipher block chaining message authentication code protocol. This strong encryption protocol confirms message integrity and confidentiality. CCMP is based on AES and is an improvement on TKIP. WPA2 no longer uses TKIP but has a setting that can make it compatible with older TKIP devices. This is good for compatibility reasons but still risks making a network unsecure, since TKIP is disapproved (Hoffman, 2014). WPA2 uses similar EAP authentication methods as discussed in the WPA section.

WPA2 is more secure and advanced than the earlier wireless security protocols. It eliminates worries about man-in-the-middle (MitM) attacks and packet and authentication forging. PMK caching allows the client to easily reconnect to the AP without having to reauthenticate. It also allows a user to begin making his or her next connection while still connected to the first AP. WPA2 supports all of the older WPA features but adds stronger encryption and authentication with less overhead.

Like most technologies, WPA2 is not perfect. Physical layer attacks are still an issue, and Layer 2 session hijacking is a concern as well. While attackers may not be able to read the data in packets, they can analyze the unencrypted control and management frames to gain valuable information. WPA2 is also vulnerable to DoS attacks and MAC address spoofing (Arana, 2006). The most significant vulnerability with WPA2 is called Hole196. This vulnerability allows an insider who knows the GTK to insert and send false GTK packets to unknowing users. Then, the attacker can decrypt other users' data, find holes in their Wi-Fi, and put their entire devices in jeopardy.

Other Security Considerations

Aside from the widespread protocols, some basic techniques to secure a wireless network include modifying the default SSID configuration and MAC address filtering. To secure a wireless network, the SSID should not be broadcasted. This way, the user has to know the name in order to try to connect. The default SSID should also be changed to prevent any hackers from guessing the name. MAC address filtering involves configuring the AP to only permit certain approved devices based on their MAC addresses. This is not foolproof, however, because an attacker may be able to discover an approved MAC address and then spoof (or pretend to be) that address.

Other techniques that are not specific to wireless but can still be implemented on wireless networks are virtual private networks (VPNs), firewalls, physical security, and wireless intrusion detection and prevention systems (WIDPS). VPNs allow an organization to have its private network on a public network. This means that even though traffic is being sent over the public network, it's acting as if it were the company's private network, with its own security and so on. This is done through virtual connections with tunneling and encryption.

Firewalls are designed to look at all incoming and outgoing traffic and determine what traffic is safe and what is not, based on its configurations. The two main types of firewalls are host firewalls and network firewalls. Host firewalls are implemented on the edge of a single device, while network firewalls are placed on the network, monitoring traffic going across. Routers can implement firewalls, and firewalls can be used in conjunction with VPNs.

Physical security is a basic consideration that is crucial. If a wireless device is not secure, then the wireless network is not secure. First and foremost, every device should be out of reach, if not locked up. Security cameras should be placed on important devices to monitor any suspicious activity. Geographical location should also be considered, since natural disasters may be a threat to networking equipment. There are many ways to physically secure wireless network equipment, but it's important that there's at least some physical protection.

Finally, a WIDPS should be implemented to monitor traffic on networks and alert the administrator of any suspicious activity. There are different types of intrusion prevention and detection systems, but a WIDPS is specific to wireless. These systems are able to look at traffic and protocols to determine if the traffic is legitimate or not. If it detects unusual traffic, it can be configured to try to stop the traffic. If nothing else, it at least keeps logs of the traffic's activity. Some jobs that the system is capable of include resetting connections, blocking certain traffic, or dropping packets.

Threats of Wireless Networks

Not following the accepted wireless security protocols discussed in the previous section can make WLAN infrastructures vulnerable to attack. Due to wireless networks utilizing radio frequencies (RF) as the medium for transmitting information, there are many threats to both secured and unsecured WLANs (Waliullah, Moniruzzaman, and Raham, 2015). It is no surprise that wireless networks have become as popular as they are today because of the mobility of connected devices, their low cost, and the fact that they involve less hardware; however, with the popularity level of wireless networks in corporate and personal environments, there is an ever-growing challenge of network threats due to the nature of the infrastructure. Wireless security grows just as much as the technology itself. Even with the standards of securing WLANs through WPA2 as referenced in the previous section, attacks will be an inherent problem in our society. This section of the chapter will touch specifically on the risks of a weak network that does not have security safeguards in place and the types of common attacks that are present today with WLANs.

When searching for networks to hack, attackers will commonly search for the networks that have not secured their 802.11 WLAN with WPA2 or the other security protocols that have been discussed previously. Their hope is to discover the exact network information in which those very security protocols are used to encrypt and protect. The common goal of an attacker is to associate with the wireless access point, which can allow for the launch of several different attacks. SSIDs, MAC addresses, default configurations, the network encryption protocol used, and weaknesses in physical security are all common categories of information that attackers will look to obtain or discover.

There are a variety of attacking methods used to obtain private network information that will allow attackers to gain access to a WLAN. Typically, these attacks can be placed into five categories: confidentiality, access control, integrity, availability, and authentication. These five categories help to split up the types of attacks, but there will be overlap between categories due to the combination of attacks, depending on what type of information is to be obtained. This section will unravel some of the biggest vulnerabilities to a wireless network and the most common types of attacks that can threaten the WLAN.

Confidentiality Attacks

The goal of a confidentiality attack is to gain access to private information that is being passed through the WLAN by using either passive attacks or active attacks. Once hackers are able to gain access to this sensitive information, the attack only worsens.

In order to intercept the sensitive data that is being sent across the wireless network, common passive attack methods are used. A passive attack is very difficult to detect because of its non-intrusive nature. The attackers utilizing passive attacks simply observe the transmitted data over a period of time without making any alteration to the data. Eavesdropping and traffic analysis are common types of passive attacks in which hackers will utilize various "sniffing" tools to intercept information from weak or unsecured networks (Chakravarty, 2014). This is a significant issue seen today with public wireless networks or hot spots, where attackers within range of the RF signal can pick up on transmissions across the unsecured networks from just outside the building.

Differing from passive attacks, active attacks are a type of attack whereby hackers will actually take the intercepted data, manipulate it in some fashion, and embed it into a network or communication stream. Two very common active attacks on a WLAN today are the MitM and the evil twin AP. Both of these attacks are usually based on the setup of a rogue AP in which an unauthorized AP is established to a network that typically shares the same SSID information and configurations as the legitimate AP of a wireless network. This has become a challenge in the corporate setting as rogue APs aren't always set up with malicious intent.

Employees will often configure a rogue AP connected to the enterprise network because they are receiving weak signals from their desk location in comparison to the company's legitimate APs. The evil twin AP is just a name used for a rogue AP that has malicious intent. The attacker will attempt to get an STA, any device connected to a network, to associate with the rogue AP. Once this happens, the attacker may be able to obtain sensitive credentials or information from the communications between the STA and rogue AP. Due to the difficulty of being able to discriminate between the evil twin AP and a company's legitimate AP, the end user or STA is vulnerable to associate with the fake AP. Most companies now frequently monitor and audit any setup of rogue APs on their network because of the inability to discern that the configuration's intent is different.

As previously stated, if an attacker is able to successfully set up a rogue AP on a wireless network they can perform a MitM attack. This is an active attack in which hackers will actually place themselves, as a fake AP, between two communicating nodes and wait for sensitive information to be transmitted, allowing them to intercept the message. In doing so, the attacker usually goes unnoticed and the communicating devices think they are still talking to each other.

Access Control Attacks

Access control attacks are used to gain unauthorized access to a wireless network by a series of attempts to get through the filters and firewalls of the network. As previously stated, some of the attacks will overlap between the five categories, and access control attacks show this overlap. Due to the nature of attacks requiring access into the AP, the evil twin AP setup could very well be placed into the access control category as well as confidentiality. With that being said, for the

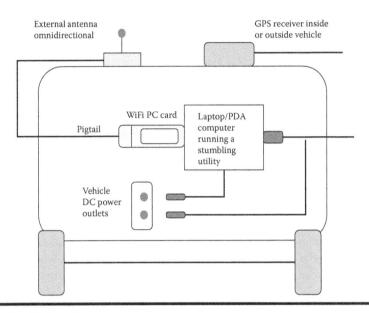

External antenna omnidirectional

GPS receiver inside or outside vehicle

WiFi PC card

Laptop/PDA computer running a stumbling utility

Pigtail

Vehicle DC power outlets

Figure 19.5   Wardriving kit.

sake of this discussion, if attackers are looking to obtain confidential information once they have gained unauthorized access to the network, we will consider that a confidentiality attack.

One of the most common types of access control attacks is wardriving. This type of attack involves the attempt to access unsecured or poorly secured networks by driving around in a vehicle sniffing out networks. Wardrivers will typically map out an area, often by utilizing a global positioning system (GPS), in order to sniff out the APs from that particular area. Following the completion of mapping the area, they can then go through the route and identify the vulnerabilities or weaknesses of each network. The vehicle will typically be equipped with a laptop that has software installed, often free software, that allows the attackers to listen for the wireless network's broadcasts and then capture that data on their device. NetStumbler, Kismet, and Kismac are a few of the software tools available today that are used in wardriving. It is important to note that wardriving or sniffing out wireless APs is not a crime, but when the actual theft of information or unauthorized access onto a WLAN occurs, this practice becomes a criminal one. Figure 19.5 shows a typical wardriving kit that can be found in any vehicle performing this attack.

Another access control attack is MAC spoofing. This particular attack allows an attacker to use previously mentioned sniffing tools to find and access the network. The goal is to search for the MAC addresses of the network that are communicated out from the AP and to "spoof" them. If the attacker can successfully spoof the MAC address, they will attempt to have packets routed to their device rather than the actual network host (Mandal and Saini, 2015,). Similar to the other discussions regarding this topic, this attack can be avoided by using effective port security methods. Figure 19.6 depicts how MAC address spoofing is carried out.

The two access control attacks that have been discussed to this point can also be referred to as unauthorized access attacks. This attack is seen as sort of an umbrella to the others within the category because they technically all involve gaining unauthorized access to a WLAN prior to carrying out the attacks. The attack is as simple as the name implies. It is an attack whereby an individual gains access to a network without the proper authentication.

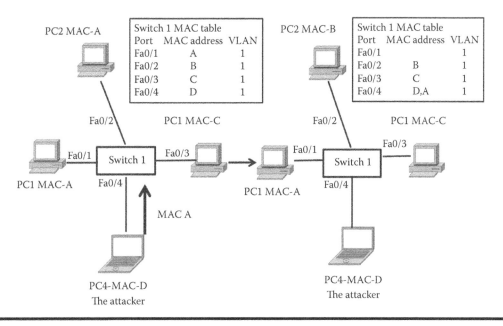

Figure 19.6   MAC address spoofing example.

Conclusion

Wireless technologies have exploded in popularity in the past couple of decades. Since so much of our data is now online and can be transferred wirelessly, it's crucial that the security is impenetrable. The CIA triad outlines expectations for security: confidentiality, integrity, and availability. These things are becoming increasingly harder to achieve but increasingly important for wireless networks to protect. As of now, the best way to protect a network is through a combination of the different efforts outlined here, the most important being WPA2 implementation.

The attacks discussed and case studies presented illustrate why wireless security must be strongly and correctly implemented—a single, minor configuration error can expose an enormous vulnerability. This is why risk assessment is so important. Frequent penetration testing and constant monitoring are simple steps that an organization can take to make sure their security is up to par. No matter how secure a network is, someone will always be on the other end trying to infiltrate it. It's up to everyone in an organization to keep a network secure; after all, a chain is no stronger than its weakest link.

QUESTIONS

1. What are the components of a WLAN?
2. What is the core of every secure network?
3. What are smart cards and why are they changing?
4. Explain the disadvantage of the WEP wireless security protocol.
5. What is the Temporal Key Integrity Protocol process?

Chapter 20

The Stuxnet Worm and the Vulnerability of the U.S. Electric Power Grid

In the realm of information security, there are always new predators who present ever-more-advanced threats to the operation and control of our infrastructure. These types of attacks are stealthy and may employ both simple infection techniques and advanced approaches to malware to be spread after an initial infection has occurred. There are a variety of motives behind these advanced threats, which include political, national, and individual reasons. One of the most sophisticated of these advanced persistent threats emerged in the form of a worm identified as the Stuxnet worm. And Stuxnet is not alone. There are also a number of other infamous destructive threats, among which are Ghostnet, Aurora, and Night Dragon.

The Stuxnet worm presents an infection that is quite simple in its means of initial infection, which occurs when a personal flash drive carrying the Stuxnet worm is inserted into a target personal computer or process controller, containing a sophisticated spread mechanism. For example, a systems technician from the target site would have his personal computer infected by standard means. The technician then passes that infection to a flash drive, which he carries to work and inserts into one of the computers connected to the business corporate network of the target enterprise. The ultimate target of the worm is the system control and data acquisition (SCADA) network, which is isolated from the business corporate network. However, the technician also carries the flash drive across to the SCADA network, which then moves across that network to the various controllers and data acquisition processors, infects them, and begins the programmed mischief.

The Stuxnet worm was first discovered in June 2010. The worm was originally designed to attack Siemens-produced programmable logic controllers (PLCs) and data acquisition processors that control electromagnetic processes for industrial control systems (ICSs). Stuxnet was a Windows-based worm and was designed to operate as a digital weapon. The worm is estimated to have destroyed up to 1000 Iranian centrifuges (10%) sometime between November 2009 and late January 2010. It affected thousands of computers in Iran, specifically targeting Iran's nuclear centrifuges. Different variants of Stuxnet targeted five Iranian organizations, with the probable target widely suspected to be Iran's uranium enrichment infrastructure. While the origin of the attack remains unacknowledged, most believe that it was created and deployed through a joint effort by teams from the United States and Israel.

The worm operates by exploiting four zero-day flaws in the Windows operating system. A zero-day flaw is a security vulnerability wherein the vendor of the software is unaware of its existence, and its exploitation may result in potentially disastrous effects. Hackers take full advantage of this vulnerability before the vendor even becomes aware of the flaws and can install a patch or version update. For Stuxnet, there are four exploitable vulnerabilities, which include (1) exposure to the use of personal USB flash drives by system technicians, (2) three network techniques employed in the system, (3) the use of common Siemens Step 7 project files, and (4) Siemens' WinCC command and control (C&C) database and connections. SIMATIC WinCC is a (SCADA and human–machine interface (HMI) system from Siemens. SCADA systems are used to monitor and control physical processes involved in industry and infrastructure on a large scale and over long distances. One aspect of this worm proved most dangerous. Although it was specifically targeted at Siemens PLCs deployed in Iran, it quickly spread to the business systems network. From there, it emanated through the Internet to countries around the world, infecting not only Siemens' PLCs but also many computer systems employed outside Iran.

The worm was initially introduced to the target network via the insertion by a system technician of a Stuxnet-infected USB flash drive. The technician inserted the drive carrying the worm into the target business operations network of the target, which was physically separated from (and not network-connected to) the SCADA centrifuge control systems. However, that technician later carried the infected flash USB drive across to the SCADA system as well, as he performed his normal work activities. After the insertion of the flash USB, the worm self-installed, propagating across the SCADA network and scanning for specific Siemens Step7 software on computers that communicate with and control the PLCs of the target technology of the victim (the centrifuges in Iran's nuclear materials manufacturing facilities). If any of the infected computers are not connected to a PLC, the malware will lay dormant until such a connection becomes available. When it does reach these specific computers, the worms install a rootkit to make the virus undetectable by most virus scanners. Not only was the worm undetectable by virus scanners but it also silently updated and redistributed itself. When the worm was active, it would monitor the PLCs and gather information about them. After collecting data about the centrifuges, Stuxnet would then take them over. And once the PLCs were taken over, the Stuxnet virus would cause the devices to overwork themselves (spinning out of control) into failure (in effect, producing another version of a denial-of-service attack by means of a worm infection). Furthermore, Stuxnet would provide false feedback about the failure of the controllers until it was too late for human intervention to fix them. It is this level of sophistication that leads many to believe that it could have only been done by U.S. and Israeli software experts. The fact that there were so many variables involved with this level of attack implies that a new, advanced level of attack has now become the norm. As of 2010, the Stuxnet virus has affected many computers globally. Table 20.1 shows the distribution of all the estimated number of computers that the worm has compromised.

Clearly, the Stuxnet worm embodies the next generation of information security threats. The sophistication and targeting of this worm is absolutely unprecedented in the world of information technology. While this attack may be one of a kind in the present world, it is a glimpse of what may be to come in the future of information security attacks. Among the children of Stuxnet are the Duqu worm and one created by the Equation Group.

Table 20.1 Estimated Percentage of Computers the Stuxnet Worm Has Affected Globally

Country	Infected Computers (%)
Iran	58.85
Indonesia	18.22
India	8.31
Azerbaijan	2.57
United States	1.56
Pakistan	1.28
Others	9.2

More Details of the Stuxnet Worm Used for Cyber Warfare

The Stuxnet virus was a significant attack from a political, economic, computer science, and cyber-warfare perspective. The virus is a Windows-based worm that used a then-unprecedented zero-day exploit. The specific purpose of the worm was to ruin centrifuges that were electronically controlled by an ICS. The target was an Iranian government–owned nuclear facility. What was most interesting about this act of cyber warfare is that it is believed to have originated from sources based in the United States.

Attack Process

As an ICS virus, Stuxnet was designed to target the specific controllers in use at that facility. The controllers were designed, built, and installed by the industry-leading supplier of such technology, Siemens of Germany. The worm, once installed, modifies the code on the PLCs, the industry versions of what many enthusiasts are currently employing.

An Arduino and a raspberry programmable logic unit are similar in nature, with input/output (I/O) pins capable of carrying out the industrial control functions of motors and other devices. The Stuxnet virus attacked three separate components: the Windows OS, the Siemens PLC software, and the PLC board itself. The nuclear facility had a network that was separated from the business network and from the public Internet. It was isolated and considered "localed down." The design of the infection mechanism anticipated that technicians would bring information back and forth by means of portable USB flash drives (including those provided by Siemens) loaded with software, technical specifications, and instruction manuals. The designers anticipated that if the worm was installed in the USB drives at Siemens or on a technician's personal computer—or especially on a computer in the more vulnerable business network of the enterprise—eventually, a technician would bring the infected USB drive across to the isolated SCADA management and control network. The process depended on an understanding of how technicians currently operate and perform their tasks. If one loads the worm onto a USB drive and the potential victim technician plugs it into an operational machine, it can spread within that closed but networked environment. Later, the worm can once again infect another inserted USB drive and be transported to the business network, where it can spread through the Internet. The worm quickly began to propagate internationally onto home and non-target industry business machines as well as other SCADA controllers. However, the worm very likely began its journey at the Siemens factory, where it was transferred to a flash drive and then transported around that factory either through the factory network or by a factory employee using a USB drive, where it could propagate and seek appropriate means to be transported to the target enterprise's location and networks.

Both PLCs are conceptually similar to the Siemens logic board attacked by the Stuxnet virus. These boards use I/O pins that open up digital control functionality of analog technologies such as sensors and actuators. The nuclear facility had a local area network (LAN) that was locked down, so the attack vector was able to propagate the worm through USB flash memory drives. The attack goal was for an infected flash memory drive to make its way inside the facility to plug into a computer on the LAN to spread to centrifuge controlling machine(s). The worm itself was quite effective at spreading undetected, and it propagated internationally into home and non-target industry business machines. Eventually, the worm spread to a flash drive of a facility employee where it could propagate through the close LAN and infect the desired target machine(s). Once a machine within the LAN is infected, Figure 20.1 outlines the architecture that the Stuxnet worm is capable of navigating through and around.

USB flash memory was used as a secondary "Sneakernet" into private LANs such as the Iranian SCADA system. Once it reached a machine connected to the vulnerable Siemens hardware and software, it performed the following operations:

1. A kernel rootkit is installed on Windows to spoof digitally signed drivers
2. Stuxnet inserts itself into "Step 7" Controller Software by Siemens
3. A PLC rootkit inserts code to hide its presence in the Siemens PLC

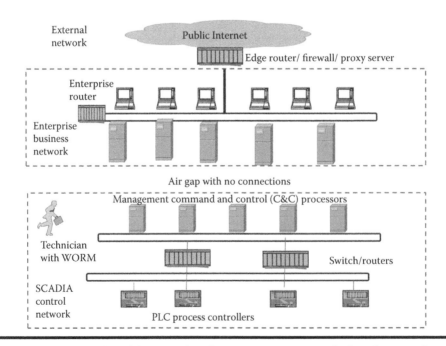

Figure 20.1   The network architecture that the Stuxnet worm was designed to travel around.

Table 20.2   Four Steps in the Stuxnet Attack Procedure

Step 1	"The core of Stuxnet was a large .DLL file that deposited onto machines. This came packaged with dozens of smaller .DLLs and components inside of it, all wrapped together in layers of encryption that had to be cracked and removed before they could decipher the code."
Step 2	Stuxnet worm would "first check if 32 or 64 bit, only 32 bit was fully vulnerable."
Step 3	"If Stuxnet decided to proceed, the second driver then got activated. This one had two tasks—the first was to infect any USB flash drive that got inserted into the machine, which it would do for only twenty-one days after Stuxnet infected the machine. The second, and most important, task was to decrypt and load the large .DLL, and its various components, into the machine's memory."
Step 4	"Once the large .DLL and its contents were all unpacked and loaded into memory, Stuxnet searched for new machines to infect and called home to the C&C servers to report its new conquest—but unless it found the Siemens Step 7 or WinCC software installed on the machine, Stuxnet would go dormant on the machine once these steps were done."

This layer-based attack embedded the malicious code deep within the operational layers of the Iranian nuclear facility, granting significant control and reporting its capabilities. Table 20.2 describes its attack procedure in greater depth but does not dive into the logic programming that took place. The computational science behind Stuxnet is addressed under the section "Stuxnet Deconstructed."

Worms operate with a form of artificial intelligence (AI) or simple decision-making logic on how it might best be able to replicate and continue its survival and infection goals. The AI that was built into Stuxnet, after performing the prioritized activities listed in Table 20.2, would perform the secondary goal of replication. Stuxnet searched out channels whose details hardcoded into it, and its success depended on detecting one of the vulnerable avenues it was coded to look for.

The malicious hacker knows that the paths to success are often defended against, making success dependent on the art and creativity of detecting new attack vectors that are not anticipated and thus the most difficult to detect and defend against. The seven Stuxnet paths listed next were obtained from two information security researchers, Paul Mueller and Babak Yadegari at the University of Arizona.

Path 1: Via WinCC

Stuxnet searches for computers running Siemens' WinCC as an interface to their SCADA systems. It connects using a password hardcoded into WinCC, and attacks its database using SQL commands to upload and start a copy of itself on the WinCC computer.

Path 2: Via Network Shares

Stuxnet can use Windows shared folders to propagate itself over a local network. It places a dropper file on any shares on remote computers, and schedules a task to execute it. ESET says the task is scheduled to run the next day, whereas Symantec claims it is scheduled for two minutes after the file is shared.

Path 3: Via the MS10-061 Print Spooler 0-Day Vulnerability

Stuxnet copies itself, places the copy on remote computers via this vulnerability, and then executes the copy, thereby infecting the remote machines. In brief, Stuxnet 'prints' itself to two files in the %system% directory on each target machine, using the 0-day privilege escalation. It then executes the dropper file to infect the computer.

Path 4: Via the MS08-067 SMB Vulnerability

If a remote computer has this vulnerability, Stuxnet can send a malformed path over SMB (a protocol for sharing files and other resources between computers); this allows it to execute arbitrary code on the remote machine, thereby propagating itself to it.

Path 5: Via Step7 Projects

Stuxnet will infect Siemens SIMATIC Step7 industrial control projects that are opened on an infected computer. It does this by modifying DLLs (Windows Dynamic Link Library; a library of shared objects: code, data, and resources) and an .exe file in the WinCC Simatic manager, so that they execute Stuxnet code as well. The additional code will insert Stuxnet into Step7 project directories.

Stuxnet Damage

While reports and estimates existed for the damage and effectiveness of the Stuxnet worm, official public recognition of the cyber attack did not take place until November 29, 2010. The president of Iran, Mahmoud Ahmadinejad, announced in a public statement regarding the cyber attacks' damage that "They succeeded in creating problems for a limited number of our centrifuges with the software they had installed in electronic parts."

Although a reliable primary source from the International Atomic Energy Association (IAEA) said that estimates of damaged centrifuges were around 1000–2000 units, the damaged centrifuges did not stop, but the attack did significantly slow the progress of the Iranian nuclear program. However, a secondary, hangover-like effect exists with worms that autonomously propagate and infect. In order to prevent a worm from continuously infecting new machines, updated definitions must be downloaded to the operating systems. Businesses and personal users are slow to update their computing equipment, leading to the same challenge that an unvaccinated individual would encounter when matched with a contagious viral infection. Although Iran was the specific target of the attack, worms do not recognize geographic boundaries of countries that openly participate in the Internet Corporation for Assigned Names and Numbers (ICANN) and domain name servers addressing shared through the Internet Assigned Numbers Authority (IANA). The list of countries infected by the spreading Stuxnet worm (including the United States) were

- Iran
- Indonesia
- India
- Pakistan
- Uzbekistan
- Russia

- Kazakhstan
- Belarus
- Kyrgyzstan
- Azerbaijan
- United States
- Cuba
- Tajikistan
- Afghanistan

A recent article by Michael Kenny, "Cyber-Terrorism in a Post-Stuxnet World" explains the lasting damage of cyber warfare on a global scale. Once a worm is introduced into the digital landscape, it acts as a model from which derivatives of similar code can develop. Politically, a damaging aspect of Stuxnet was the revealing information of a U.S.-sponsored or "state"-sponsored cyber-espionage project. Prior to this, involvement of the United States in cyber espionage was not recognized, and citizens heavily patronized the efforts of state-sponsored hacking.

Stuxnet marked a watershed in cyber warfare, not only demonstrating the United States' willingness to engage in offensive cyber attacks against its most intransigent adversaries, but also revealing a level of physical destruction with computer code that was previously reserved for kinetic bombings and physical sabotage.

Cyber Terrorism after Stuxnet

Once malicious code is used in an attack, the shrapnel of code it leaves behind is quickly dissected, analyzed, and repurposed by both malicious individuals and white-hat defenders. Unlike smart bombs that have millions of dollars of technology invested in them yet are rendered inaccessible upon detonation, intangible code lives on throughout systems. Once the Stuxnet virus was intercepted, new variations using the same mechanism emerged. Worms, viruses, and malicious code can often come back to haunt their own creators. From an economic standpoint, the lawlessness of the dark web will repackage and sell malicious exploits to the highest bidder(s) multiple times over.

The Stuxnet virus was innovative in its targeting of ICSs. But due to the release of a blueprint of this type to the world, new vectors of attack have become a reality. Much of the U.S. infrastructure is managed by means of industrial control systems such as the SCADA system provided by the Siemens Corporation. SCADA-controlled and managed smart grid technology has been implemented across the United States to manage electricity delivery where needed in a cost-effective fashion.

In December 2007, Congress passed, and the president approved, Title XIII of the Energy Independence and Security Act of 2007 (EISA). EISA provided the legislative support for the Department of Energy (DOE)'s smart grid activities and reinforced its role in leading and coordinating national grid modernization efforts.

Stuxnet Attack Summary

The Stuxnet worm provided distinct lessons and mitigation techniques in the information security arena. Often, drastic security problems must be experienced to provoke others to implement the necessary measures to prevent such attacks. One such lesson is that even "air gapped" systems with heavy physical security can be breached when user behavior has not been secured.

Clearly, people are the weak link in security. It can be easier to trick people than to hack into computing systems by force. Social engineers exploit people's natural tendency to trust and be helpful. These malicious social engineers also take advantage of our tendency to respond when faced with a crisis, acting quickly, sometimes to our own detriment.

Since this attack, a greater emphasis on the dangers of flash drives has been ever present in the computing environment. Many companies now operate with the assumption that they have already been breached and have not yet discovered what is leaking out. Monitoring three critical areas can assist with understanding when malicious activity is occurring inside a company:

1. *Authentication*: A mechanism, analogous to the use of passwords on time-sharing systems, for the secure authentication of the identity of network clients by servers and vice versa, without presuming the operating system integrity of either (e.g., Kerberos).
2. *Authorization*: A process ensuring that correctly authenticated users can access only those resources for which the owner has given them approval
3. *Accounting*: Provides the methodology for collecting information about the end user's resource consumption, which can then be processed for billing, auditing, and capacity-planning purposes

Response and Industrial Control Security

With this framework in place, companies have at least a base protection and monitoring level. To provide ample defense, it is recommended that public entities such as governments and private entities create partnerships. These partnerships provide opportunities to share strategic security information about their breaches and mitigation techniques to provide better defenses for all. These threats will only increase in the future. Best practices exist for nearly all technical infrastructure, and these best practices need to be rigorously enforced and audited at a minimum. As more physical aspects of the world are controlled by information and communication technology, greater physical harm upon malicious activity can be inflicted. Seven techniques can assist in providing a base level of invasion prevention and a deterrent to malicious reconnaissance of potential target systems:

Whitelisting bans all software from executing unless it is on a maintained list of corporately approved applications.

Advanced firewalls: *advanced* security properties that can be configured in Windows *Firewall*.

Unidirectional one-way only gateways: one gateway to exit and another to enter.

Advanced intrusion detection software employing behavioral analysis.

Security information and event management (SIEM) software combined with log analysis software observes all activity and events that have occurred in the system and examines the log tapes containing a before and after picture of each instance of activity on the complete computer system.

Compliance managers on duty 24/7 to be consulted when any abnormal activity is detected.

The operation of an internal monitoring system observing all activity in real time as it occurs and comparing that activity to a maintained file of normal activity that is specific to certain individuals at certain times of day and days of the week and occurring against certain defined and approved systems.

Stuxnet provided an example of the entirety of what it takes to launch a relatively successful cyber attack. Once malicious code is released, it can be deconstructed and repurposed, much like obtaining the blueprints for a physical weapon. This was the first publically known malware designed for "real-world damage." The lasting effects of this attack are still represented daily in the information and data security arena.

The U.S. government acknowledges the challenges a networked infrastructure can bring, which is why it developed one of the world's largest "hack labs." The National SCADA Test Bed (NSTB) was created in 2003 to help detect and block vulnerabilities such as the Stuxnet virus. The NSTB provides "a core testing environment to help industry and government identify and correct vulnerabilities in SCADA equipment and control systems within the energy sector." This testbed offers significant resources for these industry and government stakeholders to use:

- More than 17 testing and research facilities
- Field-scale control systems
- 61 miles of 138 kV transmission lines
- Seven substations
- Advanced visualization and modeling tools

The most updated cyber-security legislation relating to infrastructure within the energy sector was an executive order released in 2013, "Improving Critical Infrastructure Cybersecurity." Like most science-based hobbies, there comes a time when technologies transition outside of the hobbyist world into mainstream production and are then leveraged as a platform for political means. Much like the adoption of social media, the malicious use of computer programming followed this same path.

The Vulnerable U.S. Electronic Power Grid

The U.S. electric power grid is divided into three regions. The Eastern Interconnection connecting the East Coast states, through to the Midwestern states ending in the Dakotas and down to Mississippi. The interconnections are made at many points and do not depend on a sole interconnection junction (Figure 20.2).

Figure 20.2   The U.S. electric power grid with interconnecting points displayed.

The Western Interconnection covers those western plains states all the way through to the West Coast states. A third region, the Electric Reliability Council, encompasses and serves just the State of Texas.

These three regions are then interconnected between themselves at multiple spots, leading to a completely interconnected national electric grid.

Within those three grids, there are a number of regional subgrids and regional governing authorities (Figure 20.3).

More than 17,800 generators are involved in providing more than 1,100 GW (gigawatts) of power to their interconnected set of connections. The system contains more than 211,000 miles of high-voltage lines and over 6 million miles of low-voltage lines. These lines serve over 125 million residential customers, more than 17.6 million commercial customers, and more than 775,000 industrial customers, plus local, state, and national government agencies.

The electric grid system is managed by a set of ISCs and SCADAs. It should come as no surprise that these management and control systems are constructed, deployed, and operated in the same fashion and with either similar or exactly the same control equipment. Siemens is both the primary designer of such control systems and quite frequently the provider of the specific ISC and SCADA hardware and software deployed on most systems that are dependent on processors controlling electric facilities, whether they be grids or centrifuges. If one knows how Siemens PLCs work, one can apply this knowledge to the entire infrastructure.

Components and Operating Elements of the U.S. Electric Power Grid

1. Generators and substations composed of protective relays, circuit breakers, transformers, SCADA remote terminal units (RTUs), surge arresters, phase shifter, flexible alternating current (ac) transmission systems, phasor measurement units, and sensors.
2. Lines and cables, including extra-high-voltage AC lines, high-voltage direct current (dc) lines, superconducting lines, fault current limiters, and dynamic line rating systems.
3. To control the electric grid network, a set of control centers incorporating the following energy management system components: state estimation, economic dispatch, unit commitment, contingency analysis, automatic generator control, phase monitoring and alarming systems, oscillation detection, and constantly updated system modeling systems.

A whole connected network of electricity providers including coal, wind, hydroelectric, and nuclear plants are used to provide energy to the power grid itself and through it the end users of supplied electric power across the United States.

There is a growing appreciation as to the importance of the intercommunication and information delivery networks for supporting the operation of this national power grid, including supplying information to the controlling components, data acquisition components, and the people who manage, support, provision, modify, fix, improve, extend, and modernize this smart electric power grid network. It is the information conveyed to the grid control components and the PLCs, monitors, and data acquisition and storage processors that make it a smart electric power grid. The foundation of a smart grid is the communication infrastructure, and the role of this infrastructure is to expand its functions to cover an increasing number of aspects of the entire power grid.

Key applications for communications technology in smart grids include enabling the efficient operation of solar cells, detecting faults in grid transformers, managing power peaks, monitoring

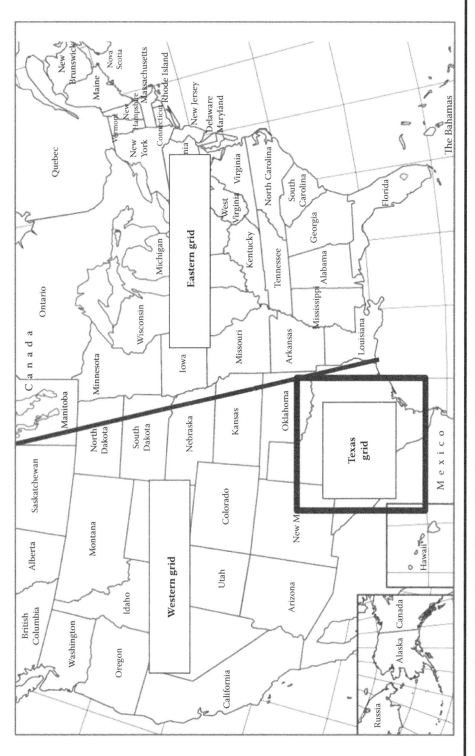

Figure 20.3   The three grid regions of the overall U.S. power grid.

power consumption in businesses and homes, controlling equipment that uses electric power, and communicating between the different pieces of equipment and management processors. The communication format can be selected to match the application, with possibilities including wired communication, wireless communication, and power-line communication.

Wireless communication simplifies installation because no wiring is required, and a variety of wireless technologies is now available with transmission capabilities ranging from near-field to long distance. For example, remote meter reading (in which power usage is monitored at regular intervals) can be accomplished by incorporating power meters into a wide-area wireless network. It also seems likely that power-line communication (which uses existing electric power wiring) will become widely used for applications such as communications among different pieces of equipment within a single building.

A smart grid uses communications technology (networks) and information systems (computers with applications) to interlink and control all components of the power grid, including generating stations, distribution facilities, transformers, businesses, and households. It is a system intended to enable the stable supply and efficient usage of electrical power. The latest technology is used to give "intelligent" functions to the entire power distribution grid, making it a "smart" grid that is capable of reducing emissions of greenhouse gases and boosting energy efficiency.

The idea of the smart grid is not merely to bring innovations to the power distribution system. Its scope of application is broad and multibranched, and it is hoped that the adoption of smart grids will give rise to a variety of new services and industries. Businesses related to smart grids that are considered to have high growth potential include the following:

1. New systems for storing and managing energy
2. Sales and billing systems for solar energy, and so on
3. "Visualization" of power usage and AMR using smart meters
4. Household appliance control (demand response, demand side management, etc.)
5. Security (antitheft), fire alarm systems, and so on

Power plants, power-transmission towers, smart grid networks, smart grid operations and management centers, green power generation units, windmill transmission fields, and all the high- and low-power transmission lines comprise the electric power delivery system.

Irreplaceable Large Power Transformers and Our Smart Grid Risk

Ted Koppel's new 2015 book *Lights Out* describes the danger of having tens of thousands of almost irreplaceable large power transformers (LPTs) installed across the United States. These transformers are on average 38–40 years old and are the most critical component in the bulk power transmission grid, sending electric power across large swathes of the country. These LPTs cost between $3M and $10M to replace and are manufactured overseas. As such, they must be transported by rail or truck to a shipping port, shipped to the United States, and then transported by flatbed truck across the country. The transformers are the size of a small house, and the trains and train tracks can no longer handle them. A road path must be cleared for giant special-purpose, 70-feet-long, 12-axle, extra-wide platform trucks to carry these transformers across country to the installation site. Then, specially trained and skilled technicians must test, update, and connect them to the SCADA networks and controlling PLCs, and then connect them to the power grid.

These transformers come in a variety of voltage classes, some in the 345–500 kV or 230–500 kV ranges, and many others, none of which are interchangeable. If you only have one variation available, you have to modify the whole transmission center to use a different one, rather than use one at the same capacity as the damaged one.

The LPTs are used to ramp up the power for distance transmission, and there are also an array of step-down transformers used to extract power from the high-powered grid and drop the voltage to the level required for local distribution. The local distribution center then controls the flow of lower voltage electricity to businesses and residences in local cities, towns, and villages and for use in the countryside: on farms, in barns, and in rural homes.

Although the LPTs themselves are not directly connected to the Internet, they and the step-down transformers are, by necessity, connected to the SCADA C&C systems for delivery of management commands and operational information feedback. These C&C management systems and the PLCs are networked together and are connected via a network to drive the transformers.

This is the same design as occurred in Iran, where it was assumed that isolating the SCADA C&C and PLC devices (which were on their own isolated network and were connected to and driving the centrifuges) provided security, due to their separation from the Iranian government network and the public Internet. However, as Ted Koppel points out, all it took to infect the Iranian PLCs and thus damage the centrifuges was for an unsuspecting technician to plug a thumb drive carrying the Stuxnet worm into the server on the C&C system network.

In the same manner, it would take only a power grid technician carrying his installation instructions, transformer specs, and step-by-step installation process (specific to that version of the transformer technology and PLC) on a USB flash drive for that SCADA system to be infected and for the LPTs to be damaged.

Those will be an attractive target for destruction similar to the centrifuges in Iran. They are controlled by the Siemens PLC processors; these are part of a Siemens SCADA network that is updated over the Internet, as well as being vulnerable to a tech plugging in a thumb drive containing instructions, pictures, and… a variation of the Stuxnet worm.

Smart Meters

Power companies have been moving forward with the adoption of electronic meters and automated meter reading (AMR) as ways to reduce the personnel costs associated with meter reading (the manual checking of the gauges of electric meters to determine power use) and to combat tampering by means of magnets and the like. By adopting electronic power meters, power companies are able to collect a variety of types of data on power usage, allowing them to provide a more fine-tuned service. For example, by offering pricing plans that make it cheaper to consume power during the times of day when usage is lowest overall, they provide consumers with a way to save on their power bills (by using electricity when it is cheapest) and reduce the load on the grid during peak times.

Now, power companies are going further by introducing advanced metering infrastructure (AMI). AMI is defined as a comprehensive power control system that, in addition to AMR and improved service for consumers, includes capabilities such as operation and maintenance of power equipment over a wide area, support for recovery from natural disasters (such as lightning strikes), and sale of power from solar cells (sale of electricity to the power company). The electric meters with the advanced functions needed to make AMI a reality are known as *smart meters*. Smart meters can measure power usage almost in real time, and, by establishing communication links with the power company via a wide area network (WAN), it is possible to implement capabilities such as bidirectional power control and bill payment by means of prepaid cards. Future possibilities include enabling power companies to adjust air-conditioner temperature settings via the network in order to reduce power demand peaks. The introduction of smart meters is already required under national or state policies in some countries overseas.

Programmable Logic Controllers

The operation and control of this national electric power grid is performed by a set of distributed PLCs (computer processors), and the primary designer, manufacturer, deliverer, and maintainer of these components is Siemens of Germany. Siemens dominates the market for the controlling processors and software used to manage and control industrial systems, including nuclear, hydroelectric, and wind-power systems, all of which contribute to the electric power and the grid systems that transport and deliver electricity to users across the nation.

Advantages of PLCs

PLCs are capable of performing the same tasks as hard-wired controllers; however, with their advanced computer processors and software, PLCs are capable of more complex applications. PLC application programs and distributed electronic communication lines replace much of the interconnecting wires required by a hard-wired controller. Furthermore, PLCs allow for connecting and reconnecting by means of software and parameter changes, correcting errors and modifying the controlling applications. They do this in an easier way than local, hard-wired control devices (which are still frequently required to connect many isolated field devices), although they provide a much less flexible approach to controlling and interconnecting a set of distributedprocess components.

Some of the additional advantages of PLCs are that they are smaller physically than many hard-wired solutions and allow for easier and faster provisioning of changes. Also, PLCs have centrally available and integrated diagnostics and override functions. Finally, PLC applications can be updated with partial or complete new versions and can duplicate and further distribute those new versions over a controlled interconnected network in a faster and less expensive fashion.

Siemens makes several PLC product lines in the SIMATIC® S7 family, including the S7-200, the S7-300, and the S7-400, which are used by electric power companies across the world.

Distribution Transformers and Controllers

Distribution transformers are found in secondary substations and connect to three-phase low-voltage lines that deliver electricity to points of supply. Electricity customers are charged for their consumption based on the measurements registered in meters present at the point of supply. PLC signals are injected into key elements. The PLC signal PRIME is a narrowband PLC band, used by utilities for power line communication distribution transformers as propagation in the distribution grids. Technology in CENELEC A communicates with meters at maximum data rates of 122.9 kbps.

PRIME technology establishes subnet works rooting at distribution transformers in secondary substations, where the so-called base nodes are installed, to communicate with service

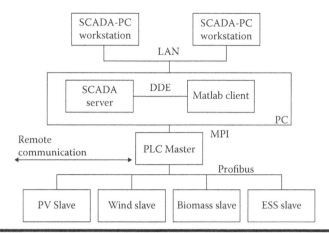

Figure 20.4 Components of a typical PLC management and control system for distributed electric energy.

nodes present at meters in smart metering environments. These are alternatives for PLC signal injection, either single phase or three phase, through different field tests, in order to improve overall network constitution and the performance of meters. The results and conclusions may be extrapolated to any other low-voltage PLC technology in the same frequency band. The conclusions of the paper make recommendations to use specific PLC injection configurations depending on the topologies under study, and they provide guidance for product development in this area, which has a fundamental influence on the results obtained for the PLC communication system (Figure 20.4).

The optimization algorithm implemented for the energy management at the SCADA outer loop control could not be implemented directly on the SCADA system, as this complex controller needs mathematical operations that are not present at usually available SCADA systems. A strategy was developed to couple the SCADA system with The MathWork's MATLAB® software.

The communication between SCADA and MATLAB was performed using the Dynamic Data Exchange (DDE) protocol. This communication protocol, developed in the 1990s but still very common, permits the exchange of data between two independent running (client and server) software programs.

In the developed application, the MATLAB software was the client, as it initiates the communication; and the SCADA software was the server, as it responds to the client's requests.

Among the different information formats supported by DDE Protocol, the TEXT format was selected, as this format was supported by both SCADA and MATLAB software.

Four different communication protocols (LAN, DDE, MPI, PROFIBUS) are working simultaneously at different levels of the developed platform.

Local PLC Inner-Loop Controller

At the inner loop of the developed strategy (PLC level), several algorithms had been developed. These algorithms were built using the Grafcet methodology—Sequential Function Chart. The designed algorithms were implemented using the Ladder Diagram Language.

The main purpose of the developed programs associated with the RES stations is the monitoring of the electric power generated. Renewable Energy Systems Ltd. (RES) is a leader in the engineering, construction, and operation of electrical energy systems including wind, solar, transmission, and energy storage projects.

A SCADA System

A SCADA system usually consists of the following subsystems:

1. RTUs connect to sensors and convert sensor signals to digital data. They have telemetry hardware capable of sending digital data to the supervisory system as well as receiving digital commands from the supervisory system. RTUs often have embedded control capabilities such as ladder logic in order to accomplish Boolean logic operations.
2. PLCs connect to sensors and convert sensor signals to digital data. PLCs have more sophisticated embedded control capabilities (typically one or more IEC 61131-3 programming languages) than RTUs. PLCs do not have telemetry hardware, although this functionality is typically installed alongside them. PLCs are sometimes used in place of RTUs as field devices because they are more economical, versatile, flexible, and configurable.
3. A telemetry system is typically used to connect PLCs and RTUs with control centers, data warehouses, and the enterprise. Examples of wired telemetry media used in SCADA systems include leased telephone lines and WAN circuits. Examples of wireless telemetry media used in SCADA systems include satellite (VSAT), licensed and unlicensed radio, cellular, and microwave.
4. A data acquisition server is a software service that uses industrial protocols to connect software services, via telemetry, with field devices such as RTUs and PLCs. It allows clients to access data from these field devices using standard protocols.
5. A human–machine interface (HMI) is the apparatus or device that presents processed data to a human operator, and through this, the human operator monitors and interacts with the process. The HMI is a client that requests data from a data acquisition server.
6. An historian is a software service that accumulates time-stamped data, Boolean events, and Boolean alarms in a database, which can be queried or used to populate graphic trends in the HMI. The historian is a client that requests data from a data acquisition server.

The basic controllers of the SIMATIC S7-1200 series are ideal for simple and precise as well as safety-related automation tasks and are mainly used in smaller, serial machines working as stand-alone.

Thanks to the integrated I/Os and flexible technology functions, the basic controllers have a minimal footprint and reduced hardware costs.

Moreover, another set of more advanced controllers are used for controlling medium and highly complex machines and for plant automation. Among these are the advanced controllers of the SIMATIC S7-1500 series, which are the standard controllers and support systems used for higher-level control, from controlling serial machines to controlling much more complex plants with high requirements. This Siemens SIMATIC S7-1500 controller series, the long-term successor to the S7-300 and S7-400 systems, which are still in use controlling the industrial environment, is the current standard for all factory automation, including complex safety-related applications.

The SIMATIC S7-1500 software controller is especially suitable for flexible control of special machines with high performance and functional requirements. The absolute independence of the software controller from the operating system has proved to increase the system availability. In addition to the new SIMATIC S7-1500 software controller, the range of the software controllers includes its predecessor, the SIMATIC WinAC.

The distributed controllers SIMATIC ET 200 central processing units (CPUs) combine compactness and flexibility.

Especially in the medium-performance range of machines with distributed intelligence or serial machines with limited footprint, the distributed controllers are the perfect solution for standard fail-safe applications. In addition to the SIMATIC ET 200SP CPUs and the new SIMATIC ET 200SP open controller, the proven SIMATIC ET 200S and ET 200pro CPUs are available as distributed controllers.

These Siemens data acquisition, operational control, and management systems are the modern prototype systems whose design, implementation, deployment, and utilization are common across the mechanized world. It is the control and ultimate destruction of such systems that the Stuxnet worm was designed to achieve.

New variations and mutations of that worm, enhanced by further transmission, infection, control, anonymity maintenance, and eventual destructive action, are entering the dark web marketplace and will soon target electric grid systems, telecommunication systems, air traffic control systems, train and road control systems, subway control systems, and the water and air purification systems of the United States and the industrialized, technology controlled world.

Conclusion

The Stuxnet worm was considered a "zero-day" threat since it took advantage of flaws and mistakes in the operating systems that are common to electric control systems, the systems themselves, the dependence on a single manufacturer to create the design, the software, and the devices that manage and control electrical systems, whether they be nuclear centrifuges or electric power grid controllers.

Furthermore, the systems are vulnerable to the simple process whereby technicians receive specification information, manuals of the operation, and repair and parts lists on digital files, which they can then carry in their pockets on USB flash drives around the standard data-processing routers and firewalls on the industrial system to isolated C&C system networks. This demonstrates the susceptibility that all systems have to simple vulnerabilities. Malware such as the Stuxnet worm has now been modified, extended, and made widely available. Ted Koppel terms it well in his new book. It is inevitable that it will eventually be "lights out" across America.

QUESTIONS

1. What is the process of infection by the Stuxnet worm?
2. What are the three target elements for a Stuxnet worm?
3. What are the five paths of the Stuxnet worm?
4. What is the vulnerability of the U.S. national electric power grid to infection and destruction by means of a variant of the Stuxnet worm?

Chapter 21

Cyber Warfare

Cyber crime and malicious attacks over the Internet are only going to increase in the coming years. As more confidential information gets transported over the Internet every day, hackers are looking for new ways to exploit that information for either personal or monetary benefits. To demonstrate this, we will examine cybersecurity trends that will only increase in the years ahead.

The first trend we will examine is that the underground marketplaces on the deep web will continue to evolve, regardless of police crackdowns, within the next few years. A perfect example of this is cyber criminals creating drug marketplaces for users to buy illegal substances using the anonymous Bitcoin Internet currency. The most famous of these is the Silk Road, which was finally located and terminated with the creator in jail. Following this site termination, cyber criminals quickly created a new version of that site. Still, the marketplace was rebooted for the third time as Silk Road 3 Reloaded. However, this is not the only type of underground marketplace service available. Many of them are now offering cyber crime as a service (CaaS).

CaaS is a booming marketplace in terms of the future of Internet security. Many of these marketplaces can show users how to create and spread their own malware or worms. One of these services is called Citadel. This service shows users how to create malicious malware and manage bots that have been infected. Figure 21.1 shows the Citadel toolkit.

While the Citadel toolkit is scary in terms of the future of information security, there are also a number of underground services that will gain in popularity in the future. These services include Mobile Hacking Service Assistant, Facebook Hacking Assistant, and even assassination services. While underground marketplaces will continue to grow, there is a specific sector of cyber attacks that has rapidly been increasing: mobile exploitations.

Mobile exploitations have been on the rise since the emergence of smartphones within our everyday lives. In fact, as we rely on our smartphone applications to perform activities such as banking, we are opening ourselves up to vulnerabilities. In fact, in 2011 alone, 1000 android malware samples were detected. Also, the increasing rate of malicious applications within the Android store has increased since the development of DroidDream. One area of mobile exploitation that will be on the rise is the exploitation of man-in-the-middle mobile browser attacks. These attacks will increase as the smartphone's computing power increases and users become more eager to do banking on their smartphones. A breakdown of mobile threats that are of importance for the future of mobile computing is shown in Figure 21.2.

Figure 21.1 Citadel spyware system browser.

Mobile threats, identified by type

1. Trojans 8.4%
2. Hack-tools 6%
3. Spyware 4%
4. Trojan- downloader 2%
5. Adware 2%
6. Malware applications 2%
7. Yet unspecified 75%

Figure 21.2 Types of mobile threats.

As one can see, cyber security is a topic that will be absolutely critical as more business becomes automated and digital in the future. Hackers and malicious coders will not stop with the plethora of options that there will be to choose from.

Cyber warfare is a reality that most information technology leaders manage daily. Companies, groups, and individuals are all affected. Most surprisingly, this information goes for a relatively low price once it is pieced out into identities, credit cards, and social security numbers. Beyond this packaged information, actual hack-based services are also available for hire, coordinated through the dark web. The universal currencies are typically untraceable or hard to trace payments, meaning that Bitcoin and Greendot disposable credit cards are primary payment methods. What makes a cyber attack an act of war is the type of entity being attacked and the reason that they are being attacked. When a government-sponsored hacking entity from China attacks a firm based in the United States, this is an act of cyber warfare. A strategy of war is to disable or hurt an opposing country's economy. Prior to digital tools, damaging infrastructure and restricting access to resources would primarily achieve this effect. In the technical age, these same effects can be produced by stealing large sums of information from corporations and liquidating the stolen assets in money.

Weapons of Cyber War

Just as inexperienced soldiers are often given damaging weapons without understanding their use, many hackers have access to freely available tools that simplify the act of performing an attack. The landscape these hackers have available to them is changing, increasingly in their favor. Prior to mobile computing, botnets with fixed locations to initiate denial-of-service attacks had a relatively limited capability, which was further diminished by the techniques of bringing the botnets on and off the network repeatedly to avoid detection. With the innovations available with smartphones and other mobile devices, and their ability to access the Internet from a changing location, their susceptibility for detection is significantly diminished. With the innovations in smartphone devices, hackers can now access always-on, highly sensitive computing devices for their disposal. Figure 21.3 displays the mobile device market shares, along with their operating system adoption rates.

The most challenging aspect of the Android platform is influencing its user base to upgrade to the latest operating system. The latest operating system usually includes a variety of bug and security fixes among the improved feature sets. This makes the platform, when viewed as a whole, much more insecure in comparison to Apple's iOS. Another example is with banking phishing software, for which some advanced toolkits have been released. Once banks recognized their customers were falsely going to web portals that simulated their own, they began using uniquely identifiable pictures as a form of capcha to allow their users to know they were at the correct address. However, the user will always be the weakest link in security.

Cyber Crime as a Service

With a variety of methods now available for using information for personal gain, information itself is becoming a fairly universal product. Criminals are not always after the information on a machine, however; sometimes, they simply use fear in order to promote a fear response–based behavior. Scareware is software that is installed with the purpose of extorting users for full access back to their device. With mobile devices, this may be a scare screen that appears on boot up saying that all conversations are being recorded. On a laptop or desktop, a screen that prevents the machine from fully booting may exist unless an untraceable form of currency is used and typed into the window. Of course, this does not mean that the criminal group is obligated to then release

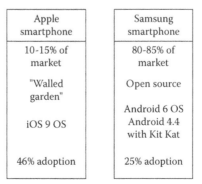

Figure 21.3   Mobile device market shares, along with their operating system adoption rates.

this scare screen; in fact, they may hide the screen and continue to record information on the user knowing that they have potential for future payouts.

Hacktivists

Groups of hackers exist that defame websites based on what communities have deemed as "bad." This means that it's common for these online groups to attack government websites and financial firms. What these groups are unaware of is that they are often being manipulated by groups that want to serve an alternative purpose. For instance, if China wants to defame the U.S. government website, they could manipulate a hacktivist group to do this task as well. These hacktivist groups will continue to disrupt large institutions with relatively unpredictable goals.

QUESTIONS

1. What is a popular service that offers a complete set of cyber-crime tools as a service?
2. How does the Citadel toolkit work?
3. What is the main source of infection that is commonly employed?
4. These six play a part in creating a secure wireless system.

Chapter 22

Conclusion

From the material covered in this book, one can see that we are currently—and for the foreseeable future will be—living in a world of malicious actors intent on diverting and destroying the rewards of the wonderful fruits of countless inventors of the integrated technology we employ when we communicate over the public Internet. The creators of our computing, network connecting, mobility, storage, and website offering systems envisioned a world of benign individuals who would use technology for their own benefit and the shared benefit of others. And that shared benefit has spread to individuals and organizations throughout the world, creating an interconnected web of a global society. Hopefully, our technologists will create encryption, monitoring, and surveillance systems that will prolong the interconnected world we inhabit for the coming generations, so that our book is only a warning that will spur others on to protecting us from predators while continuing to supply each of us with further wonders through our lifetimes.

Bibliography

Ahmad, J., Garrison, B., Gruen, J., Kelly, C., and Pankey, H. (2003). 4G wireless systems. Next-Generation Wireless Working Group.

Ahmadi, S. (2009). An overview of next-generation mobile WiMAX technology. *IEEE Communications Magazine*, 84–98.

Ahmed, B. and Feroze, Z. (2009). *3G Cellular Network*. Sweden: School of Engineering at Blekinge Institute of Technology, MEE09: 25.

Ahuja, S. and Collier, N. (2010). An assessment of WiMAX security. *CN Communications and Network* (2), 134–137.

Akin, D. (2005, May 1). 802.11i authentication and key management (AKM). Retrieved October 27, 2015, from https://www.cwnp.com/uploads/802–11i_key_management.pdf.

Andrews, J. G., Buzzi, S., Choi, W., Hanly, S. V., Lozano, A., Soong, A. C., and Zhang, J. C. (2014). What will 5G be?. *Selected Areas in Communications, IEEE Journal on* 32(6), 1065–1082.

Anritsu. (2015). Understanding 5G; A brief look back. Retrieved October 24, 2015, from http://anritsu-emea.typepad.com/my-blog/2015/04/understanding-5g-a-brief-look-back.html.

Arana, P. (2006). Benefits and vulnerabilities of Wi-Fi Protected Access 2 (WPA2).

Arora, H. (2012). TCP Attacks: TCP sequence number prediction and TCP reset attacks. January 20. http://www.thegeekstuff.com/2012/01/tcp-sequence-number-attacks/. Retrieved October 26, 2015.

Arora, H. (2014). Apple's iCloud service hit by man-in-the-middle attack in China. October 21. http://www.techspot.com/news/58514-apple-icloud-service-hit-man-middle-attack-china.html. Retrieved September 25, 2015.

Baekkelund, Ø. (2009). Session hijacking in WLAN based public networks. Retrieved September 29, 2015, from http://www.divaportal.org/smash/get/diva2:348801/FULLTEXT01.pdf.

Barabosch, T., Eschweiler, S., and Gerhards-Padilla, E. (2014). Bee master: Detecting host-based code injection attacks. www.fraunhofer.de.

Bearman, J. (2012). The rise and fall of the silk road, Part I and Part II. Wired magazine, www.wired.com/2015/04/silk-road-1/ and www.wired.com/2015/04/silk-road-1/silk-road-2/.

BEEcube: Challenges and solutions in prototyping 5G radio access network. (2014). Retrieved October 19, 2015, from http://www.beecube.com/wireless-communications.html.

Bhalla, M. R. and Bhalla, A. V. (2010). Generations of mobile wireless technology: A survey. *International Journal of Computer Applications (0975–8887)* 5(4), 26–32.

Bhargava, B., Zhang, Y., Idika, N., Lilien, L., and Azarmi, M. (2009). Collaborative attacks in WiMAX networks. *Security and Communication Networks* 2, 373–391.

Bhasker, D. (2013). 4G LTE security for mobile network operators. *Understanding Cyber Risks and Security Management* 1(4), 20–28.

Bhasker, D. (2014). Risk management in 4G LTE. *ISACA Journal*, 1, 1–5.

Bilogrevic, I. (2010). Security and privacy in next generation mobile networks: LTE and femtocells. Retrieved October 18, 2015, from http://secowinetcourse.epfl.ch/previous/09/Bilogrevic.Igor/Final_Report.pdf.

Bogdanoski, M., and Risteski, A. (2011). Wireless network behavior under ICMP ping flood DOS attack and mitigation techniques. *International Journal of Communication Networks and Information Security* 3(1), 17–24.

Boneh, D. and Bruce S. (2015). *Free Online Cryptography Course.* Stanford, CA: Stanford University. https://www.schneier.com/blog/archives/2012/11/free_online_cry.html.

Boneh, D. (2014–2015). *Data Security Course.* Stanford, CA: Stanford University. www.dado@cs.stanford.edu.

Boneh, D. (1999). Twenty years of attacks on the RSA cryptosystems. *Notices of the American Mathematical Society (AMS)* 46(2), 203–213.

Borcoci, E. (2008). WiMAX technologies: Architectures, protocols, resource management and applications. Retrieved October 17, 2015, from http://www.iaria.org/conferences2008/filesCTRQ08/CTRQ_2008_WiMAX_tutorial_EB-v1.3.pdf.

Burton, M. (2010). The 4-way handshake. Lecture. November 5. Retrieved October 27, 2015, from https://www.youtube.com/watch?v=9M8kVYFhMDw.

Bzoor, M. and Elleithy, K. (2011). WIMAX basics from PHY layer to scheduling and multicasting approaches. *International Journal of Computer Science & Engineering Survey IJCSES* 2(1), 1–17.

Cassidy, S. (2014). Diagnosis of the OpenSSL heartbleed bug, April 7, 2014. http://blog.existentialize.com/diagnosis-of-the-openssl-heartbleed-bug.html.

Chakravarty, S. (2014). Traffic analysis attacks and defenses in low latency anonymous communication. Doctoral dissertation, Columbia University, New York.

Chase, JP Morgan. (n.d.). FAQ: Chip-enabled card acceptance (EMV). Retrieved September 25, 2015, from https://www.chasepaymentech.com/faq_emv_chip_card_technology.html.

Chickowski, E. (2008). TJX: Anatomy of a massive breach. *Baseline* (81), 28. http://www.baselinemag.com/c/a/Security/TJX-Anatomy-of-a-Massive-Breach.

Chowdhary, M., Suri, S., and Bhutani, M. (2014). Comparative study of intrusion detection systems. *International Journal of Computer* 2(4), 197–200.

Çinar, H., Çibuk, M., and Balik, H. (2012). History and evaluation of mobile Wimax. *Applied Mathematical and Computational Sciences* 4, 1–20.

Cisco. (2011). The internet of things: How the next evolution of the internet is changing everything. Cisco Internet Business Solution Group. http://www.cisco.com/c/dam/en_us/about/ac79/docs/innov/IoT_IBSG_0411FINAL.pdf.

Cisco. (n.e.). A guide to defending against distributed denial of service attacks. http://www.cisco.com/c/en/us/about/security-center/guide-ddos-defense.html. Retrieved September 24, 2015, from http://www.cisco.com/web/about/security/intelligence/guide_ddos_defense.html _Toc374453052.

Cisco. (n.d.). Cisco LEAP (an 802.1X authentication type for wireless LANs). Retrieved October 25, 2015, from http://www.cisco.com/c/en/us/products/collateral/wireless/aironet-1200-series/prod_qas0900a-ecd801764f1.html.

Cisco. (n.d.). Cisco Protected Extensible Authentication Protocol. (PEAP) is an 802.1X authentication type for wireless LANs. Retrieved October 25, 2015, from http://www.cisco.com/c/en/us/products/collateral/wireless/aironet-1200-series/prod_qas0900aecd801764fa.html.

Cisco. (2015). Cisco visual networking index: Global mobile data traffic forecast update 2014–2019 white paper. February 3. Retrieved October 22, 2015, from http://www.cisco.com/c/en/us/solutions/collateral/service-provider/visual-networking-index-vni/white_paper_c11-520862.html.

Cisco prime access registrar 6.0.1 user guide—extensible authentication protocols (Cisco Prime Access Registrar 6.0). (2013). April 22. Cisco Protected Extensible Authentication Protocol. (PEAP) is an 802.1X authentication type for wireless LANs. Retrieved October 25, 2015, from http://www.cisco.com/c/en/us/td/docs/net_mgmt/prime/access_registrar/6-0-1/user/guide/user_guide/eap.html.

Chukwu, M. (n.d.). Comparative study and security limitations of 4G network (case study LTE and WIMAX). Retrieved October 29, 2015, from http://www.wsnmagazine.com/comparative study.pdf.

Cloudstrike. (2014, 2015). Global threat intel report: Know your adversary and better protect your network. http://www.cloustrike.com/global-threat-report-2014; http://www.cloustrike.com/global-threat-report-2015.

Cloudstrike. Whitepaper: Beyond malware—Compiler security checks in depth. EAP overview. Retrieved October 27, 2015, from https://technet.microsoft.com/en-us/library/cc770622(v=ws.10).aspx.

Compnetworking. (n.d.). Here's what a 'NIC' is (computer network interface card). Retrieved October 25, 2015, from http://compnetworking.about.com/od/networkadapters/g/bldef_nic.htm.

Dahlman, E., Parkvall, S., and Peisa, J. (2015). 5G wireless access. *IEICE Transactions on Communications* E98-B(8), 1407–1414.

D'Ambrosia, J. (2015). IEEE 802 LAN/MAN Standards Committee. July 22. Retrieved October 18, 2015, from http://www.ieee802.org.

Danielyan, E. (2002). IEEE 802.11. *The Internet Protocol Journal* 5, 1.

Do, T. (2001). WAP security: Wireless Transport Layer Security (WTLS) is a security protocol which is part of the Wireless Application Protocol (WAP), from George Mason University program in Secure Telecommunication Systems. Retrieved September 23, 2015, from http://bass.gmu.edu/courses/ECE636/project/reports/TDo.pdf.

Doherty, J. (2016). *Wireless and Mobile Device Security*. Burlington, MA: Jones & Bartlett Learning.

Dondia, K. M., Ma, J., and Tao, F. (2015). A CM-based model for 802.11 networks security policies enforcement. *In 2015 International Conference on Automation, Mechanical Control and Computational Engineering*. April, Amsterdam, The Netherlands: Atlantis Press.

Eddy, W. (2006). Defenses against TCP SYN flooding attacks. *The Internet Protocol Journal* 9(4), 2–16.

Eddy, M. (2015). Inside the dark web. *PC Magazine*, February 4.

Ericsson: 5G security: Scenarios and solutions. (2015, June 1). Retrieved October 18, 2015, from http://www.ericsson.com/us/res/docs/whitepapers/wp-5g-security.pdf.

Evans, D. (n.d.). What is BYOD and why is it important? Retrieved October 25, 2015, from http://www.techradar.com/us/news/computing/what-is-byod-and-why-is-it-important--1175088.

Firmino, L. (2011). WAP GAP (Wireless Application Protocol) cyber defense: Finding novel ways to apply safeguards and countermeasures. March 23. Retrieved September 25, 2015. http://www.luizfirimo.blogspot.com/2011,03/wap-gap.html.

Fitzpatrick, J. (2013). HTG explains: The difference between WEP, WPA, and WPA2 wireless encryption (and why it matters). July 16. http://www.howtogeek.com/167783/htg-explains-the-difference-between-wep-wpa-and-wpa2-wireless-encryption-and-why-it-matters/.

Frankel, S., Eydt, B., Owens, L., and Scarfone, K. (2007). *Establishing Wireless Robust Security Networks: A Guide to IEEE 802.11i*. Gaithersburg, MD: National Institute of Standards and Technology.

Gallagher, S. (2014). Chinese government launches man-in-middle attack against iCloud [Updated]. October 20. Retrieved September 25, 2015.

Gandal, N., Salant, D., and Waverman, L. (2003). Standards in wireless telephone networks. *Telecommunications Policy* 27, 325–332.

Gardezi, A. I. (2006). *Security in Wireless Cellular Networks*. St. Louis, MI: Washington University of St. Louis. Retrieved from Washington University in St. Louis.

Gartner, IT Glossary. (2015). Authentication service. http://blogs.gartner.com/it-glossary/authentication-service/.

Ge, X., Cheng, H., Guizani, M., and Han, T. (2014). 5G wireless backhaul networks: Challenges and research advances. *IEEE Network* 28(6), 6–11.

Gemini Communication Ltd. (n.d.). Mobile WIMAX architecture. Retrieved October 20, 2015. http://www.gcl.in/tsd/doc/Mobile_Wimax_Network_Architecture.pdf.

Goodrich, M. and Roberto, T. (2010). *Introduction to Computer Security*, 1st edn. Boston, MA: Addison-Wesley.

Goodin, D. (2012). 25-GPU cluster cracks every standard Windows password in <6 hours (Jeremi Gosney password cracking machine). http://arstechnica.com/security/2012/12/25-gpu-cluster-cracks-every-standard-windows-password-in-6-hours/.

Government of the Hong Kong Special Administrative Region. (2010). *Wireless Networking Security*, pp. 7–19.

Greenberg, A. (2015). Who goes there? Misperceptions about Tor and who is using it according to Runa Sandvik. www.scnagazine.com, June 2015 issue.

Greenfield, J. (2003). What the TKIP Protocol is all about—*TechRepublic*. September 15.

Greenemeier, L. (2007). The TJX Effect. *Information Week*. 10 August. Retrieved September 25, 2015. http://www.informationweek.com/the-tjx-effect/d/d-id/1058033?.

Gregg, M. (2005). CISSP security-management practices. October 28. Retrieved October 26, 2015, from http://www.pearsonitcertification.com/articles/article.aspx?p=418007&seqNum=3.

Griffith, E. A. (2004). Welcome to WPA2. September 2. http://www.wi-fiplanet.com/news/article. php/3402971/A-Warm-Welcome-to-WPA2.htm.

GSMA Intelligence. (2014). Understanding 5G: Perspectives on future technological advancements in mobile. (December 1, 2014). Retrieved October 22, 2015, from https://gsmaintelligence.com/ research/?file=141208-5g.pdf&download.

Gu, Q., Liu, P., and Zhu, S. (2004). Defending against packet injection attacks in unreliable Ad Hoc Networks. Retrieved September 25, 2015, from https://s2.ist.psu.edu/paper/cross-tr.pdf.

Hadnagy, C. (2010). *Social Engineering: The Art of Human Hacking*, 1st edn. New York: Wiley.

Han, T., Zhang, N., Liu, K., Tang, B., and Liu, Y. (n.d.). Analysis of mobile WiMAX security: Vulnerabilities and solutions. *2008 5th IEEE International Conference on Mobile Ad Hoc and Sensor Systems,* 828–833. Retrieved October 23, 2015, from http://webpages.uncc.edu/than3/publication/ WiMaxSec.pdf.

Harris, M. A. and Patten, K. P. (2014). Mobile device security considerations for small- and medium-sized enterprise business mobility. *Information Management & Computer Security* 22(1), 97–114.

Higgens, K. J. (2015). Dark reading: Analytics and threat detection. February 12. http://www.darkreading. com/security-analytics.asp.

Hill, K. (2014). How did the FBI break Tor? *Forbes*, November 7.

Hoffman, C. (2014). Wi-Fi security: Should you use WPA2-AES, WPA2-TKIP, or Both? December 12. Retrieved October 28, 2015, from http://www.howtogeek.com/204697/wi-fi-security-should-you-use-wpa2-aes-wpa2-tkip-or-both/.

HP Enterprise (2015, 2016). The collateral damage of cybercrime HPE Security Research Cyber Risk Report. http://www8.hp.com/us/en/software-solutions/cyber-risk-report-security-vulnerability/.

Huawei (2013). 5G: A technology vision. Retrieved October 21, 2015, from http://www.huawei. com/5gwhitepaper/.

IBM (2015). IBM X-Force threat intelligence quarterly, 4Q 2014, 1- 3Q, August. http://www-01.ibm.com/ common/ssi/cgi-bin/ssialias?subtype=WH&infotype=SA&htmlfid=WGL03076USEN&attachment =WGL03076USEN.PDF.

ITU (2012). Global information infrastructure. Internet Protocol aspects and next-generation networks. Retrieved October 19, 2015. https://www.itu.int/rec/T-REC-Y/en.

Jailton, J., Carvalho, T., Valente, W., Frances, R., Abelm, A., Cerqueira, E., and Dias, K. (2012). A mobile WiMAX architecture with QoE support for future multimedia networks. *Quality of Service and Resource Allocation in WiMAX,* 193–216. Retrieved October 17, 2015, from http://cdn.intechopen. com/pdfs-wm/27700.pdf.

Jain, S. (2010). MPLSVPN—Moving towards SDN and NFV based networks. May 12. Retrieved October 17, 2015, from http://www.mplsvpn.info/2010/05/wimax-architecture.html.

Jajszczyk, A. (2012). *A Guide to the Wireless Engineering Body of Knowledge (WEBOK)*, 2nd edn. Hoboken, NJ: Wiley-IEEE Press.

Jover, R. (n.d.). Security attacks against the availability of LTE mobility networks: Overview and research directions, pp. 1–9. Retrieved October 17, 2015, from http://ieeexplore.ieee.org/xpls/abs_all. jsp?arnumber=6618585&tag=1.

Jupiter Networks Mobile Threat Center (2011). Mobile devices security: Emerging threats, essential strate-gies. http://www.adtechglobal.com/Data/Sites/1/marketing/juniperwhitepapermobiledevicesecurity. pdf.

Kak, A. (2011). Lecture notes on "Computer and Network Security." Lecture 12 Public-key cryptography and the RSA algorithm, February 19, 2015 Avinash Kak, Purdue University: West Lafayette, Indiana. https://engineering.purdue.edu/kak/.

Kak, A. (2015). Lecture notes on "Computer and Network Security." Lecture 20.5 The Tor protocol for anonymous routing. https://engineering.purdue.edu/kak/.

Kaminsky, D. (2008). An illustrated guide to the Kaminsky DNS vulnerability. http://www.unixwiz.net/ techtips/iguide-kaminsky-dns-vuln.html.

Kaspersky Labs (n.d.). Unveiling "Careto," the masked APT. http://kasperskycontenthub.com/ wp-pdfpdfcontent/uploads/sites/43/vlpdf/unveilingthemask_v1.0.

Kenney, M. (2015). Cyber-terrorism in a post-Stuxnet world. *Orbis* 59(1), 111–128.

Knapp, K. J. and Boulton, W. R. (2006). Cyber-warfare threatens corporations: Expansion into commercial environments. *Information Systems Management* 23(2), 76–87.

Koebler, J. (2015). The closest thing to a map of the dark net: PASTBIN, Motherboard, February 23. http://motherboard.vice.com/read/the-closest-thing-to-a-map-of-the-dark-net-pastebin.

Koebler, J. (2015). Six ways law enforcement monitors the dark web. Motherboard, February 17. http://motherboard.vice.com/read/six-ways-law-enforcement-monitors-the-dark-web.

Krebs, B. (2014). Krebs on security blog. Anthem breach may have started in April 2014. February 9, 2015. https://krebsonsecurity.com/.

Krebs, B. (2015). Email attack on vendor set up breach at Target, February 14. Retrieved September 25, 2015. http://www.krebsonsecurity.com/2014/02/email-attack-on-vendor-set-up-breach-at-target.

Krebs, B. (2015). Krebs on security blog. 28 with stolen cards, fraudsters shop to drop. September 15, 2015. https://krebsonsecurity.com/.

Kriaa, S., Bouissou, M., and Piètre-Cambacédès, L. (2012). Modeling the Stuxnet attack with BDMP: Towards more formal risk assessments. In *Risk and Security of Internet and Systems (CRiSIS), 2012 7th International Conference on (pp. 1–8)*. IEEE, October, 2012.

Lee, M. (2011). Insecure 2G needs global fix: AusCERT. Retrieved November 25, 2011, from zdnet: http://www.zdnet.com/article/insecure-2g-needs-global-fix-auscert/.

Li, N. (2015). Data Security Course, West Lafayette, IN: Purdue University.

Liang, L., Yang, G., Du, J., Liu, Z., He, Q., Bai, Y., and Yang, S. (2014). The practical risk assessment for enterprise wireless local area network. In *Information Science, Electronics and Electrical Engineering (ISEEE), 2014 International Conference on* (Vol. 3, pp. 1936–1940). IEEE. http://ieeexplore.ieee.org/xpls/abs_all.jsp?arnumber=6946261&tag=1.

Livingstone, A. and Fritsky, L. (2003). What is a WAP browser? October 13. Retrieved September 25, 2015. http://www.wisegeek.com/what-is-a-wap-browser.htm.

Lunden, I. (2015). Target says credit card data breach cost it $162M in 2013–14. February 25. Retrieved September 25, 2015. http://techcrunch.com/2015/02/25/target-says-credit-card-data-breach-cost-it-162m-in-2013-14/.

Marks, R. (2015). Wireless MAN standards for wireless metropolitan area networks. July 7. Retrieved October 13, 2015, from http://www.ieee802.org/16/.

Matrosov, A., Rodionov, E., Harley, D., and Malcho, J. (2010). Stuxnet under the microscope. ESET LLC, September 2010. https://www.esetnod32.ru/company/viruslab/analytics/doc/Stuxnet_Under_the_Microscope.pdf.

Matthews, M. (2011). Network security attack: Active/passive comparison. January 27. Retrieved from http://www.brighthub.com/computing/smb-security/articles/104551.aspx.

McCann, S. (2015). What 802.11is doing. September 3. Retrieved October 25, 2015, from http://www.ieee802.org/11/presentation.html.

Mcclure, S. and Joel, S. Cambray, (2012). *Hacking Exposed 7: Network Security Secrets &Amp; Solutions*, Osborne Media 7th Edition Paperback, New York: McGraw-Hill.

Metz, C., (1999). AAA protocols: Authentication, authorization, and accounting for the Internet. *Internet Computing, IEEE* 3(6), 75–79.

Microsoft. (2009). Preventing the exploitation of structured exception handler (SEH) overwrites with SEHOP. http://blogs.technet.com/b/srd/archive/2009/02/02/preventing-the-exploitation-of-seh-overwrites-with-sehop.aspx.

Microsoft. (2011). How to enable structured exception handling overwrite protection (SEHOP) in Windows operating systems. https://support.microsoft.com/en-us/kb/956607.

Microsoft Developer Network (n.d.). Replay attacks (current version). Retrieved October 26, 2015. https://msdn.microsoft.com/en-us/library/aa738652(v=vs.110).aspx.

Microsoft Technet. (n.d.). Common types of network attacks. Retrieved September 25, 2015, from https://technet.microsoft.com/en-us/library/cc959354.aspx.

Microsoft Technet (n.d.). EAP overview (Extensible Authentication Protocol). Retrieved October 25, 2015, https://technet.microsoft.com/en-us/library/cc770622(v=ws.10).aspx.

Milanov, E. (2009). The RSA algorithm, pp. 1–11. June 3. https://www.math.washington.edu/~morrow/336_09/papers/Yevgeny.pdf.

Minho, S., Justin, M., Arunesh, M., and Arbaugh, W. A. (2006). Wireless network security and interworking. *Proceedings of the IEEE* 94(8), 455–466.

Mishra, A. R. (2006). *Advanced Cellular Network Planning and Optimisation: 2G/2.5G/3G.Evolution to 4G.* John Wiley.

Mitchell, B. (n.d.). What 'WPA' is (WiFi protected access). Retrieved October 25, 2015, from http://compnetworking.about.com/cs/wirelesssecurity/g/bldef_wpa.htm.

Motsay, E. (2004). Unsecure wireless networks spawn industry trying to rectify problem. *RCR Wireless News* 23(25), 3.

Mueller, P. and Yadegari, B. (n.d.). The Stuxnet worm (downloadable pdf), Department of Information Sciences, University of Arizona. http://www.cs.arizona.edu/~collberg/Teaching/466-566/2012/Resources/presentations/2012/topic9-final/report.pdf.

Multi-factor Authentication Implementation. (2013). June 17. Retrieved October 26, 2015, from https://www.irs.gov/uac/Safeguards-Program.

Narayanan, A. and Shmatikov, V. (2005). November. Fast dictionary attacks on passwords using time-space tradeoff. In *Proceedings of the 12th ACM Conference on Computer and Communications Security* (pp. 364–372). ACM. http://dl.acm.org/citation.cfm?id=1102168.

Nelson, C. (2011). Cyber warfare: The newest battlefield. Retrieved from http://www.cse.wustl.edu/~jain/cse571-11/ftp/cyberwar/.

NIST, Guide for Conducting Risk Assessments. (2012). NIST special publication 800-30, Revision 1. Retrieved from http://csrc.nist.gov/publications/nistpubs/800-30-rev1/sp800_30_r1.pdf.

O'Brien, D. (2014). Symantec, Heartbleed bug poses serious threat to unpatched servers. April 9. http://www.symantec.com/connect/blogs/heartbleed-bug-poses-serious-threat-unpatched-servers.

Office of Electricity Delivery & Energy Reliability. (2015). http://energy.gov/oe/services/technology-development/smart-grid; http://energy.gov/oe/services/technology-development/energy-delivery-systems-cybersecurity.

Paganini, P. (2012). Critical infrastructures—Main threats for 2G and 3G mobile networks. January 13. Retrieved from Security Affairs: http://securityaffairs.co/wordpress/1603/security/critical-infrastructures-main-threats-for-2g-and-3g-mobile-networks.html.

Paolini, M. (2012). Wireless security in LTE networks. Retrieved October 18, 2015, from http://www.gsma.com/membership/wp-content/uploads/2012/11/SenzaFili_WirelessSecurity_121029_FINAL.pdf.

Parks, M. (2015). Target offers $10 million settlement in data breach lawsuit. March 19. Retrieved September 25, 2015. http://www.npr.org/sections/thetwo-way/2015/03/19/394039055/target-offers-10-million-settlement-in-data-breach-lawsuit.

Patil, G. R. and Wankhade, P. S. (2014). 5G wireless technology. *International Journal of Computer Science and Mobile Computing* 3(10), 203–207.

Paul, S. (2008). Long term evolution (LTE) & ultra-mobile broadband (UMB) technologies for broadband wireless access, pp. 1–15. Retrieved October 29, 2015, from http://www.cse.wustl.edu/~jain/cse574-08/ftp/lte.pdf.

Paxson, V. (2015). Data security course, University of California at Berkeley.

PC Magazine (n.d.). PC Magazine Encyclopedia, 802.11 Definition. Retrieved October 25, 2015, from http://www.pcmag.com/encyclopedia/term/37204/802-11. http://www.pcmag.com/encyclopedia/term/37204/802-11.

PC Magazine (n.d.). PC Magazine Encyclopedia, 802.11i-2004 Definition. (2004, June 24). Retrieved September 25, 2015.

PC Magazine (n.d.). PC Magazine Encyclopedia, 802.11i Definition. Retrieved September 25, 2015. http://www.pcmag.com/encyclopedia/term/37212/802-11i .

Phifer, L. (2003). WLAN security: Best practices for wireless network security. April 1. http://www.pcmag.com/encyclopedia/term/51537/smartphone.

Ponemon Institute. (2014). Global report on the cost of cyber crime. October 2014.

Priya, C. S., Umar, S., and Sirisha, T. (2014). *The Impact of War Driving on Wireless Networks*. IJCSET.

Rani, D. D., Krishna, T. S., Dayanandam, G., and Rao, T. V. (2013). TCP SYN flood attack detection and prevention. *International Journal of Computer Trends and Technology (IJCTT)* 4(10), 3412.

Rappaport, T. S., Sun, S., Mayzus, R., Zhao, H., Azar, Y., Wang, K., Wong, G., Schulz, J., Samimi, M., and Gutierrez, F. (2013). Millimeter wave mobile communications for 5G cellular: It will work! *Access, IEEE, 1*, 335–349.

Rivest, R. (2014–2015). Data security course, MIT, https://courses.csail.mit.edu/6.857/2015/.

Rook Security, (2011). Anatomy of an attack: Identifying phishing attacks to prevent data loss. Rook Security.com. https://www.rooksecurity.com/wp-content/uploads/2015/11/Whitepaper-Anatomy-of-the-Attack-Phishing.pdf.

RSA Incident Response: Emerging threat profile shell crew, January 2014. https://www.emc.com/collateral/white-papers/h12756-wp-shell-crew.pdf.

RSA Research. Terracotta VPN enabler of advanced threat anonymity August 2015. https://blogs.rsa.com/wp-content/uploads/2015/08/Terracotta-VPN-Report-Final-8-3.pdf; https://www.linkedin.com/pulse/check-out-rsas-recent-report-terracotta-vpn-enabler-threat-dimarino.

Ruggiero, P. and Foote, J. (2011). Cyber threats to mobile phones. *United States Computer Emergency Readiness Team*, 6.

Saini, N. and Mandal, S. (2015). Wireless LAN security. *International Journal of Research* 2(5), 33–37.

Salunke, M. D. and Kabra, R. (2014). Denial-of-service attack detection. *International Journal of Innovative Research in Advanced Engineering (IJIRAE)* 1(11), 16–20.

Seddigh, N., Nandy, B., Makkar, R., and Beaumont, J. (2010). Security advances and challenges in 4G wireless networks. *2010 8th International Conference on Privacy, Security and Trust, 62–71*. Retrieved October 29, 2015, from http://gonet1.qcwireless.net/pst_paper_2010/papers/p62-seddigh.pdf.

Shankdhar, P. (n.d.). Popular tools for brute-force attacks. Retrieved September 29, 2015, from http://resources.infosecinstitute.com/popular-tools-for-brute-force-attacks/.

Sharma, P. (2013). Evolution of mobile wireless communication networks–1G to 5G as well as future prospective of next generation communication network. *International Journal of Computer Science and Mobile Computing* 47–53.

Simion, D., Ursuleanu, M., and Graur, A. (2012). An overview on WiMAX security weaknesses/potential solutions. *11th International Conference on Development and Application Systems.* pp. 98–102.

Singh, B. and Panda, S. N. (2015). Defending against DDOS flooding attacks—A data streaming approach. *International Journal of Computer & IT.* 38–44.

Skendžić, A. (2014). Sigurnost infrastrukturnog načina rada bežične mreže standarda IEEE 802.11. *Zbornik Veleučilišta u Rijeci* 2(1), 163–176.

Smart Card Alliance, About smart cards introduction: Primer. (n.d.). http://www.smartcardalliance.org/smart-cards. Retrieved September 25, 2015.

Sobh, T. S. (n.d.). Wi-Fi networks security and accessing control (IJCNIS) (downloadable pdf). http://www.mecs-press.org/ijcnis/ijcnis-v5-n7/v5n7-2.html.

Stallings, W. and Lawrie, B. (2014). *Computer Security: Principles and Practices* 3rd edn. July 18, Upper Saddle River, NJ: Prentice Hall.

Steflick, D. (2015). *Data Security Course*, Binghamton, NY: State University of New York at Binghamton.

Stefanick, G. (2010). CWSP journey (Chapter 5—Keys Post #4). September 10. http://www.my80211.com/cwsp-george-stefanick/2010/10/3/george-stefanick-cwsp-journey-chapter-5-4-way-handshake-post.html.

Stoneburner, G., Hayden, C., and Feringa, A. (2004). *Engineering Principles for Information Technology Security (A Baseline for Achieving Security)*. Gaithersburg, MD: National Institute of Standards and Technology.

Symantec ISTR internet security threat report 2014 and 2015.

Tarantola, A. (2014). What are "smart" credit cards, and why are they coming to America? February 11. Retrieved September 25, 2015.

TCP 3-way handshake. (2013). Retrieved September 26, 2015, from http://www.inetdaemon.com/tutorials/internet/tcp/3-way_handshake.shtml.

Technical specifications. (n.d.). Retrieved October 12, 2015, from http://www.wimaxforum.org/resources/technical-specifications.

Telelink (n.d.). MAC address spoofing. Retrieved September 26, 2015. http://itsecurity.telelink.com/mac-address-sproofing.

Thomson Reuters. (2010). UPDATE 2-Iran says cyber foes caused centrifuge problems. http://af.reuters.com/article/energyOilNews/idAFLDE6AS1L120101129, 2015.

Timberg, C. (2014). Apple's iCloud service suffers cyber-attack in China, putting passwords in peril. *Washington Post*, October 21. https://www.washingtonpost.com/news/the-switch/wp/2014/10/21/apples-icloud-service-suffers-cyber-attack-in-china-putting-passwords-in-peril/.

Tor Project, How the TOR Network Works. (https://www.torproject.org/).

University of California, Santa Cruz. (2014). Information technology services. http://its.ucsc.edu/security/scams.html, 2013.

US Department of Energy (2009). National SCADA test bed: Fact sheet. September 9. http://energy.gov/sites/prod/files/oeprod/DocumentsandMedia/NSTB_Fact_Sheet_FINAL_09-16-09.pdf.

USB tokens, mobile soft tokens, dual authentication. (n.d.). Retrieved September 25, 2015, from http://www.entrust.com/products/usb-tokens/.

Verizon 2014 data breach investigations report.

Waliullah, M., Moniruzzaman, A. B. M., and Rahman, M. S. (2015). An experimental study analysis of security attacks at IEEE 802.11 wireless local area network. *International Journal of Future Generation Communication and Networking* 8(1), 9–18.

Weaver, R. (2007). *Guide to Network Defense and Countermeasures*, 2nd edn. : Australia: Course Technology.

What is a security token? Retrieved September 25, 2015, from https://www.techopedia.com/definition/16148/security-token.

What is a security token (authentication token)? (n.d.). Retrieved September 25, 2015, from http://searchsecurity.techtarget.com/definition/security-token.

What is TKIP (Temporal Key Integrity Protocol). (n.d.). Definition from WhatIs.com. Retrieved October 25, 2015, from http://searchmobilecomputing.techtarget.com/definition/TKIP.

What is Wired Equivalent Privacy (WEP). (n.d.). Definition from WhatIs.com. Retrieved October 25, 2015, from http://searchsecurity.techtarget.com/definition/Wired-Equivalent-Privacy.

What is a Wireless Local Area Network (WLAN). (n.d.). Definition from techopedia. Retrieved October 25, 2015, from https://www.techopedia.com/definition/5107/wireless-local-area-network-wlan.

White House. (2013). Office of the press secretary. *Executive Order – Improving Critical Infrastructure Cybersecurity.* https://www.whitehouse.gov/the-press-office/2013/02/12/executive-order-improving-critical-infrastructure-cybersecurity.

Wi-Fi protected setup (WPS) vulnerable to brute-force attack. (2012). January 6. Retrieved October 27, 2015, from https://www.us-cert.gov/ncas/alerts/TA12-006A.

Wikipedia, Many of the protocol definitions. www.wikipedia.com.

WiMax Forum. (n.d.). About the WiMAX forum. Retrieved October 11, 2015, from http://www.wimax-forum.org/about.

WLAN configuration guide. (n.d.). Retrieved October 25, 2015, from http://www.h3c.com/portal/Technical_Support___Documents/Technical_Documents/WLAN/Access_Point/H3C_WA2200_Series_WLAN_Access_Points/Configuration/Operation_Manual/H3C_WA_Series_WLAN_Access_CG-6W100/02/201009/691527_1285_0.htm.

WPA2 Hole196 Vulnerability - FAQs. (n.d.). Retrieved October 27, 2015, from http://www.airtightnetworks.com/WPA2-Hole196.

WTLS. (n.d.). Retrieved September 25, 2015, from http://www.webopedia.com/TERM/W/WTLS.html.

Wu, Z., Cai, M., Liang, S., and Zhang, J. (2014). An approach for prevention of MitM attack based on Rouge AP in wireless network. *Sensors & Transducers* 183(12), 162–171.

Wu, Z. (2014). Rogue AP in wireless network. *Sensors & Transducers (1726–5479)* 183(12).

Xuan, D. (n.d.). Mobile handset cellular network. Retrieved from October 17, 2015. http://www.cse.unt.edu/~rdantu/FALL_2015_WIRELESS_NETWORKS/2G_3G_4G_Tutorial.pp.

Yadav, R. and Srinivasan, S. (2013). Evolution of WiMAX technology, security issues and available solutions. *International Journal of Computer Applications (0975–8887)* 66(2), 44–48.

Yang, N., Wang, L., Geraci, G., Elkashlan, M., Yuan, J., and Renzo, M. D. (2015). Safeguarding 5G wireless communication networks using physical layer security. *Communications Magazine, IEEE* 53(4), 20–27.

Zetter, K. (2014). *Countdown to Zero Day: Stuxnet and the Launch of the World's First Digital Weapon.* New York: Crown.

Appendix: End of Chapter Question Answers

Chapter 2: The Anthem Break-in Case Study

1.
   a. Spear phishing
   b. Waterholes
2.
   a. Enterprise Compromise Assessment Tool (ECAT) scanning software
3.
   a. The China Chopper web shell
4.
   a. They use the Sticky Keys trick to modify the registry on the target's system server.
5.
   a. It's a network of virtual tunnels that is used to hide websites from each other and outsiders.
6.
   a. Control and relay packets. Tor packets set up an anonymous path. The path sets up links in sequence, and when it is finished, hackers send relay packets containing malware, code, and software to the target site.
7.
   a. The process of encapsulating a transmitted message in a series of encrypted IP addressing layers is called onion wrapping.

Chapter 3: Anonymous Persistent Threats

1.
   a. Altering/poisoning web pages maintained by an organization
   b. Exploiting systems using different SETHC.exe methods accessible via Remote Desktop Protocol
   c. Extensive use of time/date stamping of malicious files to hinder forensic analysis
2.
   a. Involved in global cyber espionage in 2007, The Mask is malware. It is an advanced threat actor that attacks and infects victims.
3.
   a. What makes The Mask special is the complexity of the toolset used by the attackers. This includes malware, rootkit, bootkit, and Mac and Linux versions.

4.
  a. Government institutions
  b. Energy, oil, and gas companies
  c. Private equity firms

Chapter 4: Creating Secure Code

1.
  a. The purpose is to isolate modules so it becomes difficult for malware to transmit their effects across a confinement chasm
  b. Physical confinement
  c. Virtual confinement
  d. Operating system confinement
  e. Isolation of threads

2.
  a. Physical confinement is the most primitive method. This method uses an "air gap," which is a network security measure. It physically isolates the device from unsecured networks. If one device is attacked, the others will still be safe.

3.
  a. Chroot: An operating system separating it from the main operating system and directory structure. Essentially generates a confined space with its own root directory to run software programs.
    i. This provides security to the base system.
  b. Jail kit:
    i. A set of utilities to limit user accounts to specific files using Chroot and specific commands.
  c. FreeBSD
    i. Confines stronger mechanisms by binding sockets with specified Internet Protocol (IP) addresses and authorized ports.
  d. All of these are forms of network security.

4.
  a. Yes, only specific types of programs can run in jail-restricted environments, and Chroot and jail routines tend to have coarse, inflexible policies.

Chapter 5: Providing a Secure Architecture

1.
  a. Isolation and least privilege
  b. Access control concepts
  c. Operating system isolation
  d. Browser isolation and least privilege

2.
  a. Fix bugs, concede overflow, and add run-time code to detect overflow exploits

3.
  a. Passwords: Hackers use graphics processing units to calculate various character combinations to eventually crack the password.

4.
  a. Compartmentalize

    b. Utilize defense in depth

    c. Keep it simple

Chapter 6: Hacker Strategy: Expanded

1.

    a. Surveillance

2.

    a. Spear-phishing e-mails: Commonly used in an effort to trick the target into giving information

    b. Watering holes: Where hackers create an attractive website catering to the target's behaviors

3.

    a. Binary analysis can uncover potential vulnerabilities like the basic data flow from the network, or the use of bad application programming interface (API).

4.

    a. *Zero day* refers to an unknown software vulnerability that the developers are unaware of that can be triggered on day "zero." This can result in potential damage to your computer/personal data.

5.

    a. Using buffers and buffer overrun. Hackers are able to determine the return address in the memory stack by guessing the approximate stack state and inserting a no-operation line of code.

6.

    a. Address space layout randomization

7.

    a. Four

    b. Fix bugs

    c. Concede overflow but prevent code execution

    d. Add run-time code to detect overflow exploit

    e. Data execution prevention

Chapter 7: Malware, Viruses, Worms, Bugs, and Botnets

1.

    a. Honeypot

2.

    a. After a computer is taken over by a bot, it can be used to carry out four tasks:

        i. Sending

        ii. Stealing

        iii. Denial of service (DoS)

        iv. Clickfraud

3.

    a. Worms self-replicate and spread across networks, exploiting vulnerabilities. They don't need to latch onto another computer program.

        i. Example: An e-mail worm or the Love Bug worm

    b. Viruses are self-replicating but insert themselves into other computer programs, hard drives, and data files.

        i. Example: Through USB, e-mail, pop-up message

4.
   a. Polymorphic code and metamorphic code d.
   b. Polymorphic code encrypts its original code to avoid pattern recognition. Metamorphic code reprograms itself to different versions.
5.
   a. Host-based instruction detection systems (HIDS)
   b. Network-based instruction detection systems (NIDS)

Chapter 8: Cryptography and the RSA Algorithm
1.
   a. Cryptography
2.
   a. Cryptography is the study and practice of applying encryption techniques for ensuring secure communication.
   b. Encryption is the use of a process or algorithm (cipher) to make information hidden or secret.
3.
   a. Block ciphers.
   b. In symmetric-key encryption, the sender and receiver of a message share a single common key. Symmetric is simple and faster, but the two parties must somehow exchange the key in secure way.
   c. Public-key uses two keys: a public key and private key. Public-key encryption is more secure.
4.
   a. Hashing is another form of cryptography. Hashing stores passwords, and it is very difficult for someone with access to raw data to reverse the hashed data back to the original. It is great for usage where you want to compare a value with stored value.

Chapter 9: Browser Security
1.
   a. Website, victim, and attacker
2.
   a. To execute untested code or untrusted programs from unverified third parties
3.
   a. Port scanning is important in managing networks.
   b. However, it can also be malicious if someone is looking for a weakened access point to break in.
4.
   a. Frame busting: Preventing a web page from loading in a frame

Chapter 10: Banking Security, Zeus, and SpyEye
1.
   a. Eavesdropping attack that occurs when a malicious actor inserts himself as a relay into a communication session
2.
   a. Money mule

3.
  a. Steals personal data such as e-mail passwords and financial information such as online banking passwords. Hackers use Zeus Trojan to steal information.
4.
  a. Can delete its own installation files
  b. Injects itself into dynamic link libraries
5.
  a. A file encrypting ransomware that encrypts personal documents on a victim's computer and makes them pay a ransom.
  b. Distributed through several means such as malicious websites that have been hacked and can infect your machine. Spam e-mail is another method.

Chapter 11: Web Application Security
  1.
    a. Scanbox software collects information and compromises user's machine.
  2.
    a. A language for updating, deleting, and requesting information from databases.
  3.
    a. Select, where, pwd
  4.
    a. Web-browser behavior such as cookies and Hypertext Transfer Protocol (HTTP) authentication
    b. Knowledge by attacker
    c. Application session management
    d. Existence of Hypertext Markup Language (HTML) tags

Chapter 12: Session Management, User Authentication, and Web Application Security
  1.
    a. Confidentiality
    b. Integrity
    c. Availability
    d. Common attacks
  2.
    a. Border gateway
  3.
    a. A program that can see all of the information passing over the network it is connected to
  4.
    a. Unfiltered: Captures all of the packets
    b. Filtered: Captures only those packets containing specific data elements
  5.
    a. Eavesdropping
    b. Disruption
    c. Injection
  6.
    a. Attackers want to hide their identity, so they change the source address while attacking the victim.

7.
   a. MAC addresses, Dynamic Host Configuration Protocol (DHCP) servers, Internet Protocol (IP) addresses, and other Transmission Control Protocol (TCP)/IP settings.

8.
   a. Because there is no authentication or authorization takes place during an exchange between DHCP server and DHCP client.

Chapter 13: Web Security, DNS Security, and the Internet

1.
   a. Short for IP security, this is a set of protocols to support secure exchange of packets at the IP layer (Layer 3).

2.
   a. Transport and tunnel

3.
   a. Tunnel mode encrypts both the header and the data portion

4.
   a. Secure socket layer is used to provide the security protocol used by the Internet to provide easy access to websites.

5.
   a. Unlike a firewall, Snort has the ability to detect hostile intent.

Chapter 14: Network Security and Defenses

1.
   a. Confidentiality
   b. Integrity
   c. Availability
   d. Common attacks

2.
   a. Confidentiality: Packet sniffing
   b. Integrity: Cross-site scripting (XSS)
   c. Availability: Denial-of-service (DoS) attacks
   d. Common attacks: Address translation poisoning attacks

3.
   a. Border gateways. Because it is an area network and another area network bridged through use of border area gateway.

4.
   a. Address Resolution Protocol (ARP)

5.
   a. It presents vulnerability because it is easy to spoof ARP requests and replies.

6.
   a. Creates stop-and-start flooding, making it difficult to identify the source of attacks. Normally used through distributed denial of service (DDoS).

7.
   a. Eavesdropping (sniffing)

8.
   a. Source and destination addresses

9.
   a. Blind spoofing

Chapter 15: Network Security Protocols and Defensive Mechanisms
1.
   a. Relies on standard private/public-key cryptography.
   b. Adds cryptographic signature to Domain Name System (DNS) answers returned.
   c. It is important because DNS uses User Datagram Protocol (UDP) for packet transport, so when you query, any returned UDP packet could be the answer. The returned UDP packet has to have the right source IP, destination IP, and port.
2.
   a. Authentication header (AH): Allows authentication of sender of data.
   b. Encapsulating security payload supports both authentication of the sender and encryption of data.
3.
   a. Authentication using preshared secret
   b. Authentication using Rivest–Shamir–Adleman (RSA) encrypted nonces
   c. Authentication using RSA signatures
4.
   a. An intrusion detection system (IDS) collects and analyzes information in its database that contains patterns called signatures.
   b. An intrusion prevention system (IPS) blocks attacks itself and sits directly in the line of network traffic.
5.
   a. No, it is commonly mistaken for a firewall or substitute. They are similar in that they both relate to network security but IDS differs by looking out for intrusions in order to stop them from happening.
6.
   a. Misuse detection model
      i. Analyzes the information it gathers and compares it with large databases of attack signatures.
   b. Anomaly detection model
      ii. Monitors network segments to compare their state with the normal baseline and look for anomalies.

Chapter 16: Denial-of-Service Attacks
1.
   a. Two
2.
   a. Bugs and floods
3.
   a. User sends several authentication requests to the server; all requests have false return addresses so the server can't find the user when it tries to send the authentication approval.
4.
   a. Set up a filter or sniffer on a network before a stream of information reaches site web servers.

5.
   a. A client repeatedly sends synchronize (SYN) packets to every port on a server using fake IP addresses.

Chapter 17: Mobile Platform Security

1.
   a. Cocoa Touch layer
      i. Top layer. Contains key frameworks for building iOS apps.
   b. Media layer
      i. Upper middle layer. Contains graphics, audio, and video that you would use to implement in apps.
   c. Core services
      i. One of the middle layers. Key service is core foundation frameworks; contains iCloud, social media, and networking.
   d. Core operating system (OS) layer
      i. Bottom layer. Contains low-level features that most technologies are built on.
2.
   a. Activity
   b. Service
   c. Intents
   d. Content provider
   e. Broadcast receiver
3.
   a. Creates an environment with strict limitations, allowing a program to be hosted on your computer and you want to provide an environment where the program can run.
4.
   a. Byte code verifier
   b. Applet class loader
   c. Security manager

Chapter 18: Cellular Access Security: 4G LTE, Mobile WiMAX, 5G, and MIMOs

1.
   a. IEEE 802.16
2.
   a. 3G
3.
   a. DoS
4.
   a. Strong encryption
   b. 1G
5.
   a. 67%
6.
   a. Base station (BS)
7.
   a. Packet-switched network implementation
   b. Device to device (D2D)

8.
    a. Orthogonal frequency division multiplexing (OFDM)

Chapter 19: Wireless LAN Security

1.
    a. First component (important) radio card
    b. Antenna
    c. Ability to operate under the 802.11 protocol standards

2.
    a. Confidentiality
    b. Integrity
    c. Availability

3.
    a. Magnetic strip lacks security reliability. It will be equipped with microcontroller that carries its own encryption protocol and authentication.

4.
    a. Designed to provide the same level of security as wired LAN but it is vulnerable to tampering and is not as secure.

5.
    a. Encryption through use of preshared-key technology. Each packet creates a different 128-bit key.

Chapter 20: The Stuxnet Worm and the Vulnerability of the U.S. Electric Power Grid

1.
    a. A simple infection by means of a personal flash driving carrying the worm, which then spreads onto the next machine.

2.
    a. Windows OS
    b. The Siemens programmable logic controllers (PLC) software
    c. PLC

3.
    a. Path 1: Via WinCC, interface to system control and data acquisition (SCADA) systems.
    b. Path 2: Via network shares: Stuxnet uses Windows shared folders to propagate itself over a local network.
    c. Path 3: Via the MS10-061 print spooler 0 day vulnerability: Stuxnet copies itself, places the copy on remote computers.
    d. Path 4: Via the MS08-067 SMB vulnerability: Stuxnet can send malformed path over SMB.
    e. Path 5: Via Step 7 projects: Stuxnet infects Siemens.

4.
    a. The SCADA command and control system uses the same Siemens devices as the Iranian centrifuge system.
    b. The means of infection by insertion of a contaminated flash drive is available.
    c. The Stuxnet worm has been reverse engineered and is now available worldwide in a much more advanced form.

Chapter 21: Cyber Warfare

    1.
        a. Citadel toolkit

    2.
        a. It creates a hidden connection to a control server from the infected computer.

    3.
        a. A citadel is spread through drive-by exploits.

    4.
        a. Government regulators
        b. Network infrastructure providers
        c. Equipment providers
        d. Service providers
        e. End device users

Index

Printed and bound by CPI Group (UK) Ltd, Croydon, CR0 4YY

22/10/2024

01777636-0017